Praise fo

"A fiercely honest, wickedly humorous, ⹁⹁⹁ insightful look at the heart of a poet. *Mi'ja* takes the reader on a transformational journey. We witness how scars become jewels, how compassion and wit are the best revenge, and how a river of passionate words and stories can soothe the worst injustices. Gómez dances with her ancestors, despite the stale cookies and slaps of childhood. What a harvest! *Mi'ja* will make you take a deep healing breath."

 —Beverly Naidus, author of *Arts for Change: Teaching Outside the Frame, One Size Does Not Fit All*, and creator of the Pandemic Healing Deities
  series; Professor Emeritus, University of Washington, Tacoma

"Mi'ja" belongs on your bookshelf between *I Know Why the Caged Bird Sings* and *The House on Mango Street*. Pure passion, pure life, pure New York City. We thrill watching the narrator survive, thrive and tell her tale. Brilliant!"

 —Lisa Aronson-Fontes, PhD; psychologist, professor, Fulbright
 Scholar, global speaker and author of *Invisible Chains: Overcoming
  Coercive Control in Your Intimate Relationship* and *Child Abuse and
  Culture: Working with Diverse Families.*

"Magdalena Gómez's searing honesty excavates what is dishonest within us. What she allows us to witness here is catharsis—hers, and ours—we will not carry the weight of abuse and oppression on our chests any longer. We will sing, and our liberation will terrify tyrants."

 —Diana Alvarez, PhD (a.k.a. Doctora Xingona) award-winning
 poet, songwriter, and opera composer, *Quiero Volver: A Xicanx
  Ritual Opera*

"At once irreverent and true, Magdalena Gómez writes with the prose of a poet and the soul of a survivor. You'll find yourself savoring each playful turn of phrase and philosophical rumination. By excavating and (re)writing her coming-of-age story, Gómez gives her younger self that voice and full humanity the adults in her life too often denied her, growing up. *Mi'ja* is thus a masterclass in the art of reparenting one's inner child. Heartbreaking and hopeful, this memoir stays with you long after the final page."

—Li Yun Alvarado, PhD, author of *Words or Water*

"The language dances.

The stories sing.

My heart broke and was mended, over and over again.

Magdalena, the wise elder, offers healing to Magdalena, the wiser child, and in turn opens a path, brimming with love and compassion, to heal all our child selves. *Mijá* is for those who have endured much suffering at the hands of those who couldn't or wouldn't love us in the ways we needed and, more importantly, in the ways we deserved to be loved. Her stories are hers, particular in time and place: various parts of New York City in the 1950s, 60s, and 70s. The stories are also universal in the best ways; they travel the world, they speak many languages, they weave connections, and they show us how empathy, courage, and creativity are deep wells from which we all can draw as we soldier through this maddening world. Gracías a Magdalena por tus palabras y tu corazón tiernisimo."

—Priscilla Maria Page, MFA, PhD; University of Massachusetts,
    Amherst Multicultural Theater Certificate Director,
        Dramaturgy Faculty

"Funny, painful, wickedly smart, and the definition of *real*."
    —Bob Spivey, PhD, Founder of SEEDS (Social Ecology Education and
        Demonstration School), a Revolutionary Activist Art Group

"This book will be of historical and literary interest for decades to come."
    —Anonymous

MI'JA

MI'JA

Magdalena Gómez

Ⓗ Heliotrope Books
New York

Other books by Magdalena Gómez:

Shameless Woman

Co-editor with María Luisa Arroyo, *Bullying: Replies, Rebuttals, Confessions, and Catharsis*

Bilingual CDs:

AmaXonica: *Howls from the Left Side of My Body*, poems, co-produced with Rotary Records, MA; Ted Levine, saxophone

Bemba y Chichón, songs of resistance and *Poems*, co-Produced with Abraham Gomez-Delgado, featuring Juancho Herrera and Reinaldo Dejesus

Limited Edition Chapbook, *Window Shopping in America: Poems for Performance*; Teatro V!da Publication

Heliotrope Books LLC
heliotropebooks@gmail.com

ISBN: 978-1-956474-05-3
ISBN: 978-1-956474-06-0 eBook

Cover Image courtesy of Sarah Haviland;
"Aviary 9: Volcanic Rock" (steel mesh, brass cage, obsidian, beads)
www.sarahhaviland.net

Cover photo: Naomi Rosenblatt

Designed and typeset by Naomi Rosenblatt with AJ&J Design

To my immortal parents:

Virgilio Gómez Fernández, you infused me with Duende,
tu salero Xitano, a profound love for the sea and humor to thrive
in the worst of circumstances. "Don't follow. Lead"—the hippocampus
tattoo that gave me the spine to stand alone and speak truth,
no matter the price.

Lydia Lajara, you gave me the furia that became an inner
strength to fear no one or anything. Not even Death.
"If your pantaletas should fall, step out of them
and keep walking, head held high, eyes straight ahead."

For all of the teachers, tías, cousins, friends, and strangers,
who by their actions and words, from the smallest
to the greatest of kindnesses, kept the child alive.

I offer my childhood as a portal for your pain. Release.

My soul a wick
welcomes ancestral flame.
I am reborn from secret tongues.
I write to you from a nether world.
A place that is no place.
Where Time has all the properties of Water.
Life's inverted star secures our best for battle.
Memory,
trickster third cousin of Knowing
Tells it like it was.
And like it wasn't;
Dances in peripheral shadows
mocks our diadem of eyes.
We Speak from the Dark
Invoking Light to Rise.
Hell. Truest name of
that friend to some
enemy to all:
Time.

ONE/FORMICA

I looked too much like Papi for Mami to ever really love me. "Every night your father rapes me." She said it with the calmness of a midnight Mass, as coffee pulsed in the percolator. "That's how we got you." Mami assumed I knew what that meant, even though I was only six and she never told me anything about sex except to keep my legs closed.

I did know a few things. The stork delivered babies; men delivered trouble. I learned that everything bad in the world was on account of Satan. Mami said his name a lot. Satanás made Mami's rice get amogollao. Satanás gave Papi bunions. Even farts were from Satan; especially the kind that smell like rotten eggs. Whenever I said his name, a high-pitched "¡Señor te reprenda!" preceded a slap, a yanking of hair.

I knew that Mami was lying about Papi so that I would hate him as much as she did. Maybe she was lying about Satanás too.

When Mami sat down in the kitchen to tell me a story of some horrible thing, there were always expired Stella D'oro anisette cookies and cold milk for me, black coffee and soda crackers for her. If she was feeling motherly she'd splash a little coffee and sugar into my milk. I did my best to dunk those treats quickly, so I wouldn't get smacked for making cookie sludge. I was safe from cocotasos once Mami got rolling on a story, dragging me into her haunted house of mirror shards, my eyelids pinned back, unable to look away.

Mami spoke the language of her experiences and DNA. A sancocho of her own inventions and accents, Spanish, Arawak, Taíno, Garífuna, Dominican, Arabic, Creole, Nigerian, El Bronx Spanglish, and a few words in U.S. English, most of which originated somewhere else. Snobs called Mami's language "broken"; I still call it original. She could never understand Los Americanos, as they leaned into her thick accent with over-enunciated vowels and jaggedly-pitched voices laying down words like uneven bricks in a clumsy stack.

The kitchen ceiling paint, mouse gray from window-blown soot, cracked and curled into lenguas rabiosas; little raging tongues that caught chispas of hot Crisco splatter. A fitting soundtrack to Mami's mayhem. I counted each of them in my head and gave them names like Chucho, Pingo, Dingo, Chiringo, Pipiripingo. I figured that spells had to rhyme or they wouldn't take. "Fall on her. Fall on her. Please Jesus, silence her." You can do or say just about anything in the name of Jesus and get away with it. Papi always scraped, cleaned, painted and repainted that ceiling, thwarting my spells and maledictions. He didn't know I was trying to save him too.

As Mami went on about rats in the subways and diabetics with leg rot, a renegade bluebottle fly crapped on her frilly pink flamingo dishtowel from one of the jonkería stores on Southern Boulevard, where women sluggishly tossed cheap and toxic household items into carts, mocking their poverty; "Humph, better than nothing."

TWO/CERAMIC

What lives on a coffee table is seldom coffee. The week's *TV Guide*. A jar of Vicks. Porcelain Lady ashtrays—"Naughty Nodders." Their wombs crematoriums for unfiltered Camels and Lucky Strikes. Rust-colored hair, suggestively rocking legs, a red fan where breasts should be, cherry lips perfectly painted within the lines by a steady hand somewhere in pre-war Japan.

The Artist sits by a tiny, cracked window, squinting from slivers of the only available light. This painter (who can find no other work) readies one special Porcelain Lady for the cargo ship that will take her to America. (Mami called all of her various female figurines from jonkería stores "Las Damas de Porcelana.") The Artist is determined that this Porcelain Lady will not be a forgery of other forgeries, tucked into little wooden caskets, protected on beds of shredded news and classifieds for the long overseas journey. The Artist chain smokes to stave off hunger.

The Artist grows intimate with his creation. "You will be an undetected stowaway, your name in Ainu, painted on your insides. Only you and I will know. The other ladies, all the same, like tiny North American pin-up girls. You will be in a proper, well-buttoned teacher's dress, someone to be respected. I have mixed the paint for your skin with a drop of my blood, so the ancestors will find you."

Porcelain Lady's legs rock in a shorter arc than the others, as if marking time. "You will not be a midnight doorway for lost men." The Artist conjures a tiny book from stamps he has steamed from envelopes that hold letters from a forbidden love. He hardens it with cornstarch, paints it tenderly. "A book for your heart." It replaces what was going to be a red fan. "You will look like a mistake to mediocre eyes and go to a poor family for a lower price at a seconds store. You will become a friend to a child who has no friends. They make greatest friends of all."

The Artist knows from experience that hungry children often steal half-smoked cigarettes. He knows of the secret life that awakens inside the most mundane object when it is loved and protected by a child—a doll, a blanket, a button, a rag. "To be different is the only way to survive the living death, my tomodachi. You and a child shall find each other. An outsider. Like us." In this way, The Artist imagines, that he too might be remembered. He knows that children carry youthful friendships to the grave and beyond; it is a part of humans that never dies, like the memory of a first kiss.

The Artist gently swathes Porcelain Lady in a furoshiki that belonged to his Great-Grandmother. "I am sorry to separate you from your legs and book on such a long journey, but it is the only way to hide your true nature. You must appear to be like all the others." The Artist does a final check, making sure that all of Porcelain Lady's separate parts would be safe for the journey. "One day, you will be revived by unknown hands. May those hands belong to a heart filled with books, to eyes that have known love." The Artist resists walking away.

"Seven cigarettes paid for your freedom, little friend. Seven, so we might never be parted." The Artist whispers their secret names gently over Porcelain Lady; the embroidery of his loving breath over her stillness seals their bond. Abiogenesis; the ultimate triumph of impossible desires.

"You will survive the discovery of your difference and never be discarded or broken before your time. You will know a little something of love." The Artist seals the tiny coffin-like box, tapping on a small nail with a sun-bleached river stone that has lived deep inside his pocket since he was a boy. He gently places and hides his little tomodachi into the large crate, which he safely fastens for the endless journey. It holds 7x7x7x7 nameless sisters that Porcelain Lady will never know.

Southern Boulevard

Saturday stroll
to the junk store for mousetraps
I become Executioner
steel wool for gnawed holes
set the cheese
with reverence
before the snap
the squeak
the bulging eyes
Cousins screech
run into each other
swear into sofa cushions
mouse tail whips
like Mami's belt
across my back
I release the broken body
into a kitchen match box
for one last breath
Cousins look up to me
gather, push, rise to salute
Taps, a lip—trumpet foam
of serious stillness
we march to the gravesite
our layered hands
push down on the oar of Charon
the tiny fetal-like bundle drops
from his casket, swirls
on one last ride
to places unknown
no coins small enough
to cover his eyes.
On his behalf,
I cover mine.

A *Popeye the Sailor* cartoon blares a song about "those dirty little Japs" from the living room console TV. My instantly bored little shit cousins run to secure the best spots on the sofa. The usual Saturday giggles and gum snaps return, "Yew, I hate spinach!" A chorus of gagging sounds as they squeeze out arm muscles the size of Swedish meatballs. "I don't need spinach." We eat chocolate-covered jellies from the penny candy store. Mami calls it "Jew candy." Welcome to America, Porcelain Lady. I touch her little book that doesn't open. I rock her legs and count in my head. She makes me sad and I don't know why.

THREE/VELVET

There are many words for female genitalia. Vagina is not my favorite. Too imperial. "Enter, Her Royal Majesty, Vah-gina." All powdered wigs and beet-stained cheeks; back stabbing bitches in suffocating baleen corsets. My cunt is working-class and loyal, not royal. I am no Queen, nor do I want to be. Little good has ever come from The Court for any of my people.

What is your favorite word for the Holy Hole from which you made your sloppy entrance? Say it out loud seven times and then you will be ready to continue reading this book. Mine is "toto." toto. toto. toto. toto. toto. toto. toto. My toto has always been a portal for the best and worst of life. Cunt is my favored daughter of three consonant words. From them arises a beast that is both tender and barbarous. Toto-Cunt-Toto-Cunt-Toto-Cunt. There. I find the strength to lift my pen.

When I wet the bed as a child, Mami, a seamstress, threatened to sew up my toto. Please take note of the lower case t of my toto. I never want my Puerto Rican Romani multilingual toto to be mistaken for Dorothy's dog or industrial Japanese bathroom fixtures. The part of my toto that is Gitana is still a virgin. Should you host a séance, and my parents show up, make sure to let them know. Don't bother telling them anything else about me, since the purity of even half of my toto would make them the most proud. You will hear Mami utter, "Better than nothing."

Nothing is impossible since there is always something. As long as we can question its existence (Nothing) it continues to exist. When it finally arrives none of us will exist, no one will give a shit about Zero Point Energy, as we will all be absorbed into the void with Billy Preston having the last word: "Nothin' from nothin' brings nothin', you gotta have somethin' if you wanna be with me."

I offer my experiences as a trampoline for your fear of falling. The tightrope of my guts for your fear of heights. Let my body break your fall. Step into my cosmic toto and balance your way to my pituitary, where childhood innocence waits to know itself again, if ever at all. There is room on my bench. We have a better chance of boarding that runaway train if we lift each other onto that first step. My life has made me ready for anything. May our children, all children, and the Post Nothing generation never be so fortunate. ·

Mami didn't notice I was casting spells on her when she told her kitchen stories, but sniffed the air for my thoughts, staring at the stove. She would conjure some kind of saying like: "Never think impure thoughts while frying a sausage and you will grow up to be decente." The Pipiripingos clung to the ceiling. It wasn't time for my spells to work. Besides, if the ceiling caved in, my life would be an even bigger mess with the splash of upstairs neighbors and their dogs. There was no one I could turn to in times of mess.

Most fairytales are horrible beneath the surface; Mami just ripped off the scabs and skipped over the fairies. When Mami told a story it was like watching an opera, all tears and snots, perfect makeup, with upswept hair trying to keep pace. Several octaves of swearing and anemic euphemisms; dainty, conceited hands waved like frantic pigeons fleeing nasty school boys, slapping the oxygen out of the room. Someone was always mutilated or disfigured into una vida de jamona, or murdered into the sanctity of martyrdom; usually a servant stabbed while fending off the unwanted advances of a married man. Infants found suffocated between a wall and mattress, or garroted by their umbilical cords on their way out, blamed for inheriting the stubborn ineptitudes of their fathers, betraying their suffering mothers. "Poor womens with their ungrateful bastards. You were una bestia in my womb; you tried to kill me before you were born." I hated myself for not finishing the job.

Where we lived, pigeons had names like Lucky and Machito, rooftop penthouses, good eats and gang protection. They got love and respect. In return, they attended to airmail on the wire. Pigeons are a lot smarter than people give them credit for—they invented GPS, don't snitch, and always come home on time. Mami hated pigeons and told me with scientific certainty that breathing around them would give me tuberculosis or leprosy. Those daily talks were Mami's version of homeschooling. I knew there was no leprosy in the Bronx, but worried about my nose falling off just the same.

The Mami monologues were thematically consistent: why I shouldn't marry a Puerto Rican; that she'd slit my throat before she'd let me marry "un cocolo"; that having children is a life-long sacrifice that causes wrinkles, gray hair and heart disease. The importance of virginity to escape the fires of hell and snag a unionized, blue-eyed husband, so if I "caught the cancer" I'd have insurance or at least leave behind a cute little blanquita grandchild for her. "If you can, you should marry a Jew, they make the best husbands. Not the ones with the curlies; the regular ones. They will even wash your pantaletas and you will never go hungry."

Mami had flirted with and charmed neighborhood Jewish merchants for years, always snagging the best price on all of her sewing supplies, especially textured and natural fabrics. "I can make something nice for your wife and you can surprise her. What size she is?" The men seldom knew. Mami always guessed the right size just from their gestures

"I am too stupid for men with brains, so I ended up with your father. You should do better so you can make your Mami proud." She got really quiet, then reached for grape jelly to spread on her *Gitana* crackers. She stage whispered how her step-sister, Altagracia, practiced evil magic rituals on children's genitals with silk cord and a Zippo lighter and made Mami watch; what it means when your turds are yellow; and that she wouldn't let me shave my legs or wear pantyhose until I had my high school degree. Never a word about why women get periods, what it means, or what to do when it happens.

When it finally did arrive, she handed me a bulky sanitary napkin, safety pins and told me "Now you could get preña, so be careful. You come to me with a belly and I will kill you, I swear to my mother, en paz descanse; te mato a tijerasos." As far as sex education, "Your husband will teach you. Cierra las patas until you marry and everything will be nice. Jesus likes young ladies, no little putas con bembas pintá y toto gasta'o. Jesus likes you to keep down there fresquesito like a little flower. Like snow." She gave me weird thoughts about Jesus and almost ruined toto for me. Had I said anything or asked a question she would have busted my lip, just in case I was blast-feeming. Next I knew she was sobbing hysterically about how her baby was now a *Señorita* and something about a rooster crowing. Stroking my wiry hair as if it were cutting her hand, she would assure me that she gave up smoking while pregnant and that my *pelo malo* came from Papi's side of the family.

The scratching of mice inside the walls of the apartment amplified in my head, their claws burrowed into the meatiest parts of my brain, slipping out on the jelly of my eyes. Everything just went away, until Mami would smack the trance out of me. When she said "te mato" I pictured a tomato, and would disappear in ways she would never know.

As Mami told stories, her unblinking eyes dragged my thoughts through crazed mobs at public hangings. We humans become sick or monsters because of a deficiency in the asking of questions, mostly for never having learned how to ask, or getting ignored (or worse) for asking. Those of us who see and feel things most people don't, spin like tops inside, and learn to count floor tiles.

FOUR/SATIN

"Now I lay me down to sleep. I pray thee Lord my soul to keep. If I should die before I wake, I pray thee Lord my soul to take."
—18th Century New England Primer

Eyeballs and hardboiled eggs suspended in glass jars everywhere. I chew on sea green marbles and shatter all of my teeth. I wake up in a cold sweat, screaming in the darkness with no sound, for fear of a beating from Mami for being "exajerá." After that first night of terror (that she noticed), Mami told me that I was born with *nervios*. According to Dr. Mami, it was a strictly female affliction.

"You will be cured when you accept Cristo as your Lord and Savior and stop being so *delicagada*. Some of Mami's cruel invented words have slipped into in my lexicon and live in the boxing ring part of my dreamworld set aside for street battle—where it's safe to fight back. According to Dr. Mami, nightmares reveal a moral deficit of unbelief. "Jesus will fix you, if you ask nice and stop being so engreída."

The terrors hung on like a pervert uncle, showing up in the dark, forcing me to look. I fought back with punches and curses into my pillow, I didn't think of asking Jesus for anything since obviously "now I lay me down to sleep..." wasn't working. I figured for *that* prayer to take you had to drop dead in your sleep. Mami warmed up some milk with honey and cinnamon. "Leche, miel y canela te quita la pena." She served it in her special second-hand English teacup, all pink roses and gold rim. Her Tía Amparo had given it to her for Christmas with a handful of Jordan Almonds wrapped in pink tulle tied with a matching ribbon. Matching things, like purses and shoes were very important to all of the women in the family. "Drink slow and don't spill. I just washed those pajamas. Drink it all; I need to sleep. Y si rompes la taza, te mato. Sueña con los angelitos." Tomato.

One time, I tried some Boo-Doo with blue food coloring and water in a glass jar. I dropped in my rubber goldfish that I'd rescued from a crate of peaches at the Hunts Point Market. He told me his name was Binx as I wiped baby dribble from his tooth-marked head. So, I reminded Binx that I had rescued him and now I needed him to rescue me. He floated belly-up in the blue water, pretending to be dead. I held my breath with him so we could both be dead. I wouldn't miss myself much, but I would miss Binx. No more talks. No more badmouthing the little fat freckled kid who, eh-hem, *lost* him at the market. No more subway rides protected in my pocket as I slipped beneath the turnstile. No more sleeping under my pillow. Binx would play dead for as long as it took.

Weeks later I threw him out of a window to see if he could fly. I have outlived him. Binx taught me to make something bad happen so that bad things could never surprise me. "It's the worrying before it happens that will kill you." Like nervios. I started biting my nails after that, until they almost disappeared. I prayed Binx would forgive me, as I hunted for hangnails, stripping skin until I could see blood and feel the sting.

FIVE/LINEN

While other toddlers picked at their Cheerios, figuring out where their mouth was, I ate plump Spanish olives and hoarded the pits. I'd steal them during family holiday parties from colorful little glass bowls on coffee tables reserved for grownup snacks. Teeth arrived early, as if my ancestral DNA knew how much I would need them to survive. The pits were my bullets and my nose was my gun. I ate the casings off my bullets first. I covered one nostril and blew out a pit from the other, always going for the fattest cockroach, because Mami said the fat ones were preña; they kept coming. They were hard to kill and even harder to impress. Mami paid the exterminator to spray poison everywhere and then made him a spiced ham sandwich and coffee. I got a beating for being asquerosa.

Everyone in our building complained about all kinds of bugs, no matter how clean and nice their apartments were. I think they came in Tarzan style on the clotheslines that ran on pulleys from outside the kitchen windows to the fire escapes. I thought everyone had mice and bugs. I didn't know expressions like "absentee landlords," "arson for profit," "redlining," "ethnic cleansing," or "urban renewal." And I didn't know about divide and conquer highways that c-sectioned the life out of poor neighborhoods. Mice and roaches were the least of it.

Saint Térése of Lisieux held her roses like a pageant queen from the top of Mami's immaculate refrigerator, staring out of the grimy window. No matter how much Mami fought it, armed with Windex and yesterday's news, she couldn't fight the soot. Not sure why Saint T was hanging around, since Mami believed saints were false idols. I'd heard that Saint T, who the older women called the Little Flower, was born wanting to be a nun and that her parents loved her and she loved Jesus. Mami loved roses; that had to be why Saint T got a pass. Before coughing herself to death, Saint T promised to spend her "time in Heaven doing good on Earth." She also said that people would know she'd been around because she would leave a rose. I loved Jesus more than T did since I wasn't doing it to pay him back for anything he did for me, or bribe him for anything to get better. It was way too late to get another mother and I was nobody's Little Flower. I was unwanted and born anyway. Stitch that on biker leather, bitches. Kid brains are wildfires. And Saints still make great action figures in my head when I pray, like St. Jude, the human torch.

My Name is Jude Not Judas

Mami's crocheted stars
spread across a table of misery
intricate webs touching point to point
unappreciated
no praise in Papi's glances
silent as Mami serves
obligatory prayer
no talk in the presence of food
too many hours stolen
from Papi's life
just to pay the butcher.
Mami thanks herself
for all the things she makes
by yanking on my braid: DON'T SPILL!

SIX/GLASS

When Mami talks about her stepsister's Boo-Doo, she mentions Orishas and calls them demonios. She says they have powers like to make lightning and that they're conceited about it. I think that if they can do magic, they have something to be conceited about, and that Mami as usual, is just jealous.

She took me to a Botánica one time because the farmacia was out of Agua Florida that she used to cure her famous headaches. She told me to hold my breath as we walked in the door and squeezed my arm to pull me close. I stretched my eyeballs as far as they would go to look at all the statues. My favorites were a Cinnamon Lady in a blue and white dress, and a Black Gentleman wearing a gold crown. The smoky air made me think of what Heaven might smell like. I only pretended to hold my breath. Mami got her Agua Florida, grabbed her change and hustled me out the door. I felt a little less alone after that; a part of me floating on a warm, turquoise sea.

Tía Amparo, Our Lady of the Jordan Almonds, had lots of colorful statues on her bedroom dressing table: olive wood, ceramic, plaster, metal, clay, jade, stone. There were seashells and pennies everywhere and lit candles burning inside little cups from all over the world. The candlelight reflected in the big round mirror; a parallel universe where my twin called to me. Her breath, seawater and cinnamon.

The one time Mami left me alone with Tía Amparo, was so she could go to the Laundromat in peace "pa' que no me fastidies." I prayed she had lots of Papi's boxer shorts. She liked to run those through twice.

I asked Tía about the statues. Her face lit up, as if I'd been the first to ask. "Well, the Seven African Powers are very important to us. They are some of the many faces of God. They are Orishas, and are represented by the saints here. Our Black ancestors from West Africa had to hide their religión after los jankees brought them here by force." I wanted Tía to know I was smart. "You mean the slaves that were chained into big boats, whipped and had to row, and had no food, no bathrooms, and no water, right?" Tía shrugged out a yes like it made her weak and too sad to imagine. "What does Orisha mean, Tía?" She leaned in to whisper. "It means supernatural. It means a being that can do things humans can't, like fly into your dreams and give you their wisdom." I loved the sound of the word, Orisha, and noticed that my mouth stayed open when I said it, like prayers were coming out on their own. Vowels are like that, consonants, not so much. My favorite words all have k's in them since I found out there's no k in the Spanish alphabet. I don't know who took it away from us, but I wish they'd put it back. Kulebra. AguaKate. CoKí. Karajo. Koño.

Or. Ree. Sha. It was still the consonants that made it sound so good. Or, is like a little prayer. Ree, feels like the slow spin of a carousel. Sha, feels like the quiet before battle. Orisha. I didn't dare say all that to Tía Amparo; I wasn't sure if it was respectful to think that way about holy words.

I found out that Cinnamon Lady and Black Gentleman from the Botánica are very famous Orishas, Yémaya and Changó. "Tía, I know them, I saw them when I went with Mami to buy her Agua Florida. They are so beautiful! I think they noticed me too!" Tía did a little happy dance with me, and then her face dropped. "Never tell your mother how you feel. Her pressure goes up when anyone talks about the Orishas. Hide them in your heart, like our ancestors hid them inside the Saints, okay?" Tía gave me a kiss on the forehead and La Bendición.

I learned that Yémaya's skirt is the foam of the sea; that she is the guardian of all waters and Mother of all children. Changó has a two-headed axe that kind of looks like Papi's second-hand meat cleavers that he got as a present from Mr. Sammy, the Kosher butcher.

Papi had really nice friends. Mami never had any for too long because mostly she scared them away, always predicting bad things would happen, like constipation or pus, or telling people the worst things that happened in the building, like "the little puta was preña and did suicidio off the roof" or "Did you hear that la jamona, Doña Fonseca got a mugging by a tecato for two dollars? She's at Lincoln Hospital." Everybody in the building knew how bad things were, they just didn't want to eat it for dinner.

Tía Amparo opened a blue bottle of *Evening in Paris* perfume and put a little on my wrist. "Now, rub them together—the heat from the friction wakes it up to smell nice. Smells good, right?" It did. It made me feel a little grown up. I closed my eyes and imagined what an evening in Paris would be like. Papi had taught me that some of his people lived in the Pyrenees. I figured it was the same as Paris. Tía slipped my hand between hers, as if to protect me. Their wrinkles settled like waves made in deserts by wind. "When you see lightening and hear thunder, never be afraid. It is Yémaya and Changó arguing about who loves you more." All the hairs on my neck became soldiers. "They know who I am?" Tía Amparo leaned in close. "Of course they do, you are a good girl and so smart. No one would believe you have only seven years in this life. I light a candle for you every night and they tell me that no matter what happens, they will protect you. Remember that."

Tía looked into my eyes as she removed the blue crystal rosary that was hiding under her soft orange blouse. "The Orishas and Saints and Angels, and every God and Goddess all work together as if they were the different parts of the same body. You see this?" The crystals sparkled. "It's so pretty." "Yes, it is, and I'm giving it to you. It is filled with many years of prayers, and I bring them all when I light my candles and pray. Each bead is a whole world of prayers, many of them for you." "Is it magic, Tía?" "Yes, that is exactly what it is. Talking to God is magic. Never let your Mami know I gave it to you. She doesn't like my religión or the different ways I talk with God." She looked at me with warning eyes. Feeling a little scared of Mami, I asked: "Do you do Boo-Doo?" Tía's eyes sparkled a little less. "Vudún is a religión from a place where your Mami was always sad. She doesn't understand, because she had a very bad teacher. Many bad teachers. All ways to talk with God are good and everyone has their own way. You'll find yours." Mami rang the doorbell. "Quick, hide the rosary in your pocket and never let your Mami see it. Never. Entiendes?" "Yes, Tía. I promise." I stumbled out of her bedroom so fast I tripped over the living room coffee table, "¡Coño!" flew hard out of my mouth, just as Mami pushed open the door. That C was as good as a K. No. It was better.

"´¡Coño! ¡Puñeta!" Mami's battle cry before washing my mouth with Ivory soap. Mine was a world of mixed messages and enforced secrecy punishable by strap or broomstick. Mami's loose grasp on reality was brought on by a hijacked childhood as a recyclable five-year-old virgin to male tourists at the Dominican-Haitian border. She could suffocate me in my sleep for a snore, then munch on her galletitas dipped in black Bustello, as she pondered how to discreetly dispose of my body. She often reminded me that Papi had access to a pizza oven at work.

Before anything, even prolicide, Mami would set her hair in pink sponge rollers, pluck her eyebrows swearing at each pull, glaring at me, like somehow that pain was my fault. When she sprayed on her green perfume, she'd point it towards my toto, making a face like I stunk. "¡Fo! Cover up that bacalao! Never leave this house looking like a cualquiera, someone will always see you, no matter where you are going or what you are doing." Nothing I wore felt right on my body, no matter how dressy, or how much I scrubbed, I always felt like the outside of the kitchen window.

Baby sounds are a highly developed and simply misunderstood global language. Given the beatific glow and profound human emotions that infants evoke, I would guess it's the language of a higher intelligence lost over time by human imprinting. When you look deeply into an infant's eyes, you know they're trying to tell you of something infinite, unimaginably beautiful. They arrive beyond the taint of words. The fragrance of their newborn heads fades over time, returns to some original, infinite source. Before infants can even grunt as they poop, some idiot parent is either squeezing a lawyer out of a cellist; beating the genius out of them, or taking orders from a fledgling narcissist.

Mami ruled with an iron chancleta. I don't think she ever understood anything I said and she hated everything I asked. "What's for dinner, Mami?" She bared the orange lipstick on her teeth. "Eat and shut up, puñeta." As much as I hated being yelled at, the sound of puñeta captivated me. Primal. Vulgar. Piercing. Forbidden. Like the K inside my Coño. Like the mysteries and secrets within the languages of infants. It isn't the sounds or words of languages that inspire or offend, but the different listenings.

> Every star will grow dim.
> Do they know?
> Death's power:
> Being known.
> New England is calling me home.
> *You will know your home by the willow tree.*

The only excerpt of any poem to survive my prolific childhood before the age of 12. Written when I was 8. Mami burned the rest, sending them down an incinerator chute. She continued to find them until I buried them deep inside, where Mami would never think to look.

EIGHT/SEAM BINDING

The dress factory. Fifteen minutes for lunch. Florescent lights flicker with nervios. Unwrapped from a paper napkin: white crackers, yellow cheese. A bummed cigarette tucked over a sagging ear. Cafecito in a red plaid thermos bought with Green Stamps. Furry pink slippers rest on a wrought iron peddle where a needle turns Quinceañera satin into rice and beans and a scrap of meat. Flowery Woolworth fabric shoes peek out from a worn leather purse. Underwear gets sucked into sweaty cracks, a rebel forces open a window, hacks out the evidence of a tired lung. Two women compare fingernails, another cuts a raspberry Danish four ways; smiles surround her.

La Sucia, as Mami calls her, tells a dirty joke that includes the dimensions and density of her husband's bicho and and how every Sunday she makes sancocho for her two sons and their "childless" wives. "One time, the boys left us for Yankee Stadium, so me and the girls hit the Barrilito hard and laughed till we pissed ourselves and dried our panties over the shower rack. Life's better without the men around." That was never true at my house. Days were longer without Papi.

Mami's doing piece work on the sneak from Papi. She can smell it on him when he owes his bookie and she'll be damned before "we have to live on the street or take the Welfare." Mami promises to slit my throat if I snitch.

The factory foreman and the Puerto Rican kid. The fifty bucks in singles in that dirty envelope could feed the kid's family for a month. His Papi dead from a seven-day work week; he became the man of the house. Accelerant. Insurance. A faceless, forgettable brown boy.

The friendships and alliances, a scorched rubble of grief. Only the stories remain. After that, Mami talked her way into a gloves factory where she got what she called her martillaso headaches. She got the hammer idea from an Excedrin commercial. Every night she grimaced and squinted and wrapped her head in a white hankie soaked in Agua Florida or Bay Rum. "If you was a good girl, I would not get these headaches. God is going to punish you." She moaned and sighed and shuffled to the kitchen in flattened chancletas.

With mortar and pestle, Mami mashed black tea leaves, valerian root, linden flowers, chamomile, and passion flowers to mix into water just before boiling; an aromatic ancestral garden. Lemon and honey crowned her necromantic concoction. (I highly recommend; it will help you sleep. Mami had skills.)

Potion in hand, she would carry herself as if dying towards the plastic upholstered teal rectangular couch. If sofas were superheroes, Mami's would be The Hulk. She commanded me with facial gestures to bring her a perfect white sheet to keep her thighs from sticking to the plastic. "Te voy a despellejar si no arreglas bien la sábana." I smoothed out the sheet like an acolyte setting the altar for Mass. Mami snorted her disapproval to remind me how I could never do anything right, and uncurled herself on the sofa to watch La Novela on the Philco that swiveled. She moaned as I turned it, until I got the angle just right.

Mami's looks of disgust always left me belly-up, bleeding in some desert, dreaming of water. She referred to telenovela heartthrobs and cowboys as her "boyfriends." Mami liked hero types. She insisted that Papi was a good for nothing who couldn't get a nail to anchor into a wall. "Mira, Hoss Cartwright, a humble, real man." She never cared much for John Wayne, "too many teeth, not enough bite," and she was sure he tried a little too hard, "puro maricón" and she hated pilgrims; until she got la religión. Mami was the original Siskel and Ebert. Middle fingers replaced thumbs. Actors were either Caca or Coco. "You see beautiful Mejicana next to John Wayne? That's Miriam Colón. Mujerota Boricua. Esa mujer es puro Coco. Ese John Wayne es pura Caca." I remember she went nuclear every time Miriam didn't get to play herself as a Puerto Rican, which was most of the time. "Why? Why? Puñeta. Why everything is Mejicanos y Cubanos? And why everything is Rita Moreno? Pendejos en Hollywoo think only one Boricua has talentos? Lemme tell you. She's no Lolita Lebrón. That's why she got money."

It was of little consolation to Mami that Dominicans didn't show up in Hollywood or TV either. "Fuck, Dominicanos. They don't wear socks." Fighting words on the street. Comedy in the living room. All Dominicans would pay the debt Mami's sex trafficking stepbrother owed her. "Wear socks, mi'ja, talk nice, go to school. No Hollywoo for you." Giving directives without snapping her belt was a way of showing affection.

Papi expressed love by putting maraschino cherries in my Coke whenever he picked me up from school and took me to the Crosstown Bar where he poured long and took bets. His code: No dogs; no bare knuckle or cock fights. To Papi, gambling was a gentlemen's sport. He'd had experience as a numbers runner for a bolitero in Harlem and he knew what it meant to owe your bookie.

Everybody trusted Papi, from cops to politicians, laborers and priests. He never took bets from women. The Crosstown was known as a men's hangout, so Papi knew that women who came in there to drink were usually desperate. Papi was known in the neighborhood as a "soft touch." When a woman slapped down money for a drink, Papi would slide it back, whispering: "Save that money for you and your baby and don't tell your husband. Is good for women to have insurance just in case. Capiche?" (Mami taught herself about that kind of insurance.) "One in the bush is better than two the gutter. Better two dollars for sure, than four dollars maybe. Come by in an hour; I make a nice pizza pie for you and the kids. No cooking tonight." (Like Mami, Papi liked to mix it up in the dichos y refranes department. My favorite was, "a bird in the hand means you should wash them.") Papi would slip a few bucks into an envelope and slip them under the pizza for the women who wore sunglasses after dark.

It was mostly a drinking place, but Papi always kept a few supplies around for the neighborhood kids who strayed in to use the toilet or try to steal cherries out of Papi's special tray. He could always tell who the hungry ones were. He'd had plenty of practice staving hunger away with cigarettes and rage when he was a kid on the streets of Sevilla. He swore to me on his mother's "virtue and eyes" that he never stole and did whatever job he could to earn a few pesetas for her and his siblings. It was fun to be with Papi. Sometimes. He was never home enough and worked long days on his feet. They were big, and flat and his toes criss-crossed over each other. He complained a lot about his bunions. For a long time I thought he hated onions and I wondered why Mami was so mean to put them in everything she cooked.

Mami was convinced that Papi's glass accidents had cursed her with three lifetimes of bad luck: the pearl framed photo of their City Hall wedding; the tipped dark amber Dominican rum bottle bleeding out on her yellow floral Korvette's throw rug; and the cracked emerald green tinted Chinese vase. About the vase. She'd splurged at Macy's on 34th Street during a big sale. "Downtown is better. They have things for people with money." The vase held plastic red roses Mami bought for herself at the jonkería store; ten for a dollar. If you wanted an even dozen, you had to buy twenty. Mami wasn't having it; ten would just have to pass for a dozen. As for my future with roses, Mami persisted like a shadchanit. "Mi'ja, marry a Jewish man. They smart, know to make money, buy their womans real flowers and don't beat them. These men are decente. They believe in God, read important books and work hard. With your father I have to buy my own flowers. ¡Borrachón huevón!"

Mami scratched her head and picked her nose for effect. Checked and re-checked her perfect, home done manicure, until she chipped it. Looked at me with a sigh of blame, as if my looking at her was some kind of ongoing curse. "Go make me some cafecito negro. This tea tastes like agua tindanga." She had made the tea, but of course its weakness was my fault, all the way back to the Yunnan Province from where it and its whore mother came. "Pero, Mami the doctor said no cafecito...your blood pressure."

Her limp, dismissive hand wave meant shut up before I smack you and break every tooth in your head, pendeja. "What does a gringo jincho jipato know about Boricuas and our coffee? They're all a bunch of bicho mongo hijos de su madre. Un bonche e' mamaó."

Mami was the very definition of contradictions. Men were limp dick thieves and mama's boy tittie suckers all. Unless, of course, they were Jewish. In the Book of Mami, to marry a Jewish business owner or doctor would be the pinnacle event of my life. It would mean a full lunch at Saks, not just coffee and a shared slice of pound cake for the chance to rest and stay out of the cold.

"Usa el cola'ol." El cola'ol was this old-school coffee filter that looked like a dirty gym sock hanging from a metal ring on a wooden handle. I could never figure it out, terrified that I would ruin Mami's café. The old grounds stains wouldn't wash out no matter how hard I scrubbed. The one time I used bleach Mami chased me and beat me with a broom screaming that I was trying to murder her. This time, after handing her the cup, terrified of spilling, I sat watching with a fisheye, awaiting her verdict for twenty minutes; her unblinking eyes never left the television screen, even when she pulled the raging red nail polish bottle out from under the sofa cushion. The coffee sat, staining the green melamine cup. Finally, she threw a chancleta at me for serving cold coffee. "¡Idiota!" I had not yet learned how to keep coffee warm by sheer will.

I did learn to use el cola'ol, though. Heat the milk, add sugar and you're back on a balcón rocking in a cane bottom chair, grateful for the salted air and sun. Sipping untold histories, especially the ones with blood on their roots. El cafecito offers a few moments of relief and remembrance; warming the heart. Boricuas make the best Baristas, without machines.

NINE/MUSLIN

"Mami, were there any Puerto Ricans at the Last Supper?" "Yes. They did all the cooking and cleaned out the escupideras." Mami shook like a wet cat. "Always with the stupid questions, sangana."

Mami didn't like questions that made her think about being Puerto Rican. She wanted people to believe she was from Spain. "But not like your father. Like a real Spaniard with good hair." I thought about those spittoons at the Last supper. I asked her why the word for exploited sounded like the word for exploded. I asked her how come Jesus was white. I asked her if they had coquito and pasteles at the Last Supper since the Puerto Ricans were cooking and how come we weren't in any of the paintings and how come Jesus didn't do Palm Sunday in Puerto Rico where all the best palms are. "¡Señor te reprenda! Leave these things to the adults. For what all these questions? They won't get you a husband. All that matters about the Last Supper is that Jesus died on the cross so that people could go to Heaven." "So, is there really a Hell too?" "Por supuesto, because Eva was a puta and she spoiled everything for her poor husband. You will find out too late where is the real Hell if you don't obey Jesus now."

My seven-year-old brain was spinning, and I forgot what I was asking in the first place. I thought about how Mr. Spitoon was always ready for the worst. Puke, plagues, pandemics and parasites. Mr. Spitoon and I didn't talk much or have much in common. He wanted it all to come out, and I had to make it all stay in.

I was sad that Jesus died for me. A little angry too. I wanted to die for myself. The calendar from Mr. Rosario's liquor store had a picture of Jesus wearing a crown of thorns and all streaked in blood, like window grime. If you tilted it just right Jesus's eyes would open and close. He was pretty skinny and had pelo bueno. I thought he was supposed to be a Black man since we learned in Sunday School that his hair was "like wool." Papi's face was white but he had hair like wool too. I wondered if Jesus had been drinking a lot at the Last Supper like Papi, to feel better?

Did all the Puerto Rican servants at the Last Supper go to Heaven? Does anybody know their names? I had to memorize all the names of the Apostles for Sunday school and all the names of the Bible Books. My favorite book name was Doo-Doo something. "Mami, do Puerto Ricans get special names in Heaven, like Señor Pagán el Piragüero or Doña Elba the Lunch Lady who got fired for giving out extra chocolate milk in the school cafeteria?" They both were really important on our block, cooling us down on hot days and trying to keep our bones strong. That's important work and I don't know why people don't know that and why they don't give them special names for all the hours they work standing and taking orders, and obeying Jesus, like Papi in those kitchens so steamy and hot that sometimes his eyes hurt.

How come people who make lots of money get awards for just doing their job, like business big shots, mayors and movie stars? The person who has to scrape gum off of school floor tiles should get an award. The people who sell hot dogs and beer and soda at Yankee Stadium in the hot sun should get awards. Soldiers get awards, but all the best stuff shows up after they're dead. Like my cousin Joe who taught me hoola hoop and bought me pistachio ice cream. His eyes exploded from their sockets and I hope they're rolling on the moon taking memory pictures for his ghost. He loved the moon. Every time I jump rope I think of his tripas.

I have all my questions written down on loose leaf, folded up in a shoebox with socks on top so no one knows. So many questions and no one to ask without getting into trouble. I don't want to forget them because I know some day I'll get the chance to ask them without getting punished. I ask them after prayers and ask the people who live on other planets to please come down and talk with me. I promise not to snitch on them and that they should make themselves invisible. The Earth isn't safe for visitors.

Children know and sing things into being that only they can hear and see since they're born intuitive particle physicists. If they were all encouraged, we'd be time traveling and healing our own bodies from disease by now, and those tools wouldn't be just for the rich. "Mami, if matter cannot be created or destroyed, how come we're born and die?" Smack. Mami, the human fly swatter. "Go make some chocolate milk for yourself." Without adults to tell them that what they think is important and good, the depth of what children know can make them feel desperately alone. Or worse; their minds and bodies become the burial ground of their most essential self.

Firefly

tiny lantern of the night
let me crawl the tall grass
gently in light
see how you dress
in search of love;
wear your shadow face
in daylight
please help me find mine
so I too might keep safely
out of sight

Difficult for most to conceive how a five year-old might cut herself just to be sure she's real and not something imagining itself that can't imagine itself because it isn't. Matter not created. Matter not destroyed. I never stopped asking and braced myself for the beatings. "Is that where God lives, Mami, in the things that are but cannot be known? Is God the light inside a firefly? You know Mami, the beautiful luciérnaga." Silence. "Qué carajo are you talking about? You need to think about school and get an education, no be thinking about boberías." I pull up some courage from my quivering stomach. "Pero Mami, I just want to know if God is in the middle of all matter, or, in the space of not here, not there?" I fell into an existential abyss muttering to the heavens that seldom went beyond the ceiling.

It began before I got to grade school. These ancient thoughts were drowning my child mind without anything or anyone to hold onto. Suicidal ideation took place in the bathtub with a razor blade, in the kitchen with oil and matches, on downward glances from fire escapes, by the medicine cabinet, iodine bottle in my hand, in the smell and hanging length of leather belts, in the knotting of bed sheets, on subway platforms— jumping onto the tracks, falling through, believing in a soft landing on the featherbed of another world, a different time. A place with fruit trees where children were loved. Where they could speak endlessly, and be heard. Where they could shamelessly sing their invented songs and dances. I had yet to see that place, but I knew it was somewhere between worlds, between what is and what isn't. On the mystical sides of walls and ceilings. On walks with Mami I stepped hard on cracks and wished for my freedom as she yanked me by the arm into docility. Invisible telegrams passed between my brain and feet. Slow down. Stop. Shut up. Stop. Disappear.

The adults around me cringed and wondered if such a mind (and I revealed little of it to them) was controlled by something evil. In between Mami's café carajo and bendito sea guava con queso, the hard slaps came. Mami's tiny fist slipped into the brass knuckles of malos recuerdos; memories that clung to her, like emasculated men desperate over lost power, cannibalizing innocence in some deeply perverse baptism, diving into her flesh. Mami dove into mine, driving away "demonios" and silencing possibilities. To Mami, memories, and those big questions from her little nothing daughter, seemed like a wet foot on the third rail. Who did I think I was? If God were forgiving, well then, perhaps I could become the wife of a clean house with red peppers in the garden and white gardenias in green window boxes. Mami had no clue what it takes to grow gardenias, nor the price of a too clean house, which she paid daily. Her analysis of society: "Only God is good." The only commitment to our bodies, to "keep it clean, especially downstairs, you ears, your sobaco and the back of your neck."

TEN/NYLON

The first time I sewed by hand I was five. Titi Angela taught me how to use a thimble. I wanted to stitch the little square of blue cotton all around but was running out of thread. I was sure that if I just sewed faster, the thread would last. Miss Thimble betrayed me and I cried so much from the sting that Titi gave me ice cream and Mami gave me a dirty look. At five, Mami's body had been for rent on the Dominican-Haitian border. Capitalist imperialism, the father of her castrated familial pimp. ¿Qué carajo did I have to cry about?

The lemon yellow oil painted kitchen walls matched the dishes. Bubble gum pink matte bedroom matched the "Hollywoo" stuffed vinyl headboard. Retiree beige living room to match everything. White bathroom to reflect light and expose dirt wherever it would try to hide. The assimilated hues of my 1950s world. The matching of colors and mixing of prints. An American dream palette of the only paint we could afford; El Super's sloppy leftovers for the price of a shot of rum and a high-end Dominican cigar. Inside that prison of seething and muffled screams, I ate my way through the rooster sugar bowl. Just like a rooster, I lived to breach into one more day. Staring into the white medicine cabinet mirror, I learned to hate the words *beautiful* and *blanquita*.

My favorite spot was the cool, marble hexagon-tiled bathroom floor, where I'd press my skin in the middle of steamy summer nights to survive the torpid air. My naked belly temporarily tattooed with a blank periodic table. Table fans were no match for the sad heaviness of asphalt exhalations. I imagined how Mami would react if she found me face down dead in a pool of my anemic blood. The thought of her gritos y mocos and all the sympathy she would get pumped my will to live.

Secretly, I resented Papi for marrying Mami. No. I hated him for it. I thought he was stupid and cruel to stay with her and then say he did it for me. I did the shotgun wedding math, but that would have meant it took me ten months to kick my way out of Mami. While snooping through

Papi's bureau drawer, as if it would help me know him better (sometimes it did) I found a photograph. He was sitting shirtless beneath a tree, and my Titi Angela, Mami's sister in bathing suit, their arms touching. Their usually sad faces were lit from the inside.

Titi's daughter, who thrives on the misery of others with that "just kidding" smirk that often comes with cruelty, told me her version of the story of how Mami and Papi met in the Catskills resorts of the Spanish and Puerto Rican Diasporas, known as *Las Villas*, in Plattekill, New York. It was the Cuchifrito counterpart to the Borscht Belt. Too little has been documented of that magical place.

Papi was the cook at Villa Madrid, the poorest of all the Villas, with its rusty swings and beautiful apple orchards. The weekly price was right for the working poor and included meals. Papi was friends with my Titi Angela, who was married. According to Titi's daughter, Papi was in love with her mother and married mine just to be close to Angela, who I do believe was the love of his life. *Like Water for Café Con Leche*, (all respect to Laura Esquivel) romantic and heartbreaking all at once. Toxic Cousin thought it would hurt me; but in fact it made me happy to know that Papi had known real love.

Mami, being one of thirteen children, was the one whose birth would end the life of my grandmother; guilt from which she never recovered. All of the children were parceled out; Mami ended up on the Dominican Haitian border, and Titi Angela was sent to distant relatives in Caracas, Venezuela. They didn't know of each other's existence. Both of them were sewing factory workers who took vacations at Las Villas, and that was how Papi got to know Angela, her husband, and three children. One summer the sisters both happened to be at the Villa Madrid at the same time. Papi, always the picaro coqueto, got to know the guests—his charming stories brought in bigger tips at the end of their stays. After speaking with Mami and getting to know her a bit, he realized that she was Angela's sister. It was Papi who introduced Mami to her sister. I used to fantasize that Angela was my true mother. Mami lived in Titi's shadow, and grew to hate the sight of me, as my face looked more and more like Papi's.

ELEVEN/DOTS

One morning I woke up to a baby grackle on the bathroom windowsill. She couldn't fly so I made her a bed out of one of Mami's cardboard shoeboxes and an old dishrag, snuggling it next to the hamper. Even Mami looked like she felt bad for the little creature looking so helpless and trapped, but it was Papi who let me keep her. I fed her water with one of my doll's tiny baby bottles, and I mashed up some sunflower seeds, carefully taking each one out of its salted shell and rinsing it. Lucky for my new feather baby that sunflower seeds were a big time snack in my neighborhood. They were cheap and cracking open those shells was a good release for those of us with undiagnosed or untreated anxieties and OCD that had nowhere to go beyond the sugar bowl or a nickel deck.

When I was at school all I could think about was how bad I felt leaving my little friend with Mami, who had made it clear it was my job to take care of her. "You want to get sick from birds, go ahead. Your Papi es un alcagüete. Every time I use the toilet that pendeja bird is making all these pio-pio sounds. Never any peace in this house, carajo." As soon as I'd get home from school, I'd go to Pio-Pio. I felt like that was what she named herself, and that's something everyone should have the right to do. Mami had no idea that Pio-Pio was introducing herself. On the second day, I showed Pio-Pio with my hands how to move her wings. I did it over and over with the patience of abuelas praying novenas. On the third day, Pio-Pio flapped her tiny wings, unable to go anywhere. On the fourth day, Pio-Pio was able to fly over the top of the box and onto the floor. I put her back into the box and we kept practicing to the sound of Mami's "Nena loca. Dios me libre, coño."

By Friday, Pio-Pio flew out of the box and landed on my head. I gently put her in my hand and we looked at each other for what felt like hours. I knew that Pio-Pio would soon be able to fly and I shut the bathroom window all the way. I had to be sure she was strong enough before she took her flight. I was so excited to see Pio-Pio on Saturday morning for her flying lesson. I walked into the bathroom and the window was open all the way. I ran to my mother and looked at her, wishing she would just die right then and there. Papi was still sleeping from a double shift, his snoring seeped through the bedroom door.

"What happened to Pio -Pio?" Mami looked away. I always knew when she was lying. "She fly away." My heart went somewhere without water. "Why did you open the window? She wasn't ready." Mami wiped her hands on a dishtowel. "Are you a bird? What do you know about it? Birds fly, is what they do. For what do you go to school, bruta?" There was a single feather on the windowsill. All I could do was pray like a priest at a crime scene that Pio-Pio made it when Mami threw her out the window. I knew that's what she did. Mami hated her. Thought she was dirty and full of germs. She probably wore her big yellow Playtex gloves to do it. Mami hated how Pio-Pio sounded, how she took all of my attention. How Papi let me have my way.

I would remember for the rest of my life that I had taught Pio-Pio to fly. Did I teach her well? Did I feed her the right things? Did she run out of breath and free fall where one of the half starved alley cats finished her off? Did she know I loved her? Did she care? Do birds have souls? Does anyone?

I startle awake sometimes, when Pio-Pio visits my dream world, her wings torn off at the stem, Mami's hands pushing through in their place. On those days I do too much and accomplish little.

TWELVE/COIN

Shaming. Always. Every day. Relentless. Whatever it took to keep my vagina in a state of perpetual prayer, like a tiny pinched-face nun. Wetting the bed, a sign of moral weakness. Not only did Mami threaten to sew shut my toto, but that she'd sew up my mouth so I couldn't cry about it. "¡Cochina! Use the toilet like a human being, carajo!" She shoved my face into the wet mattress. Said if I behaved like a dog she'd treat me like one. "You born trouble; three days to shit you out. You almost killed me with your patadas." And what the hell was wrong with me and all those questions, like if God is so forgiving then why didn't he forgive Adam and Eve? Mami assured me I was unforgivable, even to God.

Sold
Soliders and tourists circle
the marketplace
little girls painted
in colors of sex
one shifts from foot to foot
no panties
beneath ruffles
and talcum
stares at a lost penny
terrified to bend
dreams of bread
of never again hearing
the calling of her name
that is no name:
Nena linda.
Sweet Cakes.
Bonita.
Schätzchen
Mija.

THIRTEEN/GOSSAMER

Mami's brother was a minister, the nuanced weaponized scripture kind. Always locked and loaded, silencer on the barrel. In a poor family with low literacy and few professionals, even a self-appointed minister is like having a Ph.D. Well, I thought he'd slap me left-to-right too, for questioning God's ways. Instead he laughed and told me I'd make a good lawyer. Papi called him *El Reverendo*, but not out of respect; more like that was his huckster name. Convinced my uncle was a raquetero, Papi said he'd go to church only if he could be in charge of passing the basket. Papi threw back some Dominican rum and told El Reverendo I had a big head because I had "lots of brains and a big mouth for a healthy appetite, and a good vocabulario."

That was one of the few times I'd heard Papi brag about me that wasn't about me being "pretty" "beautiful" or fruit cup "nice." The subtext translated into my being a big headed, fat assed know-it-all, but it was better than nothing, and ten times better than "beautiful." The Sea is beautiful, but that's not all she is.

Papi looked at El Reverendo up and down and sideways. "Mi'ja is like her Papi, she doesn't like raqueteros either." I didn't think that Tío was a raquetero, more like the circus guy with the top hat, just trying to make people happy, pay attention to what's in front of them and believe in what wasn't. Papi meant well, but he put so many words in my mouth there was no room for my own. Papi stared Tío down with a bulldog tilt that looks like you're about to throw a punch. "God doesn't like people cashing in on his name. I think you should get a real job."

Sizing up El Reverendo, Papi formed a finger gun saying in all seriousness: "You look like a German with those blue eyes and movie star looks; you could get some real work a lot easier than the rest of us." Chamber roll. Click. "You make Billy Graham look like a jamona." Click. Click. Click. El Reverendo would mumble some exorcism in tongues so that Papi's liquor wouldn't take any more effect. I could tell he mostly missed

or ignored Papi's insults and liked the compliment, that in El Reverendo's world, bordered on flirtation. Televangelist Billy Graham was El
Reverendo's hero and all unmarried blancas in the family, even the "no
church, never" ones, said he could put his shoes under their bed anytime.
He glanced in Mami's oversized beveled living room mirror; his vanity
formed a dimple. When vanity or perfectionism struck in my family, it distracted you for life. I should have bought stock in spray starch, pomade,
and false humility.

El Reverendo had mumbo jumbo prayers to kill any joy in life. He
could decaffeinate your coffee, kill sexual desire with gibberish about the
eyes of God burning into every secret, drown healthy lust in the "Blood
of the Lamb" and call on Mary Magdalene to make you surrender your
vibrator to Jesus, only he'd called it something else, like "a demon's trick-
ery of Lust." Sins were always CAPITALIZED on cheery, colorful Sunday School posters. They were tacked down in the bathrooms right in our
sightline from the toilet. Pride. Greed. Wrath. Envy. Lust. Gluttony. Sloth.
El Reverendo never prayed the fat out of pork though, he chomped on
that cloven hoofed mud slinger down to the grizzle. "Pigs are very clean
and intelligent creatures of God." I had to wonder why I never saw them
in pictures of Noah's Ark.

There's nothing like witnessing a blast of selective sanctity to send you
running into the arms of the first fallen angel you meet. At least with them,
you know what you're getting. There would be a legion coming my way.

This Mami's "palomita blanquita" got chicken skin at the thought of
the Prince of Darkness, wondering what it was he did so wrong that God
couldn't find it in his heart to forgive him. I wrote a poem in his defense.
Prince of Darkness; I've written him poems. Love letters. Cards. He's the
reason I started shoplifting lipsticks when Mami lingered at the Blooming-
dale's makeup counter after her free makeover. She got one every Saturday, and never bought a thing. The price of a fancy lipstick was a bag
of groceries. The women never turned her down; Mami was so naturally glamorous, it was free advertising for the store. Not to mention that
Mami was kind of a wingman for the make-up ladies. When all 4'11" of
her curvy 90 pounds was in that chair, those upscale male browsers suddenly had shopping urges and flocked to the counter. The store should
have given Mami a commission. Her size four feet in heels and perfect
legs, wavy, thick chestnut hair and heart-shaped mouth were chicken on

the bone to the wolves in silk ties. Lipsticks, lotions and perfumes kept the register singing. Mami missed it all, with her closed eyes and surrender to the hands of her Saturday angels. "Mami look good, right?" "Yes, Mami. Like a Queen." I meant like on a deck of cards, since those were the only pretty queens I knew about. The ones we learned about in school were on the pale side and wore fancy clown wigs.

The security guards guiltily eyeballed Mami and her homemade, over-sized, roses embroidered black canvas tote bag. Wink and nod. Did they know she would never steal, or was her beauty bribe enough? I was invisible. Sometimes I wished that Helena Rubinstein was my mother, so I could always look and smell good should the Prince of Darkness ever visit. A Prince is a Prince. I stole a lipstick once I could reach the counter and hid it in my shoebox of secrets, questions and treasures beneath the socks. I painted my lips in the bathroom when I made number two, the only time I was ever out of Mami's sightline. I cleaned off my lips and timed it with flushing, so I could keep it on long enough to feel just a little bit pretty. Pretty for myself, not daughter pretty. I stayed in there so long Mami was convinced I was chronically constipated, so rectal suppository laxatives became a weekly ritual. I screamed my head off every time. Big price for a little privacy and mirror magic.

When El Reverendo had snuck some church wine (the congregants got grape juice) or Papi's rum, he'd pop some peppermint Chiclets, and get all romantic about Jesus and the Prophets. (I thought they would make a good Motown group.) He'd say things like "the Word of God was the only salt anybody needs, and Mary the only sweetness." He'd dance some fake flamenco clapping out Amén y Amén. Aleluya. Espíritu Santo, trying to win over his Xitano brother-in-law. Chapter. Verse. Finger snaps. Head bowed. A fancy turn or two. Hands to the sky, then another sip to bless Papi and pray for his soul. El Reverendo had the fear of God and wanted to make sure everyone else caught it. I could see cartoons over his head of whatever he was thinking. Some version of synesthesia not quite on the books yet. Most kids have it; unfortunately, they outgrow it. Bullshit meters slow down with age; buried alive in the grave of politeness. "¡Amén y olé!" Papi clapped, happy to see that El Reverendo's fever of fear did not keep him from dancing. His feet seemed to stamp out Klutz! Klutz! Klutz!

The way El Reverendo talked about the sixteen-year-old Virgin Mary made him sound like a lickspittle. He made sure we understood he didn't worship Mary. No "false idols," no corpus on the cross. No Saints, no Orishas. "What do you think of a religion where priests kill Christ over and over again on a daily basis and makes children look at the bloody corpse and then eat his body? Or a religion where you allow spirits of the dead into your body?" Papi wasn't offended since he liked God but "shit on religion." Any religion.

El Reverendo reminded me of cartoon missionaries and those big bellied white guys going on safari to hunt animals for heads they could have stuffed and displayed over their leather chairs. Sick cartoons that adults let kids watch, where Africans with bones through their noses cooked up those doughy white guys in pith helmets. Lots of people still think that Africa is a country and all Black Africans live in jungles. Disney seems to think reparations for the contamination of children's brains with racist crap is casting a white Puerto Rican as a Brit in Mary Poppins. Walt is probably spinning in his grave, but I'm not sure for which reason or in what direction.

Papi liked to grunt and make the sign of the cross and kiss his thumb like it was Jesus, just to drive El Reverendo nuts and remind him he was dealing with a Xitano, not one of Franco's Semana Santa sycophants. On his own since he was eight, Papi had his own religión and commandments. "Never lie. Never steal. Be a person of your word; your honor is all you have. Pick up the check when you can. Oh, and never drink white wine unless you run out of red." Papi didn't bow his head for anybody. Especially for some hustler in-law on the take, selling heavenly artillery to the earthbound powerless. Papi uttered "cabrón" like I was deaf and I knew in that moment that El Reverendo was still alive only because he was my mother's brother, occasionally entertaining and mostly because he was my Tío. For Papi, crooks and hypocrites were a cancer to be cut out at the root. "It should look like an accident."

FOURTEEN/SCALPEL

School made me think that maybe I was cancer. Teachers were saddled with at least forty kids per class and no support staff. The only way we could get attention from our beleaguered teachers was to be troublemakers or pets. I chose Teacher's Pet (a title that belongs in the shredder) so I could sit close to the front, making it a little more difficult for my sworn enemies to stab me with the sharp end of the compass or put well-soaked wads of pink Bazooka Joe's bubblegum in my "Brillo" hair. (Did anyone ever wonder why a kid with an eye patch was named after a rocket launcher?)

The raunchy soup of tenement kids (getting hot water from broken down boilers was a crap shoot); the filthy industrial school mops that moved grime from one room to another; piss warm rusty water from hallway drinking fountains, and open, unscreened windows that allowed horse flies to bite our tender skin as diesel fumes from the Bruckner Expressway settled in our lungs. Circumstances of neglect conspired to send the message that we were just part of the garbage and decrepitude that tried to bury us. By the time I was in Fifth Grade, Moses had completed the Cross Bronx Expressway that finished nailing the Bronx to the Cross with Jésus. El Reverendo explained to me that this was a different Moses, not the Charlton Heston one.

My fifth grade teacher referred to herself as Dr. T. (l wish to spare her descendants) and was a concert pianist. Perched on her desk, she crossed one pterodactyl leg over the other, hiked up her skirt, and lit one cigarette with the next. She referred to us as "shocking human beings" and taught us songs in French, hoping to "civilize" us. She pounded longitude and latitude lessons into us, insisting that like her, we should go on safari in Africa and get out and see the world. "If you should choose to not remain idiots and barbarians, longitude and latitude will allow you to always know exactly where you are standing in the world. If you are not a citizen of the world, you are a stranger everywhere." That last bite stayed with me; something in me knew she was right on that one. I decided right then and there that I would be a citizen of the world some day.

Sitting closest to Dr. T., I had a year of Chesterfield smoke blown into my face. Her hanging nylon slip, visible long-legged girdle and urine fumes made it exceptionally hard to concentrate. Her abuse had been normalized in a school where the culture was to look in the opposite direction of adult infractions. Dr. T.'s lessons were peppered with stories of the "African savages" who "with their bare hands and spears" hunted the leopard for the coat she wore indoors, even in hot weather. Aside from the lyrics of J'et Deaux Amours, schoolyard fights, finding Tahiti by coordinates, and Dr. T.'s daily admonitions to "go sit in the toilet and rot," I recall little else of that 10th year of my life, beyond President Kennedy's brains all over the First Lady's pink Chanel suit.

With rare exceptions, like my second grade teacher—red headed, freckle-faced, Mrs. McGreevy—who understood that a kid who carries around Ralph Waldo Emerson's essays and can, through her Puerto Rican accent, stutter, and lisp, explain some of his basic concepts, was exceptional. My reward? The seat closest to her desk and mob-like protection from bullies. Good thing too; Diana Rosario, relegated to the back of the room for swearing and touching boy's penises, had threatened to kick my ass if I didn't smoke cigarettes with her after school.

An ass kicking from Diana would have been a Saturday stroll compared to what my parents would do if they even sniffed a hint of nicotine on my breath. My father, smoking since age five, would give me the silent treatment. My mother had given up smoking when she was pregnant with me and she'd be damned some little "putita" was going to contaminate her virginal little muñequita. She'd take the strap to us both. It was almost worth the risk to see that little bully bitch get it worse than me. Mami would shred her like Lung Fung's Chino-Cubano 8th Avenue kitchen shredded their beef. (If you've never eaten Ropa Vieja Cuban style, you haven't lived).

Most of my teachers, even the best of them, seemed to think that the classroom Siberia of the last row would somehow shame or deter the perpetrators out of their "disgusting" behavior. They were quieter, since they were able to keep themselves fully occupied tormenting other residents of Siberia beyond detection. Or like Diana, who had a much easier time of touching boys' dicks in the last row. The ostrich principle ruled when teachers had hit the wall and didn't know if the tires would still be on their cars at the end of the day.

Administrators and my parents knew about Dr. T. and her shortcomings, but like physicians, teachers were revered in my family. Especially ones who spoke French. It was common in the 1950s for parents to tell their children some version of "your teacher is your mother when you're in school. You must respect her." Besides, what would my father, who soaked, froze, and defrosted DaNoble cigars in cognac to smoke in my face, have to say? Unconditional obedience to adults was expected in our family and any deviation from the protocol was punished, often with undue severity. "Do as I say, not as I do." The Gospel According to Papi.

I nearly had a nervous breakdown the one time Dr. T. put me out of the classroom and left me standing in the hallway for at least an hour because the kid sitting next to me was talking. Apparently, I was listening to him, the only white boy in class, instead of to her. He was the "shocking human being" but I was the one left out to "rot." Fortunately, it never got back to my mother (the doppelgänger of Torquemada) and that day I found religion. Like the great mystics, Jesus would become my boyfriend and at the end of the day, he would listen to all my troubles; the daddy pimp to whom I would promise anything. Of course, I muffled my voice with a pillow so no one would hear. The complaints of a child were considered nothing more than insubordination and speaking aloud in an empty room just the excuse needed to institutionalize an inconvenient and annoyingly inquisitive rebel. I wondered if Dr. T. had really been a concert pianist. I could see where her knotted up fingers could make her really sad. Not sure about the mean part, though.

Why I'm a Night Owl

Unkind mornings.
Papi to his coffee.
Mami to her stove.
Me to a school
that feels like a hole.
No kisses.
No hugs.
No "good morning."
No bacon.
No love.

FIFTEEN/FRINGE

Papi, Xitano to the core, had his own thing for La Vírgen Moreneta. A Black Madonna of the Andalusian Roma, who married virgins, but hid their stashes of porn, like Papi. Sí, I found it. A stack of "Flirt" magazines with black and white images of corseted bottle blondes, endless legs in seamed stockings with lace garters and over-the-shoulder seductions. Mami let Papi have one drawer in the oak dresser she lemon oiled every Saturday. I stealthily avoided beatings for both me and Papi. Porn in those days was like ads for Victoria's Secret today. Gimme a break Papi, what's the big deal? If you like blondes so much you should have married one. One of 10,000 things I wanted to say to my father and didn't. And sí, Mami would have beat him with a broom handle and reported him to whomever would listen. One more secret to keep, no matter how tempting it was to blurt out in school bathroom gossip sessions in between fart humiliations and fist fights.

On most of our hooky days, Papi would call the school and tell them I had a fever. First he'd touch my head and convince me I had one, so that I'd never peg him as a liar. He would insist we head to the New York Eye and Ear Infirmary down on 14th Street. We'd head for the #6 train, at our Hunts Point station, where Papi could get me to sneak beneath the turnstile until I was twelve. We'd ride all the way to Union Square where I would miraculously recover and we'd switch over to the #4 South Ferry express train that took us all the way to the southern tip of Manhattan. First we'd walk through Battery Park and pay our respects to all the WWII soldiers who didn't have flat feet. Papi said it was the only war that did more than just make rich white men richer. "It was the war that took down that sonuvumbiche Hitler and his boyfriend, Mussolini. Hitler's mother should have slit his throat in the womb. Flushed him down the toilet. Evil is not ready to live." Papi's proverbs didn't always make sense, but they were cinematic for sure. "Franco and Perón should get married and kill each other on the honeymoon. Now that would be an opera!" Papi talked about how we should invite his dear friend Mr. Lipschitz to come downtown with us sometime. "It is too much pain for him to be on the train for such a long ride, mi'ja. Your Papi will pay for a taxi for him, what do you think?" "I think that's great, Papi! I love Mr. Lipschitz!" I knew that meant Papi would have to work extra hard.

I loved Papi so much, especially when he said kind things. "Mr. Lipschitz still might not come. He cannot walk so much and he is always in pain. It is much worse than your Papi's juanetes." I looked down at Papi's canvas shoes, worn thin where his bunions exhaled. "Juanetes hate shoes," Papi said. I think Juan Etes was the guy bunions were named after. Papi talked up at the sky. "A taxi could be painful too, especially going over all the sonovumbiche potholes. They only fix streets in the comemierda neighborhoods where the fancy poodles make their caca and the servants have to pick it up." It was as if he was sending God a message about sleeping on the job. "Mr. Lipchitz is a good man with bad luck. A very good man, mi'ja. Decente." He said "decente" like he was telling God that he could try and be a little more decente himself. To Papi, being decente meant you were honest. That you helped people in need. It meant you told the truth no matter what it cost you, and that you never stole from anyone. Oh yeah, and for girls stay a virgin and for boys do what comes "natural" but don't make babies with bad girls. "Even if Mr. Lipschitz can't be with us, we invite him, okay, mi'ja? So he knows we are thinking of him." I wondered if God ever really listened to anybody who didn't own a poodle.

I asked Papi if all his friends from the Crosstown Bar were decente. "There's different kinds of decente. Every man must find his own meaning. My friends are good to me. I judge people by who they are to me, not who they are to someone else." I was confused. "But Papi, Hitler never did anything to you. Would you think he was decente?" Papi sighed and his eyes looked into the distance for what felt like ten years. He returned to look me dead in the eyes: "A crook will steal because he has to. A thief will steal because he wants to. Hitler's mouth was a shovel that unburied what is most evil in humanity. He and all his paisanos were the thieves of souls. These sonuvumbiches had children and grandchildren who still walk the earth. Think of all the aunts and uncles, nieces, nephews, cousins." I wondered if Papi thought El

Reverendo was a Nazi. "They could be anywhere and anyone."

Papi pointed with his lips to the tiny gold amulets around my neck: a cross with diamond chips in place of Jesus; a medal of La Virgen del Rocío; and a cornicello from one of Papi's Silicilan friends who hated Mussolini as much as he did, to ward off the malocchio. I wanted to keep it short but had to ask. "So is El Reverendo a thief or a crook?" Papi laughed and leaned in so I could hear over a fog horn. "Let's just say, since he's family, that he's a little of both. You are smarter than your Papi and that deserves a corned beef sandwich with a pickle." I knew that meant going for a ride on the Staten Island Ferry. There was nothing better in the world. My heart beat so fast, I almost couldn't breathe. The debate could wait.

Papi loved open waters and every kind of boat. His juanetes seemed to stop hurting and he walked happier. Real Irish corned beef was our Holy Communion. I prayed to Jesus for French fries this time. Suddenly the vowel cooing pigeons and consonant scarring gulls turned up the volume. Cars honked, and vendors hawked. My hand, safe inside of Papi's, I walked with my eyes closed, as my brain invented lyrics to go with the sounds. I'd open my eyes and imagine what kind of songs the people around us had inside their heads.

There was an old Irish pub walking distance from Battery Park, where Papi and I were monthly regulars. Papi used the pay phone there to call Mami and tell her we'd be home late. She knew about our hooky days, but never talked about it. Papi and me being happy made her miserable.

We only had to buy one sandwich at the pub because they would put so much meat on it for us, and throw in two pickles with extra napkins. Papi was a big shot because he was a good storyteller and left good tips. The sandwich was wrapped in wax paper and went into a brown paper bag. No French fries—no Jesus. I was done with him, at least for a fifteen-minute grudge. For kids, that's a big grudge. I held onto the bag with one hand and to Papi with the other.

The heft in that paper bag heralded a few rides back and forth on the ferry; fresh air on my face and my hair wild, shameless. Mami's industrial strength comb, nowhere in sight. I would pay dearly for surrendering to the wind; it was always worth it. Waving good-bye to Manhattan, locking eyes with snippy seagulls, and feeling the warmth of Papi's wool coat protecting me from the cold, was worth Mami yanking through "ese pelo malo" because it always meant I'd had un día bueno. We'd wait to eat the sandwich on the last ride back, to make it all last, like that last tiny salt rock on a pretzel. Papi kept my Yoo-Hoo drink next to his beer can in his big coat pocket, so they'd keep each other nice and cold.

Dream: February 1, 1998

I am in the South Side of Chicago. I am walking towards some desolate, fenced-in factory towers. I understand that these towers are where "art" is made. All art, including conceptualizations of art. A car with fins pulls up; in it is my lover, Al Pacino. He is a blue collar worker; not in character; not famous. I get in the car. As usual with my lovers in dreams, and in life, he is distracted. Distant. I tell him it is time for us to get married. He says "we'll never get married" because he's "a gambler and alcoholic." I tell him I will ignore those things and take the good days we have together. I tell him life is never perfect. Life is short; no time to fix it. He will work in the towers of art and we will have some happy moments together. It will be enough. I wake up in a sweat.

After riding the ferry three times each way, and eating our corned beef on seeded rye with pickles, we made our way back to the pub. "Papi, do you think the Statue of Liberty can see us? She feels so real." Papi smiled and frowned at once. I think sometimes he worried that I wasn't right in the head. "Yes, I think she can, but only in the dark when the government crooks aren't looking. In darkness her torch is at its best." Papi hated the government. "Can the crooks see us, Papi?" He squeezed my hand. "Remember when I took you to the top of the Empire State Building and all the people looked like ants?" "Uh, huh. But I knew they weren't ants, Papi, they were people just like us. To God we must be invisible. But I guess that's fair, since God is invisible to us." Papi pinched the tip of my nose. "Ay, mi nenita! You are not only smarter than your Papi, you are smarter than the government. God can still see us, even when we're invisible, but the crooks, they think they are higher than God, so they don't see us at all." I didn't really understand what Papi said, but it felt right. Like the docking of the ferry against the pier. It didn't always look right, but it always worked. I could feel my heart dip when the ferry gate opened and it was time to make our way home.

Papi bought me a ginger ale at the bar, asked for extra cherries on the side, and threw back a few Blue Ribbons and whiskey shots. He thanked the bartender for how lean the corned beef was and scored an extra pull on on the tap. They wisecracked and the bartender, who Papi called "Irish" like it was his name, gave me a comic book to keep me quiet. I could tell that was the reason because of the way he patted my head. "People come in here with their kids all the time. Some cute little nigger girl left it behind. Take it. It's yours." My soda went flat and Papi had a stupid smile on his face, like it was funny, but somewhere inside he knew it wasn't. He flipped the comic open, tapping it with his index finger, certain I would like it. I thought that Hitler must have liked comic books since all the heroes were white.

Papi held my hand on the walk to the subway. I wanted to skip, like I always did on my walks with Papi, but my legs felt heavy. There was a flying saucer inside my chest, wondering where it had landed and how it could get out. I was so quiet that Papi touched my forehead to check for a real fever. He was so drunk, he just cleared his throat and concentrated on appearing sober, which he did very well.

Dream: March 15, 1994

Last night I dreamt that I have a dark-skinned sister I didn't know about who appeared to me. She tells me she's always been in my life as a witness to the abuses of my childhood. I ask her why she waited so long to make herself known to me. She says: "I was inside a wooden box. I've come to tell you that my whole life I'm sick from watching your mother control your life. She stole all your dreams. Her mouth is a cage. Her slaps are a muzzle. I've come to tell you to stop blaming yourself." I tell her it's too late, that I'm forty years old, and my life is almost over. Then the dream switched to my father leaving my mother. He appears to be in his 50's. Says that my mother took the life out of him and he isn't going to let her do it anymore. In the dream I know I'm in a dream. I know he's dead. My sister appears again. "You have to get out of here. Don't live with your mother anymore. You have to get away from her." My sister has hair like mine, only curlier and darker, and there are sparkles in her hair. She's beautiful. My father looks very handsome and the features on his face so clearly defined I can see his pores. He is a Black man with a white man's face. My mother is small and shadowy...like smoke from embers. I am a child now. I wake up and write this as a forty-year-old woman. I grieve the sister of my dream world. My hair is in knots and I will leave it that way. Fuck the cruelty of combs. I will buy a pick.

Papi had no idea why I was upset, my feet ironing the concrete sheets along the way. He didn't know how to ask me what was wrong in a way that would make me feel like I could tell him. We caught the train just in time, leaping into the last car. We were alone, so Papi stretched out for a snooze. I was afraid someone would see him, or maybe a cop would poke him with a Billy club or crack his head open, and I would have to hold all the pieces of his brain. Most of all, I was scared to be embarrassed. I started talking non-stop so Papi couldn't fall asleep. Statue of Liberty this and corned beef that. I talked about the dead soldiers and the seagulls and how beautiful Manhattan is from the ferry, especially at night, like I saw on a postcard once. I rarely saw the night, except through our apartment windows. Papi finally sat up. "Let's go to a car where there's people." I'd been there before. I knew he was looking for an audience. The beers and shots were kicking in. I was terrified he'd slip onto the tracks as we went between cars. We walked to the middle of the train and The Papi Show began.

Papi was the original B-Boy, with his aerial breakdancing from defying gravity on the poles to hanging by his feet from the leather hand straps and looping his body like he was the needle and the thread. Next he'd play imaginary hopscotch on the tiles. Some looked away or hid behind newspapers, others laughed covering their mouths; the brazen clapped and cheered. He never asked for money, he just wanted to make people laugh. No matter how drunk he was, when it was time for the Papi Show, all his daredevil body memory kicked in. He had no idea how he made me feel. Or he didn't care. I was never sure. I just sat there with my face in my hands burning red, willing the train to derail just so Papi would stop. Shame is brutal in the body of a child; it can seize and hold it hostage for a lifetime.

Dream: March 24th, 2008

Recurrent dream. A mule is tethered to a leash on a pole and forced to walk a continuous circle. The lower half of his body is shaved. As he walks the circle of the pole, two men take turns whipping him. His skin is raw and bleeding. The men appear to be Puerto Ricans in Arab attire. I am watching through a window and I feel helpless. I want to go and rescue the animal but feel that my efforts will be ineffectual or put my own life at risk. There is more fear of failing than of physical harm. I have had this dream two nights in a row, that I can remember: Easter Saturday and Sunday.

SIXTEEN/BROCADE

One time, after a bender, Papi bragged to me that he "had a few dates" with the actress Betty Hutton long before meeting Mami. I don't think anybody else's father in my fifth grade class had adventures like Papi. They had met at Don Julio's Latin Dance Club in Greenwich Village where Papi was a busboy. You can be 80 years old and still get called a busboy. Papi couldn't resist a mic. He sang Cante Jondo, the Spanish Roma "deep song" that makes you stop everything and feel your life, even if the song is about death. He told me he sang on break every late afternoon while setting up for the dinner crowd. "The other workers like it—they never complain. The Mexicans join me sometimes and sing their rancheras." Papi always made me cry when he sang just for me, which was usually on an empty street on one of our hooky-playing adventures. His voice turned my whole body into a desert cave.

"Don Julio's was still closed, but nothing is closed to a woman like Miss Hutton, mi'ja." Hutton, a big Hollywood star, was having a drink at the bar, and Papi bought her next one. Papi could swoon almost anyone, except Mami. "We talked politics and movies, and I promised to cook for her my famous paella. A real lady, that Miss Hutton. And smart. She surprised me knowing many words in Spanish." Whatever happened between them after that would go with Papi to his next life.

Sometimes, after Papi had a few drinks, he would tell me things that I don't think he was supposed to. Like telling me a "real lady" can just take off a long white glove and "drive a man crazy." He talked about Miss Hutton and his other favorite, Miss Gypsy Rose Lee, like they were the Virgin Mary. I never heard him talk about Mami like that. I grew up wanting to be a movie star or a burlesque queen, but I didn't have the guts or the body. Mami and Papi had drilled the importance of remaining a virgin for the "right man" for so long, that I was glad to be chubby so nobody would want me anyway.

Dream: October 17th, 1987

A young Asian couple are lying down on grass watching a procession. The woman's head is on the man's lap. My mother stands beside me; we both think they are beautiful. Now my lover and I turn into vertical worms. I am a female worm wearing a blonde wig. I tell him: "I can't have babies. There's something wrong with my ribs. My ribs are no good." My lover says my ribs are fine. We are now inside an aquarium paradise, embraced by water, algae and trees all around us. I give birth to koala bears, fish, birds. My mother looks at us through the glass and she is happy. I am glowing in the dark, a bright florescent green vertical worm.

I don't think the Virgin Mary is a "sweet lady," not in that pink cupcake way, like El Reverendo and Los Curas like to sell it, all Magnificat and no mujerota. I don't think Mary cares much for men either. In her day if you weren't a royal or a rich man's daughter, you were a servant of one kind or another. If you were financially independent and single, it was assumed you were a prostitute, like the bochinche that has followed Mary Magdalene around through the centuries, without a shred of evidence. I think Mamacita Mary is more like Papi, and likes her coffee black and her underwear practical. I know she hates that dainty servile pink. Who came up with pink for girls in the first place? Been asking that my whole life.

How's a woman going to be the mother of a son who is also her father and sometimes a spirit, who's never around and pawns her off on a poor, middle aged working stiff, going to ever be sweet? Far as I know, Mary never consented to having a baby, she only agreed to keep it. There's a word for non-consensual baby-making, even if there's no actual penis involved. The results were the same.

Before you get all guilt-ridden for agreeing with me, trust me, plenty of women have asked themselves the same question. From the start of their miserable empire, the "Mother" Church has been preparing women for submission. How many little girls and boys pinch all of their holes shut at the sight of a priest? "Blessed art Thou among women and blessed is the fruit of Thy womb, Jesus. Holy Mary, Mother of God, pray for us sinners now and at the hour of our death. Amen." Mother of her own Father and his Son. The one who holds us in death. Secret sister of Charon, on the ferry with us as we cross the river, tenderly placing the coins for passage on our eyes. Holding our head, reassuring our souls they'll have some place peaceful to go. She's the main attraction of the Mother Church, but the men get the last word in everything.

Open Wide

A taste of wet pennies in the mouth;
inner voice, a torrential, infinite rain.
My fault, Jesus, please don't hate me.
I'm sorry.
I'm sorry.
I'm sorry.
I'm sorry.
I'm sorry.
I'm sorry.
I'm a very bad girl
Razor absolution.
Red Rosary beads.
The counting.
The ticking.
The turning of knobs.
The pulling of plugs.
The counting of tiles.
The shutting of light.

SEVENTEEN/CHARCOAL

Whispers make the rounds among the children, but no one hears or sees anything. It's another Saturday afternoon, and nothing has happened, nothing at all. I remember there is no such thing as Nothing. Men sing boleros posed on slatted folding chairs as the women serve them arroz con gandules loaded on styrofoam plates. Girls dig tiny hands into big icy coolers to bring up the coldest beers. Men point to their weekend stubble for kisses, pretend not to smell the stink of secret violations. What other men do is not their concern. Besides, there's a pile of home-fried chicken coming their way.

Dream, 1980

Pigeons everywhere. Fly into immaculate windows. Feathers singed against overheated hanging bulbs, land in the soup; shit in the oatmeal. Or are those hands that haunt my periphery? Asphyxiating grackles trapped in a silo where I am utterly naked, drowning in chicken feed. They peck at my eyes. One crawls inside me, flapping when he isn't sleeping. I do my best to keep him sedated with lullabies and Mami's secret pills. I wake up. He is still flapping. Inside my chest.

I ask general questions in the kitchen about bad things that happen to some girls. "Good girls don't get touched." Mami wipes her hands on a dishcloth as she hands me an aluminum pan heavy with potato salad. A thin veil of paprika makes it look more interesting than it is. It's August, too hot to be inside, extra muggy from a morning of Mami frying corn-meal breaded dark meat chicken parts. The elevator is on strike again, so it's four flights down to the courtyard. I want to fall on purpose, break my neck and die, but with my luck I'll just be paralyzed and become a worse burden than I already am. And easier to catch.

"Be a good girl and serve the Fathers first," advised one of the sad looking Novena Ladies in heavy shoes from Saint Athanasius. Mami wants me to make a good impression, especially on people she doesn't like. "Pull up your socks and look decente. And remember to serve your Tío first; Los Curas can wait." She sneers out a fake smile at the Novena Ladies and sticks out her tongue at them when their backs are turned.

Most people in the building think Mami is "a little off," so mostly they just ignore her, except for the bochincheras, who take great pleasure in her gossip operas. El Reverendo chats up Los Curas hoping they will see the light that going to Confession is a form of blast-feeming since God doesn't need interpreters. I offer El Reverendo Mami's fried chicken legs, he smiles, then checks to make sure his dentures are in tight. Los Curas look me over with their glaring, yellow eyeballs, and ask if Mami keeps any sherry in the house. "I don't know any Sherry." They laugh. El Reverendo blesses the chicken who died for him and then lectures Los Curas on idolatry with his mouth full.The Baptists and the Pentecostals show up late, as always, loaded with salads and cold meat platters stuck through with fancy toothpicks.

The Jewish twins, Las Jamonas, still single in their late 40s, bring string-tied bakery boxes from Cushman's and Woolworth's toys and balloons for the kids. Mysterious, magical women— no men, no children, "galavanting at all hours" according to the Hallelujah Lady who has a permanent peep hole indent around her eye. Whenever I run into Las Jamonas in the elevator they tell me I look like "a nice Jewish girl" and ask "How is your mother, the poor thing?" which I can tell is their way of politely asking if she's been locked up yet. The one who thinks we must be Sephardic, always digs deep into her purse to give me a rectangular fruit candy. Mami seems very pleased that her daughter doesn't look like who she is; I like getting the candy in its pretty wrapper, so I neither confirm nor deny our ethnicity.

Mami admires Las Jamonas and says they always dress in "high-class" fabrics and "smell like the Chanel No. 5." Papi bought her some a long time ago. Mami keeps the bottle with the last few drops on the bedroom dresser. She takes note that the Jamona's seam patterns always line up perfectly. "For such narizonas y panzonas they look nice." I think Mami believes she'll drop dead on the spot if she says anything nice about anybody without throwing some dirt on it.

Los Curas excuse themselves from El Reverendo and the oldest one asks Papi for "a little taste of the nice white meat." Papi's been "El Chef" in charge of turning all the meat on the barrel barbecue. Soon a sweet brown sauce drips from all Los Curas's wagging chins. Girls get patted on the head for doing a "good job" juggling huge serving dishes. Male relatives sit us on their laps. Los Curas pinch our cheeks a little tighter than they should. The other adults think nothing of it, not even Papi, like kids are just cute little toys for grownups. Papi draws the line at kissing. No kissing by any man, not even on my cheek, unless he's very old and feeble and Papi decides that it's innocent.

The oldest Cura with the veiny nose tells me I'm Martha and work too hard. Papi says that the only thing he ever lifts is the wafer at Mass. Mami always mutters about his having his mother lift his bicho to pee. I imagine sticking a fork in his bloodshot, yellow eyeball and twisting his optical nerves he sprains memorizing my little titties. He should at least offer me a tip. Cheap bastard. Papi always said the Church has too much gold and not enough God. Papi didn't know the half of it.

"You always obey Jesus, don't you my child?" I look around for Papi. He's busy cracking jokes and working the grill. I look at the ground, my face burning red. My toes curl and try to dig that hole to China the adults always talk about. Deep into the earth, but not so far as to touch hell. "Yes, Father." He licks his ají-inflamed lips. "Yes, what?" I look at my feet, he smells like dirty underwear. "I obey Jesus, Father." I wonder why I have to call him father. For a second I think...then the air smells like drowning seals. No. Stop thinking. My brain pushes hard against my skull. "How about a 7-Up for this poor old man, eh, Me-Jah?" I nod painfully and turn, wondering how many of Mami's achaque pills it would take to kill him.

Sí, children do think about these things. We think of monstrous things as the adults delude themselves that our lives are about toys and cheap breakfast cereals. We want to stop bad people. We collude in revenge fantasies. We want to protect other kids, especially the younger ones. I have yanked out the rope of bad men's tripas a hundred times and hanged them with it. Used them to jump Double Dutch. I have slit my mother's throat with Papi's straight razor each night before bed. I have sliced off men's dicks and tossed them in sewers every time the congregation sings "Onward Christian Soldiers." Every time I hear about another dead young soldier from the neighborhood. How else to survive?

Papi piles up meats in their fire tattooed skins on turkey platters, for us girls to serve, makes room for the cheaper cuts of meat on the grill; grabs his butcher's cleaver, separates ribs. I memorize every move. I look up at Papi, my face silently screaming. "Please kill Los Curas, Papi." I prune up my brow trying to connect telepathically with Papi to save me, so as to not officially be a snitch or cry baby or a blast-feemer. Papi, can't you see? I know you can't, or they would all be dead already. Please stop drinking, Papi, please.

Mami offers Papi an icy can of Schlitz. Papi's eyes don't hear me. I am left with a wink and his half smile that says you look just like your Papi. Why do people want me to look like them? I want to ask Papi for a sip of his beer but he'll tell me "this is only for the boys" like he always does. "Beer is not for young ladies." I wonder if any of the women in his magazines or Betty Hutton drink beer. Mami was all black coffee and cherry Kool Aid. Never saw a sip of happiness poured into her glass.

Kids from the block tell me things. Things that happen in stairwells, basements, sacristies, choir lofts, elevators, doorways, closets — the Catholics, the Baptists, the Methodists, the Seventh Day Adventists, and the especially soul-corseted, no drinking, no dancing, no makeup, no nothing, Evangelicals and Pentecostals. "If you surrendered to Jesus as your Lord and Savior you wouldn't suffer from depression. *Real* Christians don't get depressed." Pastors cheating on their wives; stealing money from the collections; bochinche destroying reputations with the same mouths that praise God and drink grape juice passing for the Blood of Christ. Wonder Bread Medallions, his Body. At least Los Curas use real wine; but only because they're a bunch of borrachones. *Jesus loves me, this I know, for the Bible tells me so.*

I believe in Jesus. It's the part about him coming back I'm not so sure about. If he is, I wish he'd speed it up with a better plan than his Papi had the last time. I want him to live on my block and never die again. "Never leave us, Little God the Father. Never leave us. I'll buy you a leather coat and boots and hat and a gun with silver bullets for any bloodsucker that tries to take you down. You can teach me chess and I'll teach you checkers." I can feel Mary's approval like a happy butterfly in the bowl of my stomach.

EIGHTEEN/MEAT

Two of my girl cousins, Cookie and Matilde and me, gossip at the everything supermarket as our mothers pick through the lemons and limes, one at a time. We pretend to be talking about hot dogs and donuts. Every Saturday you're sure to run into kids from school. Diana Rosario, who's been trading finger fucks for cigarettes since second grade, leans in close, like a jailhouse threat. "That shit hurts, mi'ja. Just sayin' what Tony's sister tol' me. When he was at Spofford, he got it right in his..." She points. I pretend to be shocked. Spofford was a South Bronx juvi hell; inside the boys got it as bad as girls got it on the outside. Diana points again. We know it isn't funny, but we laugh anyway. We know too much and we can never un-know it. We will know it for the rest of our lives.

We stick our fingers deep into packs of half-turned fatty ground chuck. "Shit, you know Satan was really a bicho in a snake outfit." Diana snaps her gum with a vengeance. "Eve was a puta, according to the Bible, so all us girls must be too." I glare right at Diana, trying not to twitch. Our mothers yell for us from a crate of overripe plantains where they swear at the fruit flies.

"Embarrassssssiiiiiing!" We quickly punch our way down the aisle, leaving a trail of violated meat and Diana snickering, "Mama's girl bitches." Pinkie swears of secrecy from sacristy to supermarket. We giggle our way back to our mothers, acting pure as cornstarch, twirling our braids. "Sí, Mami, I'm coming." Diana's nicotine breath still on my neck.

NINETEEN/LACE

The first two decades of my life moved like a pinball game. Mami and Papi were the flippers. Sometimes life rolled hard and fast, sometimes slow. IT happened. IT. More than once. Lots of ITS happened. If Mami and Papi didn't mostly keep me inside, there might have been a lot more ITS. I knew too much. Traumatic events rolled into night terrors. I was born a magnet for the cruel and the kind. Nothing in between. My body exhausted before I hit first grade.

Sacraments of Surrender rule over the bodies of too many little girls. First Baptism; Quinceañera; Wedding; Birthing; guilt ruined honeymoons. Clumsy sex in a white dress passed hand to hand, across generations. First Holy Communion, miniature Brides of Christ, rabbit-eyed saints in lacy white dresses. White shoes. White socks. White panties. White little tee shirt. White wafer stuck to the roof of your mouth. White diamond in the middle of the little gold cross you're expected to keep and wear for the rest of your life. Burial. White roses. White rosary. *All of God's children got shoes to wear. When I get to Heaven gonna put on my shoes, I'm gonna walk all over God's Heaven.* So many lives wasted proving we are saints; that we are decente. We live to bear children and burdens. We are not lesbians. We are not transsexual. We are binary. We are ordinary. We are pink. We are feathers to be plucked. Flowers to be picked. Men are a necessary inconvenience. We marry the money and the penis. Giving it up for White Jesus; taking one for the team. We are worthy of whiteness. The squandering of our time, the subverted essence of our lives, the truth of our identities, the melanin of our souls, all sacrificed upon the altar of who we are not. *When I get to heaven gonna put on my boots and gonna stomp all over God's Heaven.* If it's hell I'm going to, then I damn sure want to make an entrance and nothing about me will be white.

TWENTY/ACRYLIC

Daydream, August, 2020

In our urban backyard I imagine myself at a beach town. The weathered wood of fences, pitted and mousey gray. I smell salt that isn't there. The white curly-cue frame of the neighbor's back door screen takes me to the side streets of Provincetown. I sip cucumber water as a breeze comes in. I'm there, knowing all of my neighbors, heading to the ocean for a walk. On the way, an ice cream swirl in a sugar cone, the contagious laughter of drag queens hawking the evening shows, the straight tourists trying to act nonchalant, pull cheek muscles trying not to look. Nights I can dream my way to Yunnan Province, gather my own tea leaves to hang and dry; at a café in Sevilla I am drinking cortados after a night of dancing alone. I can always refuse to sleep and dream myself anywhere, tasting the air as it lands on my skin, the colors, flavors and fragrances of anywhere I am... cognac in mouthwash cups with John Waters as we walk a Hudson Pier, content with life's absurdities.

The first time Papi took me to Mass, was at Saint Athanaisius. The Virgin Mary statue had a way-too-willing handmaiden look. My eyes burned through the plaster agitating molecules to part her lips; free the trapped breath. I saw her wink at me, in a badass way, like she could see who I really was and had seen me pick my nose and look at my toto with my mother's compact mirror. My Bronx Mary leaned to the left of Yémaya, one foot worn down by supplications and the other dipping into the sea when no one was looking. The sea is everywhere, if you know where to look. Bronx Mary looked at me like she knew I was born special into crappy circumstances; it was familiar territory for her.

The sanctuary air is layered in fragrances centuries old, as if one burns to cover the ones that had burned before, tracing back to The Inquisition.

On my tongue, verdigris and rust, lavender and sage, beneath my feet rock salt, ash and bone. Flags of burlap and silk brush against my skin as I travel with closed eyes through deserts and gardens, courtyards and kingdoms, dark caves and musty cells, towers and moats, shoeless and wild haired in search of God.

I open my eyes, Bronx Mary winks at me like I matter. She looks me up and down with the sass of Carmen *La Maricona* with the dragon tattoos up both her legs who turns tricks under the screeching El train and calls me "pretty girl" like it's my name, her butch hair sleeked back stiff with Brillantina. "Stay nice, mi reina. Be a good girl. Listen to your Mami." The punctures from a thousand hummingbirds lace her arms. A secret sweetness; she holds me in them without ever touching me.

The #2 train screeches hard as it turns the sharp bend onto Simpson Street. Rails so close to tenement windows I can look into people's lives; stirring a pot; nursing a baby, mopping a floor, painting a wall. Some people like an audience and Mami yanks me by the hair to sit back down. "I know what you're looking at, putita. You want to be like Carmen La Maricona?" Yes I do. Better than being like you. She is the queen of all Mariconas! ¡Maricona! ¡Maricona! ¡Maricona! Our Lady of ¡Las Mariconas! I never had the guts to say it out loud.

TWENTY-ONE/PEYOTE

I was the kid who knew there was something very wrong with the "Pick a Bale O' Cotton" song they made us learn in school. I hated singing it. It was up there with *Ten Little Indians* in the classroom, which became *Ten Little Niggers* in the school yard. I hated both, I knew they were mean and nasty and I punched in a few faces who said otherwise with the Jack Dempsey left hook Papi taught me. To this day, I can't tell you how or why I knew those songs were horrible, since everyone around me thought they were just cute kid stuff. Dempsey being called "The Great White Hope" felt even worse. I had all the feelings, but couldn't find the words. Not even in the library.

Papi admired John Wayne. My same Papi who worked beside Mohawk Men on water tower projects that required fearlessness of dizzying heights. Papi who was invited into Peyote ceremony and never said when or where. Papi who watched movie star cowboys kill Indians and cheered for the cowboys. Papi was a tangle of contradictions. Papi only used *nigger* when he was angry and never when he was drunk. He revered Black icons: Mohammed Ali, Harry Belafonte, Ethel Waters, Nat King Cole, the Mills Brothers, Lena Horne, Mahalia Jackson, Malcolm X.

He never called them *niggers*. In his mind, he was setting a good example for me by separating the Colored from the Nigger. "You should be like them, good and decent. Mi'ja, these are luchadores who make the world better. They work hard and don't complain, mi'ja. Pero they fight in self defense, especially Ali." Papi threw punches into the air. "Fighting back is not the same as complaining. Anyone who tells you to never fight is like a cat stealing your breath. Never start the fight mi'ja; be the one who ends it."

Hearing Papi talk like that was confusing, since it sounded to me like "your mother is Puerto Rican, but she's so clean." Words like that get inside you. Especially when hateful things are spoken like they're compliments. I've always wanted to own a gun, which is exactly why I don't. I don't think it was Rheumatic Fever that gave Papi a heart condition; I think it was the self-loathing of his own blood and uncertainties of his lineage. The part of him that insulted people even when he thought he was complimenting them. The part of him that had to hate or die flowed through his barbed-wire veins.

TWENTY-TWO / EMBROIDERY

Sometimes I saw Carmen La Maricona on the nod in a doorway on Southern Boulevard, hanging like a sunflower that'd been picked clean. One time I tried to lift her head that was bowed too close to the pavement. Mami yanked me away and smacked me hard on the back. "Deja eso," she said in disgust. Eso. Not even Esa. Carmen was not a person to Mami. She was Eso. Thing. Distant. Not like us. Filth. Worthless. Inhuman. Monster. Nothing. Not even nothing. Eso. That sound stayed in my chest. The tiniest of words engorged, pressed hard against my ribs, pushing them apart. Mami's mala leche. ESO.

I look for Carmen every time Mami and I take the train to go *chopping* down by Union Square on 14th Street. Mami's addicted to the bargains at S. Klein's, second only to Alexander's bargain basement. A ritual at the Chock Full O'Nuts counter for coffee and a thick, moist slice of date nut bread with a slab of cream cheese. Or when we walk over to Cushman's, the last Jewish bakery in the neighborhood. Papi insists we pick up pumpernickel and rye breads. "Mi'ja, they call that white garbage Wonder Bread because you wonder what's in it. Basura. The darker the bread the better for you. White food is poison." Dark bread in my lunch box is how come the nasty kids call me "Jew bitch."

The last of the white kids in school are mostly Jewish, Irish, and the occasional Eastern European who don't eat bleached food. I used to have a crush on a Latvian boy, Ilmars; he is kind, awkward and a schoolyard exile like me. His name alone gets his ass kicked. Following Papi's recommendations for recess, like doing yoga and isometrics, gets me jumped every time. Ilmars looks away, just like his parents trained him. He never fights back, protecting his hands for the future. His parents want a surgeon in the family. I wonder if someday he'll save my life and we'll fall in love. No, not a chance. I don't go for cowards. During one of those recess beatings, I felt my Lotus petals turn into carbon steel blades.

They have never retracted or dropped since.

No amount of Murray's Pomade will slick back my greñas; wild hair is a fist-fight liability, so I grab first. The dirty street fight is a matter of survival. The gang huas come with razor blades, I bring Papi's lessons of "never let them see you coming. Show them a hand but land a foot." I still get my ass kicked since the gutter brawls are rarely one on one. I learned to act tough from watching Carmen mouth off "suck my dick" to the prissy and pretentious, to cops and curas, and how to throw that left hook from Papi. The kick came from dreaming in ballet. Mami defends me, but has never taught me to defend myself. She's the only bully I never hit back. I know I could take her, but also know I'd land myself in juvi or even worse—God's shit list.

I cover my head from the blows and take the sting of Mami's belt on the legs. I've sprouted varicose veins and cellulite curds from the beatings. Lotus is sharper, shredding only myself to ribbons in places no one can see, not even me. I eat myself into fat armor one box of Ring Dings and quart of milk at a time. Anything even resembling chocolate is my opiate. *Children, honor thy father and mother, so you may be long upon the land.* I have to find a reason to want to live upon on the land that constantly crumbles beneath me.

Once upon a time in Puerto Rico there was magic in the soil, and you could grow real roses, bougainvillea, vegetables, herbs, fruit and flowers on the tiniest patch of land. A lemon or plantain tree in a corner. Maybe even raise a couple of chickens and a goat. In those days, you always heard about la fulana de tal's abuela living to be a hundred. It was these small and well-tended fincas that kept families healthy and thriving.

Mami's Great Tía, Doña Ramona lived in a walk-up tenement on Simpson Street, where most of the Tías lived. She was our oldest living relative, and spent her days as the most respected hechicera in the neighborhood. At 101 years, she remained sharp, sassy and spiritually energetic. She had a thriving herb garden in her apartment that in warmer months she moved to El Jardín, also known as the fire escape. Even obese asthmatics braved the steps to her door, which she never locked. Her card readings and homemade herbal teas offered relief and emotional strength to her working neighbors. No matter how hard they worked, they could never keep up with the bills, especially the medical ones. Doña Ramona, with her thick waterfall of white hair was known as "La Bruja del Espíritu Santo" by the rebel women of the street, and many others thought her to be a saint. She was known for making people laugh even as they were dying, and never asking for money. She kept a large abalone shell on a little table by the door, and people left what they could on the way out. It was always enough, since Doña Ramona lived very simply and didn't eat much. With the lines of people always at her door, there was no time in her life for what she called "boberías" like watching television, going to the beauty parlor, o comiendo bon-bon.

"Your Mami always scolds me for leaving the door unlocked, but there is nothing here to steal. My soul belongs to God, and my body, well, there's nothing much here for anyone but the undertaker. Let that poor bastard make something off of my corpse to feed his children. It's the least I can do!" She laughs long and hard at her own jokes, and when she does, it's impossible not to laugh with her. The only time I ever saw Mami laugh for real was the moment I realized Doña Ramona really was a saint.

Mami rarely visits her and only out of a sense of obligation because of Doña Ramona's age. I know it's mostly from the fear of ill gossip, not kindness. She calls Doña Ramona a bruja blast-feemer behind her back. Mami won't call anyone a Saint. She doesn't believe in them. Mami always makes fun of Papi's superstitions; she's a real kettle black boomerang, since one of the worst beatings I ever got from her was for putting her big purse on the floor to make room on the kitchen table to do my homework. "Tu 'ta loca?!" She was sure she would never have money again and that I was disrespecting the sweat of her labors. Doña Ramona likes Italian cookies and Mami brings her a bag of Stella D'oro, whatever kind is on sale. Those dry cookies are as Italian as Bozo the Clown.

Doña Ramona uses espejuelos only for reading the fine print "where politicians and lawyers hide injustice." She cackles a spray of pitch pine needles that write wisdom into the air. "People who only ate from their own gardens never got sick and kept all their teeth." She runs a knotty finger through her mouth pulling back her lips to reveal perfect molars and youthful gums. "Es la pura verdad." The elder women of our family learned to live readily armed with evidence of their truths. "Bring me that plant over there." Doña Ramona plucks a leaf, extends her serpentine tongue, places the leaf on it and slides back into her mouth. "Peppermint. The best way to prepare for a kiss." She opens her arms, hugs me and kisses my cheek. Mami's been flipping through a crumpled up fashion magazine the whole time, muttering how she can sew better than any of the costura basura advertised (which happens to be true) looks up and calls Doña Ramona "una alcagüeta" smiling out the insult to avoid being cursed. She pushes me towards the door and mutters some phony blessing to Doña Ramona, putting the capper on another Christian duty done.

Days later, while chopping viandas for sancocho, Mami tells me flatly that Doña Ramona is dead. She says "en paz descanse," reheats Papi's leftover morning cafecito for herself and reminds me that everyone has to die sometime, including me. I tear a page out of an old newspaper and pull out my crayon nubs to make a drawing of Doña Ramona so that I will never forget her.

Mami makes me smell cilantro at the Hunts Point Market, and rub mint leaves between my fingers. She means well, but it always feels like punishment or blame. Like it's my fault she doesn't have a finca. "Huele. Huele. Pa'que lo sepa." She goes through a crate of yautía and finds the longest, thickest, best looking piece, insisting I appreciate it. I flinch a little; in Mami's hand tubers look like weapons. "El Árabe made a finca, nena. He had chickens and cows and a bull...oh yes, and two black goats. La tierra was so clean they say I liked to eat it. That's what they tell me. They tell me I was very bad. I remember nothing. What do we have now? Ratones y cucarachas. The price of having children."

I'm not sure how I brought rats and roaches into our lives, but Mami makes sure I know that by being born I made her's and Papi's lives miserable. I wonder if Mami and El Reverendo and all their other brothers and sisters made El Árabe's life miserable too. Why isn't El Árabe called abuelo? How come if he had a finca did Mami live in El Fanguito? Why doesn't El Árabe have a real name? I want to ask so many questions, but Mami hates questions. She tells me to mind my own business. She tells me about so many horrible things that happened to her, and not one nice thing about anybody. She did tell me that her mother was a saint and died giving birth to her. I got slapped for reminding her she didn't believe in saints. The finca story was almost nice. When I ask about El Árabe she tells me we shouldn't talk about los muertos. I tell her she talks about the dead all the time and she slaps me again. "'¡No me contradigas, malparida!"

I wish there were a photograph of El Árabe. The older hinchas in the family say that he had a "cara de Moro" like it was an insult. I see a handsome, exiled Black Amazigh Prince, stabbed to death by Americano goat thieves while he prayed to Allah facing West. His blood flowed into the soil Mami ate and it got into her blood and into mine. Sometimes my arms feel like his and a butter knife in my hand suddenly curves into a jambiya. Even the thought of camels or donkeys makes me cry, they work so hard only to be thought of for insults and dirty jokes. Mami raises a hunk of yucca wider than her arm and mutters something about Americanos destroying her island and how they call her a Puerto Rican midget.

Papi hates tubers. "I like to starch my shirts, not my liver." He asks Mami when dinner will be ready, holding his nose to make me laugh. Mami grunts that he should leave her alone unless he wants to cook. Papi wishes we had a finca too. "When I first came to this country there were still some farms in the Bronx. We drank milk in Brooklyn straight from Bronx cows. The Italians in Brooklyn grew tomatoes and peppers—fresh. We put a little salt and ate them like apples. Not like the garbage from the supermarket. Never buy tomatoes in a supermarket. Always everything fresh. Fresh. Everything fresh. ¿Capiche?" Papi repeats himself when he wants to drill something deep into my brain.

Mami bangs her pots around when she hears too much happiness. Even the water boils loud. Papi's nostrils flare like a bull staring down the matador. He starts pacing. "If it wasn't for the gardens and aqueducts of the Jews and Moors, Spain would be in the same shit like the Bronx. Franco is a comemierda who should not take credit for anything good in Spain. Take away everything those people built with their own hands and good brains and what do you have? The raquetero landlord big shots and politicians who don't see us as human. Here the poor are treated like my people are treated in Spain. These greedy bastardos shit where they eat and leave us to clean up. Ese sonuvumbiche cabrón hijo de puta Robert Moses nos jodió. Moses, Franco, Trujillo—la misma mierda. ¡Me cago en su madre!" Papi loved the Bronx and always pointed out the beautiful details of old buildings wherever we walked. "The Bronx has more parks than any place in New York City." Papi stops, takes a deep breath and lets it out nice and slow, as if we were inside the Bronx Botanical Gardens. Mami yells from three feet away that dinner is ready.

Mami force feeds me steaming plates of under-seasoned roots and greens. A smack to the hand. "No salt, you want to kill your father. Everything has to be soso because of his heart." I never understood how salting only my own food would kill Papi. A huge piece of coconut custard pie for dessert. "Eat everything I give you." I wish every meal at home could be the last supper and I could be Judas. "You eat like a pig, nena. How will you ever get a man to love you when you eat like that?" I push away the pie, she pushes it back, puts the fork in my hand.

Dream, 1971

the earth cracks open
like a supermarket strudel
me on one side
Mami on the other
I reach for her missing hands
fall into the crack
wake up screaming
get slapped for having nervios
from the lack of Jesus
in my evil heart
Mami warms milk
sprinkles cinnamon
stirs in prayers
makes me sip
holds the cup
to my lips
cooing with a mimicry of love
I cannot wake up from this

my wide straddle thigh flesh
burns across the open chasm
Jesus arrives as a numbness
that swears to never leave me

TWENTY-THREE/BUCKRAM

Every morning Mami walks me to school, dainty warm hand in my chubby, clammy one, all the way to the entrance where GIRLS has been chiseled into gray concrete. Annoyingly re-adjusting one of her many crochet hat experiments over my head of thick unruly curls, she leaves the stain of her "China Red" lipstick on my clenched cheek. Who will steal my milk money and kick my Mama's Girl fat ass today? On the best of days, I'm invisible.

Fifth grade assembly. The cavernous auditorium painted in church basement shades of industrial green where we sing cowboy and war songs. My perfectly starched and ironed short sleeved white shirt bites into my doughy armpits, steadily grown by government gold tins of peanut butter and bricks of yellow cheese that Papi gets as gifts from politicians. Mami proudly ties a pressed red ribbon into a bow beneath the tidy puritan collar. She knows that on Wednesdays I have to wear the flag colors. The association between a uniform and fancy schools has congealed in her head.

Mami looks at me as if standing in front of a mirror and reminds me that she only went to school for one day and that it had been the best day of her life. The paper with lines. The pencil. Her feet swimming in her step-brother's worn down shoes, a rag of a dress made new with bar soap and patches from the tail of an old, threadbare shirt.

"Listen to your teachers and do nice." The weekly command performance of nationalism by children, who for the most part, can't spell or define allegiance, Mami is certain, is "something for good discipline and to learn something good." It's all about the uniform for Mami. She isn't interested in anything I have to say about it.

The music teacher blows hard into her steel whistle that never leaves the pink lanyard that hangs limp, bouncing between her tetas as she makes her rounds, correcting everyone's posture. Orders rattle off the Principal's lips, who likes to make sure we all know he's the boss. "Keep formation.

Don't trip. Don't talk. Don't roll your eyes. Don't smirk." The color guard clear their throats and adjust flag poles balanced between white gloved hands and queasy guts.

Don't fart. Don't get a hard-on. Don't drip pee. And dear sweet Jesus H. Christ on the Cross, Virgin Mary Mother of God, don't get your first period or catch the diarrhea. The Principal speaks into a megaphone like a Pentecostal on Good Friday. "Do you kids have any idea how many men died so you could be here today?" Even the dumbest kid in our class knows that you don't blame soldiers for crappy schools. I was passed over for the color guard. I can be grateful for that.

My body, a cold-war bomb, ticks down to Armageddon, cringes at the overstated commands by the Principal, who fights an erection as he takes note of big nippled girls who've made their way to the front row to un-nerve him. "Place your right hand over your heart and stand at attention for the Pledge of Allegiance." I snicker inside, watching his sweat roll. I know that standing at attention and preparing to pledge were not the same thing. I'd watched plenty of war movies with Papi on our sticky sofa. I thank Bronx Mary for sending the big nippled girls. Marty Martell's tinny bugle sounds the first note.

The flag. The whistle. The bugle. As the school year drags on, my blouse bites down harder, deeper. It's a sweltering June day and the Colored Lady Music Teacher, Mrs. P., has been permanently demoted from conducting our voices, "One. Two. Three. And..." to walking the aisles demanding perfect posture and absolute patriotic devotion from all of us "ungrateful knuckleheads." She's always been strict, but never mean before today. The Principal wets and wraps his lips around a shiny new whistle at the end of a handmade yellow lanyard and almost blows himself into a stroke. Us kids figure it's because it's the first assembly for the cute new guidance counselor, Miss Bergin, who got hired just before summer vacation after the last one suddenly got married and left the country. It would be his only chance to impress her before September rolls around. Everyone gets quiet. Mrs. P. whispers into his ear, and he nods like he's agreeing with her idea. Everyone hates Assembly, but we go anyway. Notes from school about behavior don't go over big with most of our families, unless teachers have something good to say, and that hardly ever happens.

Mr. What's His Name Principal, is pretty much a disaster at everything.

I keep my hands at my side as the Pledge begins. Only Jehovah's Witnesses are allowed to abstain, since honoring the flag constitutes idolatry in their rulebook. Every assembly day I close my eyes and pray that teachers will assume my family has converted.

Mrs. P. wipes her brow and neckline with a perfect white hankie, her shoulders and face bunch up when our high notes of "above the fruited plains" cut into her eyes. She's a church-going Colored Lady who follows rules. I've seen her in the movies too. Ladling broth for ugly rich white people; opening doors with a smile, only to be used as a human coat rack. Us melanin-deprived kids have no clue what it takes to be one of only two Colored Grownups in the school building as Jim Crow's shadow looms large over the South Bronx.

TWENTY-FOUR/CHROME

Under the El train there's a neighborhood art deco diner where Papi, Mami and I go to warm up when the heat is off in our building, usually worse over the winter holidays or when it snows. Just the sight of steaming pots fogging the mirrored walls, and the gleaming money-green marbleized formica and chrome counters make me feel better. The place always smells like my favorite fresh hot open roast beef sandwich smothered in thick, hot brown gravy.

I can always tell when Papi's broke by the way he shyly opens his wallet eyeing it sideways, or Mami unlatches her purse really close to her chest. No matter how hungry I am, I order hot chocolate and load it up with extra cream and sugar. I have the oyster crackers that come with Mami's cup of chicken noodle soup. Papi checks the soup for meat and politely calls the server over. "I think the chicken only looked at the pot. Please take this back and tell the chef to make sure it gets in." Papi calls all cooks chefs, no matter where they work. Servers like his charm and his tips. Mami gets enough chicken to give me a little. Papi pretends to not be hungry and fills up on hot black coffee and reads a newspaper someone left behind.

Eating out is a weekly ritual Papi does his best to keep going. Papi says, "If you don't have enough for a good tip, you don't have enough to eat out." Mami won't go to Mass on Sundays, because she thinks that "esa iglesia tiene cosa de boo-doo" so Papi conjured a ritual he calls "Chibotz." Papi makes sure we never miss our Chibotz by winning at cards, working overtime, or from extra tips. When he worked near the Dakota on the West Side, some of the old time celebrities, like Rosalind Russell and Merv Griffin, tipped him. They knew Papi was a true chef on a cook's wages.

I still choose diners over those linen and crystal mausoleums. Don't have to worry if I dribble or laugh too loud and no limits on the coffee. Fuck Starbucks. Double fuck Le Bernadin. When Papi went "fancy," he supported the people who had supported him, like the Basque family who owned La Bilbaína in a Little Spain brownstone on West 14th Street, or some of the Chinese food places around Chelsea where the Asian waiters spoke Spanish, played the numbers with him, and always threw in a few extra ribs for "la señora y tu nena linda." I'll aways remember the sourpuss waiter Papi liked, on account of "he takes his job seriously, very professional. Good man." Mr. Sourpuss didn't laugh the time I first mistook a tiny bowl of Chinese mustard for flan. He just kept bringing me water and fortune cookies, until my tears and mocos were all dried up. Papi was right about Mr. Sourpuss being a good man.

TWENTY-FIVE/RUBBER

Shopping. One of few distractions that keeps Mami's fists and mouth occupied. Even if it's just to go and get a new batch of plastic roses at the
jonkería store; she chooses each one with a gardener's precision. She mutters under her breath the whole time she shops, talking to her purchases,
wondering at their true worth, scolding loose seams and buttons, bitching
about the 75% off the one soft wool sweater that gets away into faster
hands; the only carajo jodienda thing on sale she's sure is "made in Italy."
At home, she sprays her plastic roses with Maja perfume from Mr. Saul's
Farmacía. She closes her eyes to smell them and I wonder at the secret I
can feel beneath her eyelids. She sprays and inhales until the roses believe
themselves to be real.

Carmen La Maricona is always there near the El when we make our
way to the train for Mami's Manhattan excusions. Carmen is always near
Cushman's in case she needs something sweet, just a few yards away from
the Downtown staircase. Carmen always has a Loosie behind her ear and
one balanced on her lower lip as she calls out to me: "hey, pretty girl."
even when Mami walks fast to avoid Carmen and her fellow congregants,
who Mami calls "Jotas de la Mota." Mami always caught my eyes lingering in Carmen's direction. "¡Camina, carajo; ojos pa'lante, camina dere-
cho; te'vá poner joro'ba!"

Carmen was always there to meet the corner of my eye, until one day
she wasn't.

I wonder if Carmen had ever seen a baby red pepper on its green stem,
or the yellow skin of lemons still on the tree. Carmen looked yellow the last
time I saw her—more like supermarket lemons with no memory of trees.
She called me "pretty girl" that last time as the cigarette dropped from her
lip. Through the corner of my eye, I could see time stop all around her, as
her fingers did their best to reach that cigarette. I wonder if Carmen ever
lived where children learn to never name the goat, or make friends with
the chickens.

Cante Jondo

There's a snag in the clouds
Condor's wing catches
On loose threads
she must hover to choose;
accept and be still
or fight and fall.
Too many tangles and knots
choose for her.

Months passed; grief landed like a fist in beef, like aluminum swelling in the back of my throat, like two boxes of Ring Dings still in their wrappers. My teeth crumbled and fell out in dreams, they still do whenever I think of all the Carmens in the world. All the Carmens I was not allowed to touch or thank or love. Carmen sometimes called me "apple cheeks."

S. Klein's Department Store, Union Square. Bargain lair, below street level, windowless. I wear my plastic Minnie Mouse sunglasses that I won playing Skee Ball with Papi at the Cubano's bar and arcade on City Island. They protect me from the headache-inducing florescent lights. No one believes me when I tell them florescent lights are bad for you. I tell people they make my head hurt and make me want to puke. Mami calls me loca more than just in passing; her eyes scan me, looking for evidence of the moral deficits or demonic possession that demand a beating. "Light is light. Don't be stupid. Take off those things pareces una idiota con espejuelos dentro la tienda." Flashy discount signs in big red letters she can't read but understands, keep Mami distracted enough that I can put my sunglasses back on and avoid the usual public shaming at any sign of imperfection.

Gangs of working poor women and "welfare mothers" fight over blue light bargains. Bras, nylon panties, corsets and girdles that cut off circulation; that make you smell like vinegar and turn flesh into the texture of ceviche. Pull. Tug. Yank. Push. Push back. Bitch. Puta. Coño. Carajo. La madre que te parió. Fighting over the accoutrements that disguise the realities of their bodies from the mediocre men they long to please. The breadwinners. The blue to their pink. The ones they should fight off instead of each other. Socially coerced women, smiling and compliant, "find a man or die alone." Fulano de tal with house and car payments, would marry a "real doll." The latter being top of the list for marriage material. Don't forget a trip to La Farmacía for the Maybelline eyelash cake and brush. Thick eyelashes to flutter over the fan, the hijab, beneath the turban or Jackie O. pillbox hat; interacting with the red carnation in your hair; up from the downturned head signaling a talcum-fresh rosebud demurely awaiting the wedding night. A real doll scared shitless. Will I know how to please? Will it hurt? Will I bleed enough to stain the sheets? Will he find the bud after all the petals get shook off? Am I decente?

A rumble among the brassieres. I pull at Mami to look down and teach her how to check for extra stock beneath the bins. Those magical sliding doors are meant for employees only. I don't care. I spot a pricing gun for the unmarked stuff and shoot on the correct price. I'm a racketeer for Mami, not a thief. She finds her size in everything, triumphantly proceeds to the cashier. Next we head over to the Men's Department, and for a fleeting moment I'm a hero.

The first and only time I ever saw Diana Rosario at the library, someone had stuffed a biology book among the poems and she went straight for it. It was the first time Diana took an interest in science. "Yo, nena, inside the lady's toto it looks like one of them rides at Coney." Diana was impressed and insisted I pay attention. We got to look at the inside of a bicho and the huevos. I learned more about science from Diana than my teachers, that day. All these rows of hanging men's things and tags make my head spin. Papi owns one sport coat. I start checking pockets to see if I have some Diana Rosario luck.

While Mami mumbles about Papi's boxers and loses herself in complaints and men's underwear, I head over to the only soda machine in the whole world that pours a Cherry Lime Rickey into a paper cup for a dime that I don't have. If I stare at it long enough, I can taste it. A lifetime passes and I hear Mami yelling my name as it bounces off the counters. Everything stops. Everyone stares. My hero day is over.

TWENTY-SIX/STEEL

The next time I saw Carmen she was floating over my bed, calling me "pretty girl." Carmen visited my dream world when life was most unbearable. Those times when I fondled my father's butchering cleavers and begged Jesus for the guts to cut off my own head in one clean slice. The faster you cut yourself, the less it hurts. The edge of the blade balanced an atom above my outstretched neck, my eyes rolled in the direction of God, who, for whatever reason, was always upwards. Sometimes a fly landed on my nose to distract me, or a huge unexpected sulfurous fart from a nervous stomach to shame me. I was sure the dead could see, smell and hear everything: vitiated body functions from Mami's slimming laxative concoctions and fixation with rectal suppositories saved me more than once. No way was I ready to face the dead. "No hay mal que por bien no venga." Shame was bigger than suicidal ideation. Fart. Dissimulate. Hold in the next one. Skinny. Fat. Skinny. Fat. Fat. Fat. Fat. Fat. Fat. The battlefield where the vision of becoming thin one day fought the desire to be dead. Roller coaster body blues before third grade. Coney Island is inside me; I'm waiting to feel all the rides. I slice off my thighs with the outer edges of my hands in Mami's faded armoire mirror. How many women live in there? Died in there? If only....

Self-loathing is a huge ball of lard carried in the stomach that seeps into the places in our bodies meant for green pastures not concrete. I take back the green. My green. My beautiful chronesthesia that abhors the linear path. I braid the parallel universes to find respite in the impossible space between them that exists only for me. Inside the guts of that space is the secret of what can make one person hate and another love. It is there I learn to move those moments around, to play them like a solitary game of Jacks. To tightrope or spiral across minutes or years. To strap into my time machine and land on the parts of my life where I can breathe a little, decolonize my life, my body, my thoughts, the torments of uncertainty. Life between parallel lines, where a Japanese painter has hidden his indigenous name, knowing that when it returns it will no longer return or belong to him, yet remain his forever.

Summer at sixteen. My boyfriend, Mike, would help me sneak away to Greenwich Village. I'd lie and tell my parents I was going to work. Mike was the only boy I'd ever introduced to Papi that he trusted. I took a sick day at work so I could still bring home my full paycheck. I had heard that Theater for the New City in the East Village was having auditions for their Theater in the Parks. I wrote myself a monologue, since I couldn't find plays that had a voice even close to what I wanted to say. Winning people over with someone else's words didn't feel right to me; it was an audition, not a play. I wanted them know who and what they were getting right away so I wouldn't have to wait too long for a rejection. Like cutting off my head at the speed of light. Speed is why almost nothing hurts Superman. Besides, I'd always heard that show business isn't about "what you know, but who you know" so I figured I let them get to know me.

The audition wasn't what I expected, which was me and the director in a room alone with Mike listening through the closed door. It took place on a stage, seats filled with what some would call the competition. I don't even accept the concept. They did let me read my own monologue. I managed to mispronounce a word I'd plucked from my Thesaurus at the last minute—brothel—to replace "hua house." As I pronounced it Broth-El, the snickering of the mean girls and the convulsing shoulders of the kinder ones muffling themselves, brought me to tears, which I rolled right into my Bukowski's "Naked Lunch" and Carmen La Maricona-inspired monologue. The few drops of piss that escaped in the flight half of the flee moment, never hit the floor; Mami's insistence on thick cotton panties had paid off as my mind escaped into the biology lesson on capillary action. I don't remember anything about the boys in the audience, since the only one I cared about was Mike. Papi was right about him.

All of my previous auditions had been in school. This was the world of Bohemia, in a "real" theater far from the Bronx. Staggering out of the lobby to wait, I saw Crystal Field and George Barteniff hustle themselves into a private room. No one else noticed. I went to listen at the door, standing where only Mike could see me, watching my back, like he did with everything in life that smacked me, since the first time we locked eyes. "She's very talented, but too young and doesn't drive yet. Too bad. If she were just a little older..." I was overjoyed that Crystal Field thought I was talented. I wouldn't be performing in the neighborhood parks like mine, but I left there with half of me on a cloud anyway.

Poor Mike had to put up with the perseverations of my other half, and what I'd heard outside that door. "Sweet Jesus! I'm such a jerk! That's what I get for trying to be polite. I was so worried they wouldn't understand hua...you have to be from the Bronx to know from hua and it helps if you're Puerto Rican. Do you think there was one other Puerto Rican in that room? Maybe. Maybe. I mean, look at me, not even my own people believe I'm a Puerto Rican. History lessons! Hello! Yes, people need history lessons! I should have said hua. Hua is good, right?" Mike shrugged, his inner stand-up comic responded. "I don't judge how people make a living." I didn't want him to make me laugh, I wanted him to fret with me; to understand how devastated I was and to feel it. There were reels in my head always spinning. Only I knew how bedeviled I became. "They were so mean, Mike. They were going for the same job as me. I didn't go there to to be better than someone else. I went there to be good at being me—whoever in the hell she is. I didn't expect other actors in the room. Especially mean, ugly and stupid ones!" Mike was supernaturally kind as I escalated. "They were just jealous. Sounded to me like you did great. One screw up. Big deal. What? They never make mistakes? What do they know? The people who matter liked your work and being too young is not a fault." Mike always said the right thing, even when I needed him to say the wrong thing. I was terrible, but Miss Field could see beyond it. Had she seen the real me beneath all of my fears and insecurities, or did she know I was listening at the door? I didn't wait to find out.

In moments of suicidal ideation, the stench of chicken shit from the Vivero where Papi taught me how to wring a chicken's neck so his buddy the butcher could chop it off, floods through me as I hold the widest of his butchering cleavers. "They don't feel it, mi'ja. It is the kindest way to kill. I want you to try it so you can see how easy it is, okay? You like to eat chicken, right?" I try not to gag. "It is best to eat the fresh ones. Much cleaner meat. You must pluck each feather to the tip of the calamus." "The what?" Papi smiles. "Science mi'ja." Everything is science and everything has a name, even the anchoring tip of a feather. "Clean meat is good for health. Here, take her by the neck." Every Saturday Papi tries, and every Saturday I refuse, running out, most times puking on the sidewalk. I want to wring my own neck, not the poor chicken's. They keep running, headless. With my luck I'd stay that way forever.

TWENTY-EIGHT/SKIN

I wrote Carmen poems for her dream visitations and drew pictures that I folded and dropped, giving her a look that meant: "Please, please pick it up. Open it." There were no floors in my dreams; nothing on which to stand. She'd smile and wink, pick it up and kiss it. She saw ground, where I couldn't. There was never enough time to see her open it. I always woke up. I just had to believe that she knew how much I loved her. It only occurs to me now that maybe she didn't know how to read—in life or in the dream world. I'm glad there were little drawings around the poems too.

Carmen's stiff, slicked hair and thin, sinuous body excited me. It made her look hard, impenetrable. A woman who felt like a man and made me feel special. No man would be forcing himself on Carmen. No mother would be shaming her, beating her. On the street, Carmen called the shots. Her blue steel body resistant to blows. A razor in her back pocket. A huge silver Indio ring on her middle finger. At night, I'd kiss my arm, pretending I was kissing Carmen. My arm and my dreams were the only places I could give kisses to my crushes, boys or girls.

Carmen was somebody's baby. A stray dick found its way into a hole. Awkward. Or maybe a good and tender love. Sweet. Stupid adolescence. Incest. Mutual experiment. Rapist. Pedophile. False promise of a better life; that was the worst kind of rape. There are countless ways that dick can get in. The butcher. The baker. Perfect love. Too perfect. A silk bed. A dirty mattress. Penthouse. Basement. Businessman. Pendejo from the stoop. El gringo que corta jamón en la bodega y hab-blah-S-pa-knoll. Consensual. Doubtful. Forced to be pink by a Madre Santa. Carmen was born blue.

Carmen lusted for the spike. Wanted it no matter how cruel it was. How fast it made her old. How it shot through the back of her neck, erasing the past. How it collapsed her veins leaving her mermaids nowhere to go. Carmen knew it would kill her no matter how hard she kept herself. Sunday School promised life as God's banquet, Heaven as the reparations left unpaid on Earth. My feast seldom moved past the unspoken love in

Papi's maraschino cherries and alcohol-induced kindness. Carmen's visits to my dreams. The soul braille from Doña Ramona's pine needles.

Carmen made her way into my dreams for years, whatever it took. Was I ever in *her* dreams? It's a big job to be the only one remembering her. May there be others, God. When a prayer begins with "may" its already game over. May. You already know. Don't waste time lying to yourself. Rubber tourniquets haunt me, twist my insides; the lighter flame beneath the spoon; the bubbling; the stillness; the needle, the blood, I feel nothing then suddenly feel everything. I can feel the syringe slip the needle into my vein, the warmth of the junk slithering in my blood, pulling me into Charon's blissful ride to the other side; hours later back again, to not tell it, not tell a soul. I live to not tell. I can be where I have never been. I can do what I have never done. I can feel what I have never felt. I can love whom I have never met. I long to feel the ground beneath me.

Dream, Autumn of 2000

Three indigo doors appear and never leave. A stubborn dream that refuses to end. Those doors, suspended in the air when I look up from reading, or as I walk overly aware of creaks in the floor. Sometimes on the street, usually at dusk, when wonder and beauty are at their peak and I can, for a moment, believe that life is actually good. On the other side of the doors, Thirty-Five Ministers of Chance assure me they are always close. A gentle whistle passes my ear.

I am sober
I am clean
whatever that means
I know what I
have never known
I am who I have never been
Ride the Horse
on the river
back to home
where I know
what I have never known

I am who I have never been
whatever that means
I am sober
I am clean
When I hear bagpipes
in the radiator
I am certain I will be
better than nothing

TWENTY-NINE/BARK

Every plastic bag caught in a tree has a story to tell that will never be told. The workers who make them; who load the boxes; the trucks, the truckers who haul and deliver, the stops for coffee in paper cups that once were trees, the beans that must be sorted, the ones that must be excised, the elders who hold those bags from the bottom, who later transport roots for starchy dinners that hold families together. The landfills bulge with their unbreakable polymer chains. They'll stay synthetic for all of their days and reincarnations. Nothing will ever make them organic again. They are no paper cup. They are no bean.

And the trucks. What about the trucks? Back to the trucks. What are the names attached to every hand that builds each part, that assembles, that tests, that drills for oil violating sacred land, never giving it a second thought, as their hungry children wait by the stairs. And the children whose livers inherit sadness on Reservations stripped down to clay and dust, through which a sacred river still runs. What are their names? Those stairs and steps where children wait. Those steps and stairs that someone built from what once was a ringed, rooted trunk that grew from a seed carried on what wind, filled with whose breath, making what wish, on what day and time of the week, full of birthdays and weddings, love-making and death? Cradles and burial grounds touched each day, by whose hands, with what purpose, feeling, intent? The undertaker who wanted to be a concert pianist but his fingers were called sausages. Now they poke into the holes of the dead. Bean that will never grow as tall or wide as a word. Where are there Ministers of Chance?

Trying to win Mami's empathy, I read one of my poems about Carmen aloud to her in Spanish thinking she might be proud of me, even with no evidence of that possibility, maybe even happy that I cared about a person no one else gave a damn about. Lover of freaks and outcasts, like the Jesus Mami conjured, when convenient. Like Bronx Mary who really loves. I wrote Carmen's humanity. Carmen, who had been mythologized by dirty fingernail narratives. The self-proclaimed sanctified, disgusted by hands they never got close enough to see and would never touch. Hands that gently gathered secret poems from my dreams.

Mami ripped the poem from my hands and burned it in the sink. Fear and jealousy disfigured her face. Her eyes wild with horrified imaginings that I could become Eso. Her shame that she couldn't read or write. She was so busy imagining the thing I might become, that the *who* that was in front of her never entered her mind.

Mami slapped me so hard I still have red webs of broken capillaries hidden beneath makeup; my mouth a little off kilter every time I read a poem or speak in public. Mami destroyed all evidence of my childhood genius, my listenings, the kind of smarts that wear off as years of obstructive criticism and shaming pile on. It happens a little less to children who feel valued and seen, but there are always cracks, always something inside to rupture the soul dam, to mis-name non-conforming love, gender, beliefs and ways of being considered a social pestilence. A look. A word. A silence. A turning away. Poems ash, questions buried. Agape, Filios, and Eros chained in separate dungeons.

Mami slapped me to the floor, left me there, sobbing; stumbled toward her belt. No one was listening. I swallowed the screams that came as the leather burned me red, to blue, to purple, to yellow; my hatred making me strong. Little did she know I was not Eso. I was more ese than esa, and always had been, despite her every effort to force me into all things pink. Mami wore herself out. I stayed brutally strong. I did it for Carmen, For Bronx Mary. I defeated Mami, but the Eso she felt inside of herself, raged on.

There would be no more tears after that night. Mami would never beat love or poems out of me. I would save them all for everyone, for anyone, but her. "Science mi'ja; everything has a reason and a name." No Papi, not everything.

THIRTY/MYLAR

Loves me. Loves me not. Daughter of Mami, who to most was just another fulana de tal, only I remain to stitch the unspent tears of my fulana into something that proves she was here and that she mattered to someone. Goddammit, she mattered to me. In every piece of shattered glass, in the Maja spray on her plastic roses, in every stitch from her foot pedal sewing machine, through the beatings and insults and shaming. "I love you, Mami." Her unabated response, day after day, over months and years: "No you don't. You're incapable of love. Embustera."

I grew to believe her. That litany, more than anything she'd done to me, became an inner torment, the internalized monologue of self-loathing. My identity as one incapable of love. The worms and maggots will ravage every scrap of me, will shit into the earth, into the sockets of my eyes, unwittingly creating life anew. The screech of the rounding El, the seagulls of Lower Manhattan who make origami poems of the salty air; the old women who claim boardwalk benches as their own; the old men with sagging breasts and biker's legs playing paddle ball to sweat out the toxins of retirement and jobs that never loved them; the barker's litanies; mourners casting stones into the waves; shameless young lovers rubbing against each other inside their own time machines. Everything and everyone has a name; mine was inside, where no one could see: Mala Hija.

THIRTY-ONE/AL DENTE

What actually is and what is remembered can never be the same. All those colliding thoughts, memories, ideas—like protons defining the elements. The infinity of thought within unquantifiable or discreet realities. Your brain in constant flux. You might always know that 2 plus 2 equals 4, but your brain will never have the same things rolling through it every time you think of some numerical permutation that leads to 4. 36 minus 32; the square of 16.The ghost-life of spatiotemporal properties from the seen and unseen. Say it. Eat it like a mouthful of overboiled farfalla.

It's impossible for gas to become solid in recuerdos. Memory is a phantom haunting all the rooms of life. One time you might be influenced by the memory of ice in a tall glass. The eyeball feel of a peeled grape. A sniff of airplane glue. A paper cut in the webspace of your dominant hand. 4. The train that brings you safely back to the Bronx with Papi. 4. The legs of the clawfoot tub where your mother bathes you and your privates until your first period at the age of 4 + 4 + 4, scrubbing too long, staring too hard. 4. The daily sermons of wash it again—the dish, the cup, the spoon, the knife. 4. Father. Son. Holy Ghost. Satan; regular boarders beneath and above the bed. 4. The first time your brain learns to forget THINGS as soon as they happen. 4 the number of people who pretend to not know. 4. The number of pennies placed in your hand to shut you up. 4. The number of people you believe will be killed if you tell. 4. The number of chairs at the table where you eat every night and one remains empty at the bequest of war. 4. The number of times you're told to shut up and eat at every meal. 4. The least insults and slaps in a day. 4. The times you wish death on your mother each day. Thank you, Florentines, I can look and see myself. Thank you, Filippo Brunelleschi. Other eyes. Mine. My eyes and nose in the knife. Other eyes, mine. When I butter 4 slices of bread. Cut into tough meat 4 times just to get past the grizzle.

When I quarter an orange. Mami's face. Quarter an apple. Her heart. The wedges float out from the crescent of her slit throat; a Muppet's mouth still assuring me of my worthlessness to the 4 corners of anyone who'll listen. 4 will rise on the 4 x 10 - 16 wave that brings it.

Bile gathers beneath my tongue after co-ed gym class, where I change in a toilet stall, my jiggly thighs marked by the tight elastic of my ill-fitting blue gym suit. I take note that no one ever picks David B. for their team. I'm nice to him and he to me, and wonder who he'll become, as well adjusted girls with perfect teeth who practice gymnastics 4 times a week and plan 4 trips a year, prance with the certainty that they will see most of the world 4 times while young and healthy enough to enjoy it. Those hideous girls who with pitying big-eyed looks ask my weekend plans at lunch, not so discreetly touching their noses at the first whiff of my bacalaitos, and the overripe banana at its sweetest, that I pull from a wrinkled brown paper bag on its 4th trip to school. Papi survived the Great Depression by recycling and saving anything that had even the most remote possibility of re-usefulness.

Polite girly-girls with good hair, who never invite me into their 4 day weekends. Snickering from stealth distances is the best of their religion. Never really kind. Never really cruel. Mothers-to-be, some day. Overly concerned cartographers of their children's lives. In many ways, Mami was less dangerous. David B. no longer hears a Labrador barking murderous commands, his yellow Volkswagon Beetle, long gone, his .44 now in the hands of Jesus.

144,000. The number of Jehovah's Witnesses that will ascend to rule with God? No. The number of manipulations I have pulled off to survive. On any given week.

The Bronx Zoo. My first time. Papi meant well. He told me it was a place to see animals from all over the world. Right away I got nervous, because it didn't sound right. One of the first grade teachers had told me that her class was like wild monkeys at the zoo and that she wished they could all be like me. "You're such a sweet and quiet girl." I didn't think elephants would like the Bronx Zoo anymore than I liked school. Where could they go for long walks? Papi said, "There will be monos, cotorras like you, y focas." Saying "focas" was like being Dickens and saying "Master Bates." "Hey foca! Is that your mother, foca?" I found out fast that I could say foca in public and not get into trouble. There would be murciélagos, but focas, I was sure, would be better. Nocturnals made me all pale on the inside, because of the mice and roaches in our building that mostly showed up at night.

There would be monkeys, my favorites, and maybe popcorn; if I was very, very, very good. Love dragged by the leash of IF. It seemed like a high price to pay for some salty corn. I wanted cotton candy, but kept that to myself. I didn't want to hear about brain damage from mercury fillings and teeth rotting in my head. Papi had a rolling subscription to Prevention Magazine.

In Fourth Grade I called the school basement dentist Dr. Nosferatooth. He smelled like ammonia, was all shaky and had crooked, loose, nicotine stained teeth. Only Mr. Pagán, the custodian, ever got my jokes. Mr. Pagán, besides, Mrs. P., was the only other Black grownup at school, and as far as I could tell, the smartest of anyone. He got my jokes in Spanish and English. Talking with him was the only time I didn't stutter. He told me he was born in Loíza into the arms of a one-handed doula, Josefa, one of his Tías. "Yep. When she was a young lady visiting her folks down in South Carolina, a white man smashed the fingers of her right hand with a meat mallet for biting into one of his apples that was sitting on the ground. His were soft, wormy apples tasted like cotton. Josefa told my Mami the man couldn't tend a wax banana. He'd kill that too." We both laughed, and I thought about how Papi was funny sometimes, and passed down mostly good stories, not like Mami's scary operas. "That nasty so-and-so never even asked if Josefa was planning to pay for it, which she was. No thieves in my family."

I interrupted, excited that we had something in common. "Mine neither, Mr. Pagán." Mr. Pagán smiled, and I imagined one of the *Americana* teachers calling him "Mr. Pagan" and him reading her the riot act. "That mean old man had one of those farms where they have chickens and pigs and orchards. Kind of place where they torture the chickens by shoving them into cages up against each other. That's why I'm a vegetarian." He saw my eyes fill up with tears. "Don't cry, there's a happy ending. My doula was left-handed! She could get more done with one hand than any white doula or man could do with three." I walked back to my class, thinking about the chickens and praying I wouldn't have bad dreams about three-handed white men.

Papi and I walked through the zoo gate and the world suddenly smelled more alive. It stunk, but it was good stink. I felt like I was someplace far away, someplace where maybe I wouldn't have to see Mami again, or her big, fat red leather belt and matching lipstick on her leathery lips.

The sight of cages was like a finger poking into that hole in my heart that's been with me since before I came into this world. It wasn't right to put animals in jail. I thought about those South Carolina chickens. As far as I could tell, the animals were all really nice and hadn't done anything wrong, except to be themselves. The primates seemed happy enough, scratching their privates and smelling their fingers. Humans do that all the time, only they're all sneaky about it. The squirrel monkeys and marmosets were my favorites. They laughed at the humans, baring their teeth and showing off their little dicks like stiff cashews. One moment they were pinching lice off each other, then maniacally devouring fruit the next. Monkeys were my dream of riotous anarchy far from the starch of Mami's suffocating bitterness.

I sounded out the signage best I could. "Papi, how come the Pro-biscuits monkey has such a big nose?" Papi got that joke look in his eyes. "He's Jimmy Durante's brother." I didn't have the heart to tell Papi that was a mean thing to say and admit that I'd noticed the resemblance first. I laughed to be kind. I was asking for the scientific reason. Sí, I *was* that smart, but few people expect smart questions from a kid, only stupid or annoying ones. I always laughed at Papi's jokes, no matter what. I could tell that being funny when he was drunk made Papi feel taller to himself. I didn't have the words for it, but I knew what it was and that I should help him hold on to it. Kids mostly feel the truth, even if they can't explain it.

Papi always took advantage of having a few shots in the morning—"my liquid Wheaties, mi'ja"—on his day off. He once told me that rum was good for staying warm in winter. Every day was a Papi winter. Mami called him a borrachón, but as far as I understood borrachones, they didn't hold down jobs or speak five languages, and read three newspapers in different languages in the morning with their espresso. Papi smelled like Old Spice, or whatever other cologne was on sale for Father's Day. Papi wasn't any kind of borrachón I knew about. He told me it was medicine and I know he was right about that. He always looked happier after a few drinks and his cheeks got all rosy. The shots helped him borrar the parts of his life that hurt the most. Papa was more like a borrar-chón. Mami never drank and was a sourpuss all the time. Case closed.

At the monkey house I pressed my face up against the iron bars, and out of what felt like nowhere a Mandrill pounced to meet my face, both of us pressing against the bars. It's a good thing that six-year-olds don't typically have heart attacks. Papi bought me a nickel bag of peanuts to calm my screeching nervios. The elephants would be next.

I was the only kid alone with a grownup. There were groups of chattering and pointing school children with their beleaguered teachers who chain smoked and passed around a flask, spiking their coffee. A band of quiet kids with Down Syndrome were harnessed to a rope. They were interested in everything, eyes dancing and landing on every detail of a special day. The miserable-looking Catholic school kids in buttoned-up, sinless white shirts dragged their feet in punishing cowhide shoes. The Pentecostals had their kids in church three times a week; no time for field trips or naked animals wagging all that sin around. Those kids would be the ones craving the most field trip gossip from their friends. Especially the school bus stuff everybody got away with. The really tired drivers worked two or three jobs. "No retirement for the poor," Papi always said. I learned that retirement was mostly for white people who played golf in stupid hats and circus pants.

My first real-life porn was a zebra pounding his Billy club dick on the ground. My father turned my head away so fast I got whiplash. I had nightmares for weeks, not to mention some unreasonable expectations later in life.

Papi and I were officially playing hooky, but the law was on my side as long as Papi was—so I wasn't officially a "truant." I had missed Kindergarten which wasn't mandatory, so I'd had one less year of socializing with paste-eating, snot-picking comemocos, than other kids. Mostly, I learned to socialize with family adults and cousins, and the few neighbors Mami had on her gente decente list.

THIRTY-THREE/PORCELAIN

Mami would have kept me home till I hit thirty if it was up to her; my hymen her holy relic with a promise of dividends; she could inherit one of those post-mortem subsidized mansions El Reverendo promised just for protecting my cherry. A singular vision for her life: me in a poofy wedding dress marrying an Italian or Jew with a two-story brick, driver's license, his own cash business, and a pension. Plenty of blood on the sheets and a legacy of grandchildren. "A white Peruvian is okay, especially if he has some of that Chino blood. Very, very intelligent peoples."

Mami's view of successful people worthy of her time existed in four quadrants: Los Chinos, Los Judíos, Los Italianos and a few of Los Hispanos, preferably from Spain, but not a Xitano like Papi, "a real Spaniard, un Gallego rubio o un Cubano de los buenos." She said that if I fell in love with a Chino, I should make sure he owned a laundromat or a restaurant and that the rest of them tended to have bad breath. She'd wave her hand across her nose with a stageworthy, "Ay, fó!" She always reminded me that Christ was a Jew and that you never heard of one beating his wife. "Italianos okay, they work hard and very good-looking. You have good babies. Healthy. Los Sicilianos, especially, they know how to cook good. But don't take one too dark; not good for the baby. A Sicilian baby can look like a prieto." Apparently, being Black was more dangerous than polio. "And men has to be ambichos, not a lazy bum like you father." The worse Mami talked about Papi, the more I loved him.

After every lecture that didn't involve a beating, I begged to visit the V. family on Fox Street; their son James was 12, two years younger than me, but taller, which made him look more mature. Mami called him guapito and said his skin was olive and that he was already looking like a man. Mami never minded going there since visiting their apartment was like a vacation, with fresh flowers on the dining table in a clear vase, with colorful pebbles. There were fancy ivory lace curtains on every window, even the bathroom, and all matching everything, from dishes to furniture; a well graded palette that allowed everything and everyone to sit in their best light. Mami and James's mother had their café con leche in fragile cups; James and I sat on the stoop, passing the Orange Crush bottle back and forth with a lip-smacking whiskey attitude. His bomber jacket was a buttery leather. I was stunned and secretly jealous at how he never flinched when he spilled or stained it, or any of his clothes.

I could tell Mami hoped that I would marry him some day (if no Jews or Italians were available) since she left us alone on the stoop, without once peeking through the curtains of their ground floor apartment, or grabbing my arm to drag me inside. James was de sangre Europea de los buenos with good hair and came from what Mami considered to be "high class." Mrs. V. could actually shop at Macy's without sales going on, and at Sak's at the end of season. She was always wearing something new and soft, like summer cashmere. Mami hid her jealously from Jesus and Moses by letting Mrs. V. know how much she preferred cotton that breathes. "Better for your health."

Nothing in the Vizoso apartment was second-hand, except for the rocking chair that James's grandmother, Doña Luisa, left behind when she returned to Catalunya to help raise her other son's six children by three different women. Mami was glad to see her go, since she could never understand a word she spoke. Months after her arrival, Doña Luisa's *fill de mala llavor* had gotten his tongue removed from it's roots for criticizing El Generalissimo Francisco Franco and speaking Catalán; supposedly a mugging with no witnesses. "Em cague en la mare que t'ha parit." James told me she didn't seem to realize she was cursing herself. "It's like when my mother gets mad and calls me an 'hijo de la gran puta;' adults can be so stupid." James said everything with a courtly, easy-going flair, like he was being fed grapes. James could string together cusses in three languages and it would still sound like church on a cheerful summer day.

James was an only child and his parents had both finished college and had good jobs, could afford babysitters, sent money to Doña Luisa, and put James in an all-male, fancy parochial school in Manhattan. The building he lived in was smaller than ours and all the neighbors tipped El Super, Don Manolo, on holidays to keep the place looking good. Lots of old people, rent control, and everything in good repair. They owned a nice car and never rode the subways. James and I talked about his favorite subject, fashion design. "One day my gowns will be on a runway. Models will have white doves in rows across their open arms." He got the idea from El Parque María Luisa in Sevilla, where doves had learned that putting on a show would get the early morning tourists to give up pinches of baguettes in small beak sizes, careful not to choke such beautiful renditions of the Holy Spirit. Those white doves that made them feel special, unlike those poor patchwork pigeons, who were considered a nuisance.

As James envisioned his glamorous future, I played with a strand of blue pop beads Titi Angela had given me. I'd pop one off and roll it between thumb and forefinger, my soul leaving my body as it traveled to the heart of Chinatown where I squeezed fish heads, popping their eyes, my finger in a socket feeling for fish brains, fish thoughts, fish memory, fish dreams. Wondering what went through fish minds as they just lay there on crushed ice, their little souls shivering, waiting to be good enough to be wrapped in newspaper, carried to a home with a big steaming pot, children laughing, and an old man in a corner, rolling a cigarette, looking out onto Mott Street, wondering why he ever left his beautiful province where all the neighbors helped each other and always had time for tea. Me wondering why my toto sometimes smells like fish.

Popping two more beads, I squeeze Mami's eyes so she can't see me as I hop just beyond her reach. I am the rabbit, she is the hole. I steer clear and thank Jesus for the fish Papi and I buy sometimes in Chinatown, the place that always feels like my real home, with the younger children waiting patiently, happy to eat together from a big single bowl. The woven plastic slats on the old man's beach chair hang shredded and sound like wind chimes to the white kitten that taps at them. I hear slippers slap against linoleum. A cacophony of Cantonese. I'm certain there will be sweets at the table before bed. Moon cakes cut into little pieces sitting atop green paper napkins for good luck. A pot of tea. Sturdy cups. Steamed rice and bok choy are lovingly placed in a white bowl and carried to the old man on a hand-woven, laquered tray. He turns to smile at me as if to say, "You will live long." I feel as if there is something I'm supposed to do, but not supposed to know.

Soul meets body again and I return to the unpunished stains on James's buttery jacket and how his eyes sparkle when he daydreams. I want to roll a cigarette like the Chinese elder and instead I imagine what it would be like to kiss James right then and there. His lips full. Cheekbones high. Hair thick. Heat rises in my belly. A whiff of dried cod. Is a neighbor cooking, or am I? I hear myself say "little girl's room" and want to punch myself in the face. James follows. "Wanna play Chinese checkers?" I land flat on crushed ice. James crawled into my fish mind. He's peeking out from my eye sockets, a lobe of my brain between his perfect teeth. "Yeah, sure. I just need a minute." I needed an eternity. A fast run to Andromeda and back. Some unfiltered Camels. A peyote button. A grave. A tunnel. To be hit by lightening. Luckily, Chinese Checkers was one of my favorite games and I'd be able to shake everything off once I beat him two out of three, as usual. I always let him win one so his dick wouldn't fall off in front of his father who never lost at anything.

Depending on how much gossip Mami and Mrs. V. had to roll around in, James and I would play games inside, then return to the stoop to share stories and visions for as long as we could. Sometimes until the sun went down. The "No Loitering" sign made us feel like outlaws; we sucked our teeth at the few disapproving faces that walked by—mostly old white people who couldn't afford to leave the neighborhood. They'd mutter things like "hoodlums," "motherless little shits," "bastard spics," never knowing that someday their grandchildren would be begging for our autographs. James would run in to get us a couple of tonic waters from his father's bar cart. James always had a bottle opener in his back pocket. His parents never denied him anything, and he always had paper money. Sitting on that stoop was like visiting a Prince at his palace.

THIRTY-FOUR/VERDIGRIS

Papi had bigger plans for me than Mami, and hoped I'd see the world. A paralyzing fear of planes and the price of steamships kept him from ever returning to Andalucía. He told me the best thing I could be was a muck-raking journalist, that I should work hard in school and go to Columbia University, so I could expose all the "sonuvumbiches and racketeers," which I eventually learned was Papi-code for clerics, landlords and politicians. Papi wanted me to be someone who could take down The Man. He had a soft spot for "mobsters from the boot; we understand each other" as long as they kept it to gambling and merchandise "falling off the truck." Jugar la bolita in our neighborhood was the stuff of dreams —to hit that number so hard your kids could do better than you. Papi's friends were manicured men; ministers of chance. No drugs. No harm to women or children. A ham on every table come Christmas. The fingers of Baby Jesus always intact at every creche.

Papi arrived at Ellis Island during the first rumblings of Prohibition. He had worked as a Captain's Boy on a Spanish trade ship that first landed in Bermuda. He remained there for a couple of years picking up food service and cooking skills beyond the canned and desiccated. He cored out potato eyes and saved them for the rats. "Everyone needs to eat, mi'ja. No discrimination. I don't like them, but God made them too, just like he made us." He counted the days until I, like him, "could see what was really under the long skirt of La Señorita Libertad. It is not as clean under there as your ignorante Papi believed. But she never gives up mi'ja, and neither will we. Always stand up mi'ja, especially for the people whose legs have been cut off by injustice." Papi kissed my forehead like he was giving me a medal.

Looking older than his years, Papi was a full-fledged bartender by age seventeen. As Papi's feet met the wooden teeth of the Lower Manhattan pier, future bootleggers were planning ahead; they'd be needing extra men. When Papi overheard them recruiting, he understood just enough of their dialect to know that being an Olympian swimmer might be a good selling point. He charmed the men with half Spanish, half pantomime stories of his cliff diving days. Papi's sincerity magnetized mob-connected Italians and Sicilians who took him in. A furnished room in Brooklyn Heights on Willow Street, a job, a sense of belonging, of familia. He was soon speaking and reading the dialect of standard Italian fluently, so he could easily communicate with the diversity of Italian languages. "Italian is the wine of language, mi'jita, but Siciliano is the meat. It is the first of all the romance languages. More Arabic than Latin. A language that stays in the air after the conversation has ended. Fragrant with history, mi'ja and touched by genius. A good language for business." Papi raised a fist to God: "Long live the Moors!"

Papi was the King of Tangents. He dipped into his back pocket for a pint to make a toast. Sometimes to honor, sometimes to curse. He raised his Seagram's 7. "¡Me cago en tu madre!" to no one in particular. "I shit on your mother" was one of his favorite toasts, usually reserved for the Spanish royals of the late 1400s, and every crusader and cleric of the Inquisition—which he assured me, "Has never truly ended. When those sonuvumbiches took over a mosque, they spit in the face of God. You don't steal from Moors, because you don't steal from anyone. You steal and you are a thief, even if you are the Pope. Y mi'ja the Pope is the greatest thief of all, because he looks the other way. Most of the world lives in shit, and he shits diamonds. Punto. Finito. Il bastardi instrumenti diaboli! Salami en tu laykem! Hijo de puta!"

One of Papi's jobs was as the cook at an East Harlem breakfast and lunch grill. He'd hop the train after clean-up to bartend back in the neighborhood. Mami would take me there after school so she could run her errands and not have to worry about my needing to pee. She always insisted on wiping me afterwards. At least Papi gave me some privacy. Mami was sure that sitting on any public toilet would give me a venereal disease and that not wiping correctly could damage my insides and ruin her chances for grandchildren. She knew that Papi kept everything limpiezito at the bar. Toilet seats were the one thing I remember they could always agree on.

The bar, snuggled close to the Hunts Point Palace, was where Papi got friendly with Vinny the Chin's brother, Father Louis Gigante, a South Bronx housing rights activist and priest at Saint Athanasius. "El Padre Gigante is a good man, mi'ja. We talk politics at the bar. Very smart man and a good tipper. He helps many people. He put in a good word for us for the apartment. I didn't even have a box to drop dead in, pero el Padre told the landlord we are good people and would pay the rent on time. I don't like the Church, pero Father Gigante is a good priest; a good man. Not a comemierda. He tells you what he thinks and he knows that everybody's caca stinks. You can work for God in the street. You don't need a church to back you up. Father Gigante has a very big family that helps him do good. They do more for us than the Church and are not a bunch of hipócritas y pervertidos. When things fall off a truck and go through the neighborhood, there is justice and it is business. They are a familia who take care of their own. Even more. We are not their familia and in more ways than I can tell you, they have taken care of us. They are the reason your Papi has always had work since I got off the boat. We are not rich, but we have enough to live, even if dinner must be a fried egg on rice. Most in this world have less than us."

I always got what Papi was trying to say even if I didn't understand all of his words. I could hear what he didn't say; his whole face telegraphing, like the TV with the sound off. "Everybody thinks Father Gigante's brother Vincente is toasted in the head because he walks around in his pajamas y una bata. ¡Pendejos! He's smarter than the lawyers, and always a gentleman to me. Very respectful. Mi'ja you should always judge a person by who they are to you, not who others tell you they are; not even the newspapers. Each man knows his own heart. And God knows it even better." I was never sure with Papi which parts of his stories had an extra scoop and sprinkles for effect, but when Papi respected somebody, you could be sure they had earned it. Papi charmed lots of people, but liked or respected very few. I thought that maybe he liked me only because it was his job.

THIRTY-FIVE/TWEED

Papi said that you have to know the difference between a snitch and a whistle blower. "A snitch is like a tattletale of small unimportant things or the traicionero of a friend. A real comemierda. A whistleblower is a truth teller, about big things that can hurt many people, like dirty water from rusty pipes. Discretion is the better part of valor." I thought it might have something to do with not picking your nose in public or sweating out an itch in your privates when anyone's around.

Papi had a proverb for every occasion. He saw my open mouth pretending to understand. "En boca cerrada no entran moscas." I sucked in my lips before a fly could get in. "Better to avoid a fight than to have one. But if you're going to have one, make sure you win. If it's too many against one, run. Better a live chicken than a dead pigeon." Mami's mixed messages swirled in my head. "Métele un rodillaso en lo' huevo" and "No hagas nada; te va' derechito a la maestra y le cuentas todo." "Mami says I should tell the teacher when someone is bothering me." Papi agreed with her "knee to the balls" part, then fanned out his nose hairs "Mi'ja, God does not like a snitch. No soplones in Heaven. They go to the other place. To have good friends you have to know how to show respect y cerrar el pico. Your honor is all you have."

No problem. Keeping my mouth shut was a cinch and I had endless bouts with tonsillitis to prove it. Secrets will eventually turn into some variation of pus. "Better to walk away so there is no temptation to snitch—IF you can't, break their nose like your Papi taught you. 'Float like a butterfly, sting like a bee.' God bless Mohammad Ali. If you win, then there is nothing more to say. Punto. Finito. Amén."

Papi was a cook by trade (an autodidactic chef really, but the vitiligo on his arms and face was considered a disease in those days and limited his employability). He learned gourmet Mediterranean cuisine by reading old world cook books from the library and getting creative with the recipes. For a time he worked at an Italian bar and grill owned by a Mr. Frank

Bastone. Papi liked making an impression on Mr. Bastone, who to Papi was a big deal for his good manners and fancy, tailor-made suits— "Like the old days, mi'ja, when tailors took pride in their work, and men took pride in their looks." Papi prepared cross-hatch ricotta cheesecakes worthy of Morrone's in Morris Park for Mr. Bastone, to express his gratitude for having a job in a nice, clean place where he was treated with respect and his talents were appreciated. "If anything happens to your Papi, you go to Mr. Bastone and he will take care of everything for you and your Mami."

Before Mr. Bastone's place, Papi had a short stint as Chef de Partie on the line at the Waldorf Astoria. It was a miracle job for an immigrant with vitiligo. People knew right away that Papi could be trusted and had a work ethic. He could wear a burlap suit and still maintain a regal bearing, just like Mami did, only, for Papi it came naturally. Besides, he had what Xitanos call *salero*. To some, it means "salt shaker" but with Papi's people it unravels into layered meanings of charm.

In my nineteen years of knowing Papi, I saw him miss work only once, since our hooky days were on whatever days he had off. He went out in a -15 degree blizzard and almost had a heart attack waiting for the #2 train at the El Station. Feeling old and defeated, Papi popped a couple of Nitro pills to make it back home on foot. It was January 16th, 1972. Some dates burrow like scabies. Papi's face looked burnt by dry ice. Mami wailed "¡IDIOTA!" and I did everything I could to help him get warm. He couldn't bring himself to even look at me. His pride never recovered.

"The Waldorf was the most money I ever made pero they bought cheap food like pollo mocoso y lechuga martiguada. ¡Pollas en vinagre!" When Papi got mad in Spanish, he meant business. "I asked them nice to please bring better food. They would tell me 'yes', and then those asquerosos would bring me a crate of the broccoli rabe que parecía que se lo habían pasado por el culo de su madre." I could never eat rabe at Titi's Easter dinners after that. Just say the word rabe, and I smell culo. Big mistake for the boss to ignore the request of a man who wielded a meat cleaver with Samurai grace. "Would you feed this caca to your children, cabrón?" Papi caught the broccoli rabies.

Papi didn't like the response when he found out that "ese-hijo-de-puta-mal-rayo-lo-parta-me-cago-en-Dios" hated kids and would never have any. Papi stabbed the blade into the butcher block and walked out of the

Waldorf for good. He broke the news to Mami by telling her "those sonu-vumbiches charge people so much money for food I would not give to a dog. They wanted us to put lipstick on the chickens. Gravy on everything. Beet juice on the meat. I told them to put the gravy on my ass and kiss it, because it was the last time they were going to see it." Papi leaned in to say to me, "You have to show the customer respect and take pride in what you do, mi'ja. I could not be proud to serve caca to anyone. Food is sa-cred. I would rather clean toilets than put basura on the table. This is why I work with Italianos, they have respect in business. They understand the importance of fresh food and good hygiene. I will mop the floor for the Italianos before working for those high tone jankee mentecatos. Better to a be busboy for happy people, than a chef to the miserable."

Mami said she could go to a pantaletas factory, or get piece work, or clean houses as if she wasn't already sneaking a little work on the side when I was in school, with her crochet magic and embroidery—easy proj-ects to hide from Papi. "Over my dead body. You take care of my daugh-ter." End of discussion. Mami wasn't too keen on those sweatshops any-way, and she had her hands full, constantly seeking out roach and mouse shit in our apartment. It was a never-ending battle: Mami and her King Pine-Mr. Clean-Clorox-Brillo-Ajax-Spic and Span. I got asthma from all of it, along with smoke from Papi's cigars and teachers' cigarettes at school. A life of vermin turds and asbestos spores launched into the air from ham-mers, rags, and brooms. All of it, crammed inside whatever else is sleep-ing in my lungs. Night sounds of coquí permanently replaced by expelling gargajos from a chest doused with Vicks.

Papi never left a job without a good insult and fist fight, which he usu-ally won, even with men half his age. He once came home from working at a pizza restaurant wearing sunglasses. "I beat the manicotti out of a boss's nephew—un pendejito who didn't know how to wipe his ass." The punk was half of Papi's age and threatened Papi with throwing him in the oven and made some reference to Jews. Big mistake.

Papi thought the fight was over when the "sonuvumbiche hoodlum" jumped him from behind and tried to eat his eye "like it was an egg." Papi sponged up. "I threw him off the fire escape. He is still breathing, but not so pretty anymore. He'll have trouble finding a boyfriend now. Bastardo making jokes about concentration camps. Disgusting. I have to look for a job, mi'ja, but tomorrow we go to the track." Papi always lit up thinking about gambling; he showed me bite marks around his eye with a smile that read gangster and movie-star all at once. "I'm still prettier than him, right mi'jita?" I loved it when Papi said things like that; it was like he was trying to take the sting out of the "maricón" stuff. I felt like I was in on something that Mami would never know. Papi knew I didn't like it when he said "maricón," even if he didn't know that sometimes I kissed girls in my dreams. He didn't really mean anything by it. I got my love of hard consonant words from him.

Papi got away with things that put others in the ground. That salero of his saved him more than once. He was as good with the cops as he was with gangsters; Papi could keep a drunkard's confessions like a titanium vault. Papi told me, "Los mafiosos have honor, mi'ja. They have a code, real principios not like the hoodlums running the government. They don't like dirty fighters, especially in the family. A dirty fighter is a coward and inside every coward, there's a snitch."

Papi sucked in air, lips puckered, to issue one of his daily proclamations. "The Kennedys made their money in whiskey. Good people, mi'ja. Joseph Kennedy worked hard to make something with his life and for his familia. It was the hypocrites who made them rich. Keep your eyes on his son, Senator John Kennedy; one day he will be our Presidente. But he is too decente mi'ja. Too smart with good ideas for a better country. They will kill him. I can already see it. The politicians who survive are the ones who lack the balls to carry out impossible visions. Those people who have no honor live the longest. I think God gives them a break here, because they are going to hell on a one-way ticket. Men like the Kennedys know that nothing is impossible." Papi wasn't the only one who mistook Jack for Jesus.

Sí, some Xitanos really do see the future; especially the ones that read people; the highest and most useful form of literacy. As popular as he was at the Crosstown, a lot of people didn't like Papi. He could never charm hucksters or the big time bigots who always went "too far" and he didn't even try. "Mi'ja, never waste your time with a crook or a liar. Turn your back and do not honor them, not even with your eyes. The ones who talk bad about good people? Give them a chewing gum, they need it."

THIRTY-SIX/VISCOSE

Papi's slash and burn work history was epic and hereditary. In my own defense, mostly I fought off lascivious employers who felt entitled to steal a feel or dirty talk, as if wages included access to my body. Sometimes it was a female co-worker who stole tips. They never got to do it more than once. I left the burning imprint of my open hand on more than one man's smarmy face, and a handful of dollars that screamed "you need it more than me, bitch" slipped quietly into an apron pocket.

Just walking on any given street, or riding public transportation, or even an elevator, there were daily reminders that beautiful was dangerous. An unwanted eye fuck, a lick of the air, a hard bump, a command to smile, a cat-call soundtrack. This cat's claws remained unretracted and always sharp. Fatigue ate the rest of me. Days when Kings ran things and Queens were muzzled or beheaded.

No calls ever came from co-workers after my walk-outs. Not even the girls who'd been break-time confidantes of well-meaning unfulfilled promises to go out for pizza. Nevertheless, they always felt close; my little work families. I saved what I could and kept my grades up and did my best to remember the good days as I planned my escape from beneath the fist of Mami.

Papi's reasons for his nomadic approach to work were different, at least as far as I knew. He was classically gorgeous in that 1940s Hollywood leading man kind of way: Tyrone Power. Rock Hudson. Cary Grant. Impossibly good looks, a great physique, a sense of style, indefatigable wit, generosity and charisma. "Beautiful" might have been dangerous for him too. I never dared to ask.

For Papi, every boss always ended up a sonuvumbiche except for mobsters with immaculate kitchens and well stocked bars. The one who became his closest friend, Pietro, was a hardcore working class guy who owned Al Buon Gusto Restaurant, 143 W 72nd St, New York City. It wasn't a "chef" kind of restaurant, but Papi could conjure culinary miracles with an onion. The most simple of dishes inspired moans and groans. If a restaurant doesn't sound like a porno soundtrack, don't bother getting a table.

Al Buon Gusto, a plain, homecooking place with red checkered tablecloths, old Chianti bottles for decor, and a fairly priced menu, attracted neighborhood regulars like Rosalind Russell and Merv Griffin with two-star prices and five-star food. Ms. Russell always asked for Papi and tipped him. He proudly handed me her autograph on the back of a business card. Ms. Russell had that perfect schoolgirl penmanship we were all forced to practice back in the day. Papi always said how humble she was. I could tell from her handwriting; not too curly, no big loops. Catholic school perfect. Merv Griffin (whom I'd interviewed along with Arthur Treacher for my junior high school "newspaper") gave lots of compliments lived close to the restaurant—plenty of take out. I'm sure there were others; he told me he had lots of customers from The Dakota, where John Lennon and Yoko Ono lived. Never said who; he wasn't interested in talking about celebrities who never shook his hand. He learned to be content with their return appearances and the occasional kitchen cameo.

Years before Al Buon Gusto, Papi had heard the false alarm of happiness when an Andalusian Spaniard offered him a job at her diner in El Barrio, on a corner that was walking distance to La Marqueta. He came home so happy; he loved El Barrio. "Mi'ja, the freshest food in the city. La Marqueta and Chinatown, pero, the Chinos don't want us in Chinatown. I don't blame them. This country treats los Chinos the way that Spain treats Xitanos. Maybe even worse. They make them work like bestias and still they will not let them be citizens. Here we are,1963; even your poor Papi is a citizen. These are things they don't teach you in school, so you have to teach yourself." I checked my jacket pocket for my library card.

"Los payos want everything perfect and then ask for a discount." Papi always gave tips at the fish market; the vendors called him "Mr. Keep the Change." Papi laughed with delight when they said his nickname in Cantonese. "Everything sounds better than English. Mi'ja, no matter where you go, learn to say thank you in the language of the people you are with and your life will be good." Dor je.

"Chinese people helped to build this country. Maybe after Kennedy mops up the stupidity with Russia and Cuba, he can help los Chinos. Only God knows." Papi makes the sign of the Cross and mutters a blessing for El Presidente. He pinches my chin and winks. "You know, his beautiful wife looks a little China to me."

The only time Mami went with us to Chinatown, she embarrassed us by making her mean sounds and gestures of "¡Fo!" Papi made the universal sign for "crazy" and everyone laughed. "Crazy" is nothing to laugh about. I had to teach myself about that, too.

Mami was so passive aggressive and bitter that our visiting family was getting down to the the nub of runt cousins who needed Papi's handouts, El Reverendo, and a couple of loyal Titis who stuck around out of pity for me. I knew someday soon it would just be the three of us and I begged my father to get divorced. He insisted I needed my mother; the only thing I needed from her was for her to drop dead.

"Sí, Papi, whatever you say." There was no arguing with Papi. He would be loyal until his death to a woman who didn't deserve it for a daughter who didn't want it. "Hunts Point Market is good for the produce, pero the fish in El Barrio is the best; like Chinatown. All the Judíos y Latinos get along nice." Yeah, "nice." Little girl word for my old lady soul. Papi used it a lot. He wanted life to be nice for me but he wasn't willing to do what it would take to make it happen. There could be no "nice" in the House of Mami.

Papi's prophetic eyes never got to see me, years later, in my 20s walking from Loisaida to Chinatown and back for my weekly groceries, my Chinese shoes and clothes. The medicines in my bathroom cabinet prescribed by the alchemist who made special compounds for my ailments. All I had to do was point to the pain and she knew just what to put in her mortar and pestle for me from her vast apothecary cabinet every time. We communicated by facial expressions and body language, always ending in smiles and the exchange of whatever I could afford. Papi didn't live long enough to know her, or of my love for the chickens who played tic tac toe at the Chinatown Fair arcade. They always made me sad, but I could never resist them. They touched the deeply buried part of me that allowed tears.

Dor je. Xiè.Xiè. Ni Gracías.

The day before he started his new job at the diner in El Barrio, Papi took me there for an ice cream soda at the counter. The owner, Doña V., was there. He flaunted his virility at having such a "young and beautiful daughter" past his mid-life years. "What, she's only ten?" Doña V. nodded towards my wide hips. Papi pulled a stinker cigar from his inside coat pocket and lit it, to erase my embarrassment. I was Papi's Corvette.

Doña V. liked my curly hair. She dyed hers, with its old mutton texture, platinum blonde to hide the gray. That, with her Fanta orange lipstick and the heavy gold crucifix around the crepe skin of her neck, made me lean in to sniff. I reached for another napkin from a holder so could get a good whiff. Sandalwood, Rose Water, Maja cologne and week-long cotton panty piss stain. "Sorry, Doña V., disculpe usted." My good manners, despite the boarding house reach, got me extra ice cream and Papi a wink and a vulgar hand gesture regarding his virility.

Doña V. was payo and wanted Papi to like her as protection from the curses of the Psychic Reader/Adviser next door, who Papi had pegged as a fake. Papi had confided in me. "Many Halloween Xitanas in New York City. The only thing they know how to read is money." He kept his insider information from Doña V. "When someone is that old, let them have their fantasies and beliefs. It helps them live longer."

Papi always left for work at 3:30 a.m. so Mami thought he was on the hanky panky train, until he told us about the rats. It turned out that Doña V. was more piss than rose water about a lot of things. Papi told us he left early to kill rats in the basement that were crawling over food deliveries. He kept the perishables in the main kitchen and freezer as much as possible, keeping watch and cleaning everything with a surgeon's fastidiousness. He dropped a dime to the Board of Health, but the guy assigned to the diner, was "on the take." Papi tried to persuade him to do the right thing, but only money would talk; money that Papi didn't have. So he went in early and did his best to keep the basement and kitchen as clean as he could. Papi loved the customers, the neighborhood, and his after-work visits to La Marqueta. He felt so good bringing home healthy, clean food. He just couldn't justify working in a filthy place. It was too far gone and it would take more than buckets of bleach and King Pine to get that basement and kitchen to where it should be.

Papi urged Doña V. to get the basement and kitchen re-done. He used the money angle: how much more she would make attracting some new clientele, with new signs and shiny tiles, "maybe even a few nice paisanos from Little Spain."

"Esa Doña es una cheap-eh-skate. Rats get around when no one is looking. The sonuvumbiche from the Health Department is worse than the rats, un indecente. I want to cut off his balls! ¡Me cago en Dios!" Most would shit on God in whispers. Not Papi. If he cursed you, he wanted to be sure you heard it, God or no God. Mami on the other hand would cover my ears about anything that had to do with men's balls, but think nothing about calling me "una sucia cochina puta" when I wet the bed from PissTSD.

Papi loved El Barrio especially on sunny days with everyone speaking Spanish wherever you went—a stew of dialects—Boricua, Dominican, Cuban, Mexican, Castilian, Basque, Catalan, and so many more. He loved that some of his Sicilian and Italian famigghia friends lived on Palladino Avenue, heading towards his beloved East River. He liked the candy store where he played the numbers and bought me comic books and Turkish Taffy. He decided he had to do something about the rats.

Papi knew a judge who drank too much on the job and made mistakes. "Georgie Porgie has the goods on him," I heard Papi brag to Mr. Lipschitz about Detective Georgie during one of his borrachera speeches on "crooks and racketeers" as they ate Papi's homemade cheesecake, while Mami did her Saturday Sisyphus routine of cleaning soot off all the apartment windows—inside and out.

On Rat Day, Papi made sure to arrive at work before the garbage collectors and after all the homeless people were fast asleep on grates and doorways. This would be between him and the rats. And God. I know Papi felt bad for the rats and their babies and remembered their friendship on his trip from Spain, "pero están abusando de la confianza, mi'jita. When you give a rat a little bit once in a while, they are grateful, but if they have too much, they become like humans and keep wanting more. They get to the point where they will eat even if they're not hungry, igual que los Americanos."

Papi started a grease fire and made it look like an accident. He said something about oily cleaning rags. Papi called the direct line to one of his firehouse buddies to report it. The firetruck sirens rattled the windows up 116th Street. My veins, engorged with worms, woke me up in the Bronx. I could smell the fresh cotton morning of Papi's immaculately white apron; next, the pungent gray smoke acting cagey like a spy, finding ways out, leaving no evidence of origin. I could see Papi on the sidewalk, owl eyed suspicious for possible snitches. I could see from his half smile that no one was hurt and that maybe the rats escaped. I could see him shake hands with a man holding a briefcase. I could hear las vecinas en batas y rolos bochinchando about those handsome firemen and their spoiled, ungrateful Breezy Point wives who don't know how good they've got it; and the men placing bets on the who-what-why of the fire and how the insurance companies investigate up the ass sin Vaselina and you're lucky if you get half of what you lost.

The fire mostly damaged the kitchen and there was flooding in the basement. The fire was written up as accidental and Papi was off the hook. The place was shut down for renovations, and since we lived hand to mouth, Papi had to find another job fast. There would be no waiting for the new kitchen and clean basement. Papi knew that would be the case, but he was satisfied that the next cook would not be chasing rats and his neighborhood friends could return to a clean diner. "No more eating caca de ratas for my people." I never knew who Papi's people were from one week to the next. I know the fire fighters were his people that day.

Right after the fire Doña V. revealed that she had been diagnosed with throat cancer a year earlier. I felt guilty that I had laughed at her in secret, thinking she looked like the mushing together of George Washington and Queen Elizabeth—the Bette Davis one. I went with Papi to visit her on her deathbed. She owned an entire brownstone just blocks from her diner.

Papi rang the bell timidly, which was unlike him. A young woman dressed like a widow in a Lorca play answered the door. Holding a full bedpan under one arm, she simply pointed up the stairs with her chin, as if the rest of her were caught in curls of untamed barbed wire; her throat stuffed with dry communion wafers, struggling to swallow, afraid to cough. The possibilities of her young life drained by her employer's stinginess and excessive demands. She might have even caught the cancer. Lorca, my Lorca, if only you were here. "I want to sleep the sleep of apples."

The place smelled like Sunday Mass. Thickly carved mahogany furniture stabbed at my knees, painted plaster religious statues stared in quiet agonies, altars aflame with wrought iron candelabras and racist travel souvenirs, frankincense burning on charcoal disks in gilded tea cups, and prayer rosaries hanging from family portraits, strung with beads the size of hazelnuts as Jesus stared upward, as if looking for a way out, like the gray smoke in the diner, his eyes widened in search of an answer for which he didn't have a question. We followed that Torquemada inspired obstacle course up the Persian carpeted stairs to Doña V.'s bedroom. San Martin de Porres caught my braid; a warning. I wanted to run, but I knew Papi needed me.

The doors to Doña V.'s room were propped open by a plaster St. Jude and a wooden St. Peter; like wishes for a miracle in the presence of the inevitable. I could hear St. Peter dangling his keys, tormenting St. Jude. I think even Papi could hear them bickering. Porres kept his mouth shut. Of all the saints, he had the most repairs and paint touch ups. His face painted over after someone had tried to make him white.

We waited for Doña V.'s signal to approach and were summoned by a limp wave similar to Mami's. Her sallow skin matched the decades-old, elaborately embroidered yellowed sheets and chenille coverlet under which she disappeared. Even though she could already see the soles of Saint Gabriel's feet, all she talked about in a voice that smothered consonants was how much the renovations would cost her and how much water damage "esos 'omberos im'eciles" had caused. She never asked Papi how he was doing or if he or anyone else was hurt in the fire. She just said I looked pudgy, so he must be doing well. She begged Papi to come back to work for her, but offered nothing to get him through the months it would take to bring the place back up to code.

She pulled a rusty Christmas tin from under her pillow. "Cho'olate?" I shook my head, trying not to gag. "Thank you, Señora. Uh, it will spoil my dinner." Papi gave me his wink of approval. I was relieved to have made another good impression. Doña V. had never known hunger, had remained a virgin all of her life, dedicating herself to Christ and the accumulation of money.

Papi approached Doña V. with a downtempo of respect. He gently took her hand, knowing it would be the last time he would see her. She sniffed him: "A'ways wi' you' damn ci'ars. You though' I didn' know. I know every'hing. All it ta'es is an ember." Papi found it impossible to lie, and remained silent, neither confirming nor denying and relieved she thought it had been an accident. He made the sign of the cross, kissed his thumb and mumbled that the La Virgén del Rocío would see to her care. "Gracias, Doña V. por su bondad y por darle empleo a este pobre Xitano cuando más lo necesitaba. Lo siento, pero ya es tiempo...."

She responded to his compassion by spitting in his face for denying her wish that he return. She suspected the fire was his fault, but presumed it an accident. She had often thought of him as "a fool with some talents. Handsome enough to bring in the women and maricones. Good for business." Papi wiped himself with the perfectly starched white hankie Mami always slid into his coat pocket to catch his gargajos. His face went gray with sadness and shame. Had that been a man, Heaven's gates would have blown open without a key. Maybe not. Papi always fought fair. An old sick fart is an old sick fart, gender or species aside.

THIRTY-EIGHT/TWINE

On the way out of Doña V.'s after an abruptly polite farewell, and me almost knocking over poor San Martin de Porres, who had already suffered more than his share of insults, Papi pulled a butterscotch sucking candy out of his coat pocket and folded it into my hand. The smell of mildew, piss and frankincense followed us out the door. He thought of turning around, but Lorca's young widow was already bolting all the locks. Papi raised my face, his eyes unlit. "I'm sorry, mi'ja."

I'd never heard those words from Papi before. I got scared. "Why are you sorry Papi?" Taking the candy wrapper from me, he gave me his fake smile. "Because I will get to the bus stop before you!" I chased after him, laughing all the way, knowing it was what he needed to hear. The bus doors closed as Papi tried to wave them open, the bus driver pretended not to see us. "Forget the bus. Let's go for a nice walk." I didn't care what we did. Papi was holding my hand and being nice. The candy helped clean out the taste of stale piss that had settled in my throat. I guessed Papi had snuck a couple shots of Brujal before we had left in the morning.

"When people are close to death, they say and do things they don't mean. You hungry?" I quickly nodded yes. Anytime we ate without Mami around everything tasted good. The butterscotch defeated the power of stink. "How about a corned beef sandwich on a nice roll? You and me, half and half. First La Marqueta for a little rum for Papi and a little taste for you. I'll let you dip your finger. We have to disinfect ourselves from the evil in that house. A little drop on your tongue will do the trick. Your Papi will need much more, because I am bigger and I have to also clean my face."

We headed over to Don Ramiro's vegetable stall at La Marqueta. He always had a bottle hidden away to "warm up in the cold, and cool down in the heat." He sold Dominican avocados the size of footballs and taught me how to ripen them inside a paper bag. There was always something to learn at La Marqueta and thankfully, it wasn't far from Doña V.'s. It went on for five long beautiful blocks beneath the Metro North El train. As soon as we got close, I could hear an orchestra of sounds, like one of Papi's records spinning on the victrola. A descant of "Buenos Días" "Shalom aleichem" "Gracias" "How much?" rose above the rainbows of fish scales and fruit bins. Every now and then you'd hear "jolope" yelled over the crowd, which meant somebody had been mugged. I never actually saw a "jolope" but had heard stories from Papi, as he warned me to always stay close. La Marqueta was a library without books.

Don Ramiro had an eye for the ladies and always put a little extra in their bags. He once gave Mami a big yucca root and told her to knock Papi out with it and run away with him. Don Ramiro was 88 years old and tuerto. Papi whispered to me that people's eyes get crossed from staring as two cats pass each other. (He forgot he had told me that in our building's basement one time when he caught me staring at two humping cats as he was throwing out the garbage.)

"Hola, Don Ramiro, it looks like you're going to outlive us all." Papi and Don Ramiro hugged hello in that backslapping way, so no one would mistake them for maricones. "Looking good, my friend, looking good." Don Ramiro did a little boxing dance and thanked Papi for the compliment with a big nicotine smile from a leathery, brown face, that put some light back into Papi's eyes. They talked about the weather, complained about not having money and losing at cards.

"How about a little medicine today so we both stay young?" Papi pointed to Don Ramiro's hiding spot with his lips. Don Ramiro handed his rum flask to Papi, so he could have the first drink. Papi shivered with approval and used the cap to drop a whisper of rum onto my tongue. Don Ramiro wouldn't have liked my pinky dipping into his flask. He and Papi once caught me picking my nose and eating my boogers, but didn't say anything. Papi asked me about the rum. "Nice?"

I wanted to puke, but smiled and nodded instead. Don Ramiro patted me on the head and assured me I would be a doctor someday. "Curro, she is too beautiful to be anybody's wife and too smart to waste her life changing dirty diapers." Only a few people called Papi by his Xitano nickname. "Maybe you're right, Don Ramiro. Maybe you're right." Papi wasn't agreeing with him, he just always deferred to the elders. I wish he did agree. I would have made a great doctor, booger eater or not.

We walked the length of La Marqueta. I loved all the different fragrances from fresh red snapper to ancient sandalwood and palo santo.

Papi always stopped by the Botánica stall for advice on the numbers and horses from La Señora Isabel, who carved coconuts into faces and made rosaries from peonia seeds. Papi always reminded me to never look an adult straight in the eyes because it is disrespectful for children to do that, and especially with La Señora Isabel. "She has powers and visits with the dead. I don't want them to see your soul, they might want to take you with them." Papi didn't know that I'd been yakking it up with the dead from the time I could name colors and count to five. I could feel them, hear them, sometimes see them. Then there's something that happens between us—an exchange of understandings that are beyond words. I think that if Papi ever found out his nenita was born an Espiritista he would have had what Mrs. Goldstein called a "kanipshit." Papi always had a story before we talked to his Marqueta friends. "Mi'ja, I got through The Depression by dreaming winning numbers. One time I hit $500 and bought lots of groceries for my neighbors, including steaks for La Morena."

La Morena was the lady next door to Papi when he was young and single in a Harlem walk up. "Beautiful woman, mi'ja. We were good friends. Lots of sufrimientos in her life, three children, no husband. We never closed our doors in that building. We all took care of each other. Sometimes I cooked a big paella for the whole building. Those were good times." Papi stopped to say "ahsalamilaken" to Mr. Mohammed, who forgave Papi for never getting it right. It was a double insult since salami was involved. Mr. Mohammed always gave me some fresh peppermint and taught me how to rub it between my fingers to get the best smell and how to use it to "keep the breath fresh so when you say your prayers they arrive sweet to Allah." I knew he meant Jesus because Papi told me that Jesus had a different name in every country. Papi and Mr. Mohammed talked about yoga for back pain and where to get the best lamb. They talked about Kosher and Halal. Papi always told me to only buy meat from Jews and Muslims and that everything else was dirty and poison. He didn't have any problem when Mami made pernil she bought on sale at the everything supermarket. "God made lechones so that the poor have something nice for Christmas." All I could think about was how it wasn't so good for the pig. What about their Christmas?

Holy candles and ropes of sausage hung beside rows of cotton Dashiki's and leather caps. Miss Awa from Senegal always gave Papi a free stick of rose incense she made herself "for your little rose, God bless her. Look at those pretty rose cheeks!" Papi showed all his teeth when he smiled at Miss Awa. Mami hated her and said she smelled like "coco podri'o." I was so happy when Mami stayed home. Miss Awa smelled like the sea and I could breathe really deep around her. She hugged like a fluffy cloud. I was jealous of her happy grandchildren, but liked them just the same and stared hard to see if they would open their wings. They looked like the little holy card of a Black angel Don Ramiro kept in a tiny wooden frame in his secret spot near the rum. Miss Awa taught La Señora Isabel how to make Gri-Gri, little pouches for good luck and protection. I prayed to Jesus that someday they would make one for me. They had both met Mami and had probably figured out that giving me a Gri-Gri would probably get me a beating. I'm sure they were right, but I wanted one anyway.

Papi and La Señora Isabel were all business most times. "We play the numbers, hear about the horses and get out, okay?" I shrugged since I never got to play. Papi kept his hand near my eyes. La Señora Isabel always told Papi "Your little one is a daughter of Yémaya. She has gifts. You can't see it because you don't want to. One day you will. Maybe then you'll win more than lose." Papi placed his bets and that was the last time he took me with him to see La Señora Isabel.

Papi got real "talky-talky"after a few shots, Mami always said. "God was good and gave me the winning numbers plenty of times. Pay attention to your dreams, mi'ja. It's how God talks to us." I had never heard Papi talk about good times. I didn't even realize that until I heard the happy stories. He never talked like that at home. He hardly talked at all when he was sober. "I'm known for my meatballs and red sauce all over New York, even the Waldorf Astoria—at least the people in the kitchen know." Papi could make pizza dough spin like a UFO.

When Papi heard that Doña V. had died, he made the sign of the cross and kissed his thumb. "Since she died a virgin, en paz descanse, she will probably go to heaven, whether she deserves it or not." It made me think that maybe I could kill Mami as long as I stayed a virgin my whole life. I wondered if it would count if I had a girlfriend instead of a boyfriend. If that was the case, maybe all mariconas go to heaven. It made me happy to think that Carmen might be in Heaven. I could barely get through the steamy Bronx summers; there was no way I was going to have any stamina or fun in hell. It was settled then. I would be a maricona and would someday get to see Carmen again.

THIRTY-NINE/IRON

The Bronx Zoo was free on Wednesdays and public transportation was always free for kids under five, so we took the bus.

Being small, I got away with free bus rides till I hit Second Grade. On subways, I slipped beneath turnstiles until Seventh Grade, when the token booth attendant was distracted. Papi taught me the ropes. I had already taught myself to be invisible.

"We are not stealing, mi'ja. They are stealing from us. Taking our money and never fixing the trains. The stations smell like toilets and when did you go to the subway that you didn't see a rat? Capiche? Taking back what is stolen from us is not thievery, it is justice." Xitano Robin Hood. "One day the Indians will take back Manhattan from those white sonuvumbiches. I hope you will be there to witness and dance on the graves of evil men." When Papi was sober, it was "God Bless America and the Statue of Liberty." When he'd had a few shots it was "America is stolen land."

On our way to the elephants, I smelled hot dogs. I tugged at Papi's coat and he gave me a dollar to hold for our lunch. "Hot dogs later. Try the relish this time. Something new for the palate is good for the brain too. Even if you can't travel the world, you can still taste it. Many cultures make relishes, mi'ja, its one way to use up scraps and not waste food." He had never given me a dollar before. I was in shock and held the dollar in my fist with the ends sticking out, so the other kids could see.

An elephant's eye caught my attention. I was sure she was reading my mind. I tried to hide all the embarrassing thoughts in my brain like peeing the bed and Mami wiping my culo. It turned into a staring contest. Falling into her eye, I landed on shadows of Jupiter. Phosphorescent fish swam the rings of Saturn and gave me the eye too. My clothes slipped off. I floated upwards; passed them all. The sharp point of a falling star came towards my eyes, I shut them tight and was back again, next to Papi. The elephant dunked her trunk and sucked my dollar down (she was drawn to the peanut crumbs that were still in my pocket from weeks before). She sneezed before I could get out a cuss of protest, and covered me in elephant snot, but no dollar.

Papi laughed so hard, he dribbled. "Elefante must be allergic to money, like your Papi." He cracked himself up with that one so much his hat almost fell off. Papi never noticed I was gone. He never heard my name among the fish of Saturn or saw me naked among the stars. He didn't know the elephant like I did. Papi wiped his mouth with the back of his hand and gave me his perfect white hankie from the pocket of his Guayabera with the other. I did my best to wipe off the snot, but it just kept appearing, especially inside my thick, rough curls. We ended up working it out with wet napkins from the hot dog guy, leaving my nappy red hair full of paper lint.

There would be no hot dogs for us. All we had left was Papi's bus fare and enough to share a soft pretzel. Papi gave me the bigger part with the most salt. We sat on a bench to eat. I had learned early on to take small bites and eat slowly so that food I liked would last longer. We drank lukewarm water from an old brass fountain. To this day, I still think of elephants at the sight of hot dogs. The last little salt pebble on our pretzel sat on my tongue as Papi and I made our way to the house of cats. Papi called it "the cat house." No doubt he got a kick out of thinking he was getting away with saying it. The innocent look on my face was on an as-needed switch that I carried around all the time. I was born an old woman and understood almost everything when I eavesdropped on grownups. "Yes Papi, I want to see the cats, big ones, like tigers, not those mean skinny ones you chase down the alley behind the bar."

All my innuendos slid by, Ninja style. If I said Cat House, adults were certain I was talking about the zoo. Mami smacked me daily for other things, like not believing in Santa Claus, shooting olive pits out of my nose at cockroaches, or making a disgusted face as she slid a mojón-like brick of Spam out of the can to slice up and fry with runny eggs. "Mojón" meant death by chancletasos, until I convinced her it was also an Irish last name. As long as I put a Miss, Mrs. or Mister in front of it, I got away with saying it. Swearing was my mental stabilization plan.

I wonder how many cats there'd been in the alleys of Papi's loneliness. Those alleys where sadness soaked through cloth shoes. Where Papi took cigar breaks to look up at the sky like a boss. Where he spit loud and hard and examined the melanin patchwork on his arms that kept him out of any more fancy kitchens. Where he saw his apron needed bleaching. Where he stared at the ring finger that would deny any sign of Mami. "I don't want to lose it in the spaghettis."

As I got older, Papi shared a few of his secret stories. I had just turned sixteen and not a single boy came to my party. Papi gave me a hooky day in Washington Heights as a consolation prize.

We were breathing in the Hudson River from el parque Dominicano and Papi let it slip out that his friend La Morena from Harlem had broken his heart. Right after he said it I felt that silent regret bomb of his detonate. A butterfly fluttered in his throat. "This river used to be so clean I could swim in it; the East River too. You could see the fish. Now the fish have two heads and three eyes and the water smells like caquita." I knew Papi restrained himself from saying *mierda de hijos de puta me cago en la ostía y en los cabrones que se cagan donde comen*. Several versions of which he said a lot during political arguments and tirades about polluters. "This city has changed, mi'ja. Hunts Point used to have dairy farms. We used to see cows eating grass, now we see hoodlums pissing in doorways. Look at Harlem, it used to be beautiful during the Renaissance until los morenos went crazy. No self-control, those people. That's what happens when you don't have disciplina."

I took advantage of his gentle mood to challenge him. "Papi, please don't talk badly about Black people. It's the drugs Papi, the heroin, not the people. What about all the Black people in our family?" He turned and said in all seriousness, momentarily forgetting where he came from: "That's on your mother's side." He shrugged like I could never possibly understand what he was feeling. He was right. I didn't. Not that time. I just knew that Papi drank when he was sad, and some people shot up heroin so they could fly away from their sadness. So they could be sunflowers, like Carmen, living free like those Bronx cows used to do.

I thought about heroin a lot, but I knew that Carmen La Maricona didn't want that for me. "The Dominicans and the Puerto Ricans got together with the Coloreds and that was the end of it." Papi looked away. "The end of what, Papi?" "Forggeddaboutit. Anyway, los morenos in your Mami's family aren't really Black. They're Indios. You don't have to think about those things." I persisted. "But Papi, you said your mother was morena and I have the picture of her you gave me, remember?" Papi pulled the pint from his back pocket and took a long, hard swig.

He looked across the Hudson to the Palisades of Jersey like it was another world. "A morena Xitana is not the same as a morena Americana. Xitana women have salero; even the poorest ones know they are queens. They have good hair and aren't bembonas.

It took all my will not to hate him. "Pero Papi, Black women are beautiful. I will never be as beautiful as them. Sometimes I think Mami hates my hair." Papi's jaw went slack. He lit one of his stinky, crooked cigars and blew three rings into the air. Someday I would learn to do that. "Your poor mother; it takes her an hour to get through that jungle bush of yours." His words knotted up in my stomach for so many reasons. Couldn't he see the hate and resentment with which Mami yanked my hair before school most days? Didn't he hear me cry? Didn't he know he was insulting our people on both sides of the family? Papi wasn't a stupid man, and that made it all so much worse. Couldn't he feel the martillasos in my head? Why couldn't Papi feel my hurt? I could feel his. Even my throat and chest hurt from that swig. I could always feel when something was wrong with Papi, even when we were apart. "You do like your Mami says, you stay with your own kind, mi princesa rubia, but make sure it is like the kind on my side of the family, eh?" Princesa rubia. I hated that name. I hated being his White Princess. I didn't know what I was. I had more in common with the elephant who didn't belong in the Bronx. Papi didn't talk much about being Xitano, except when he was with his Jewish friends. "The Xitanos and Jews were all the same to Hitler. They threw us into the same ditches." We stared at the Hudson, I tried hard to see a fish so I could show Papi and he could be happy again. A scrappy looking seagull rode a gentle wake of yellow foam on gray water.

Papi and I had the same conversations and arguments all the time, for years on end. Having my own opinions and moral compass cost me in beatings from Mami and a never-ending struggle with Papi. Harlem had been his home, the place where he started his first and only business, a diner. "Mi'ja, after a year I had a gun strapped to my leg. Too many crooks coming to rob me. People I thought were my friends. I closed the place down before I killed somebody. Black nigger bastards."

I hated hearing him talk like that. He didn't know I felt like he was talking about me. The real me. Me inside. The me that knows who she is. The me locked inside of God's melanin mistake, and if you snitch on God you get jacked-up big time.

The older I got, the more Papi and I fought. It just didn't feel like him. It was like some demon would take him over and booze was the only cure. He needed a lot more swigs to get nice. More fire to feel in my throat and chest. When Papi was drunk, he loved everybody. I wanted to ask him more about La Morena that day by the Hudson but he was too sober. It was hard to love Papi when he got like that. It was beaten into me that you have to love your parents no matter who they are and what they do to you.

People who say the "N-word" are bigots too—even worse—because the real sounds of all the letters and the whole word sticks to their insides until they're dead and then its stuck to the insides of their kids—their grandkids—their great grandkids and every generation that euphemized the word into code and let it fester until it formed a hard shell. So hard you couldn't even shit it out. N's hanging from your lungs, your tripas, your heart. You can always tell which dead people had the most N's because they have the most maggots; only by then they get covered up with earth and grass and flowers and prayers and tears and only nice memories and it grows all over again.

Say it. SAY IT! SAY NIGGER! Find the roots of that tree. Cut out those roots. Kill those roots. Burn them. Eat the ashes. Shit them. Make new maggots that fertilize new life for everyone. Let the sacred ash feed sunflowers, seeds, and new grass. Make ashy crosses on your foreheads and promises to be kept. Let ghosts and the living make love in the graveyards. Let the wetness of their joy become a new day. A Tree of Knowledge embraced, standing tall beside the River of Wisdom. No more twisted roots. No more strange fruit. Some day, but not today.

A Bigot's Secret Prayer

it is never today
it's why I don't stay
nothing changes
stuck in yesterday
tomorrow the same
before I die

may I please for just
one day
one hour
one moment of grace
live today
free of hate

FORTY/PANTIES

I cover my doll, Negrita's, ears whenever Papi gets the Demon and we cry together late into the night. Three of El Reverendo's six kids live with us when their mother, who Mami called "La India," needs a break, as he goes around preaching and building orphanages. The Castro convertible sofa, is hell as my primas snore, kick and sweat up the sheets. They talk about babyish things like bows for their hair, blue-eyed dolls and lipstick. Candy is the only thing we can agree on. They imitate El Reverendo, quoting scripture and verse when they can use it, like to prove to me I'm going to hell because I like boys. They don't know I like girls too, especially tough ones, like Carmen. Not the mean ones like Diana Rosario, or the pinky-pink girly-girls like my sofa cousins. Papi stays up late in the kitchen and kills the Demon over and over with shots of Dominican rum. The Demon always comes back the next day. Sometimes it just get really quiet like a closed book or a broken TV.

Negrita always consoles me after Mami's beatings and humiliations. Mami hates Negrita. Mami's sister, my Titi Angela gave her to me on one of her visits. Negrita came inside a cardboard box, on a bed of what looked like big flakes of a torn up letter. She fit just right, like in a little crib. Titi made her a blankie out of a crocheted potholder. "Esa muñeca e' diabolica." Anything that has to do with Blackness is diabolical to Mami.

Mami never badmouths Negrita it in front of Titi, just to me. I know she's jealous of Titi and of how much I love my Negrita. Titi told me she is a very special doll because she isn't like any others. So what that she doesn't have fingers or toes, and that all those skankie blonde webfoot doll bitches judge her? We have ESP, me and Negrita. She has a little sky-blue head wrap, and tiny gold earrings pierced into the sides of her head where her ears are supposed to be. Her eyes are just like the buttons on Papi's shirt collars, so it's almost like Negrita is always with him too. She's his daughter too, even if he doesn't know it. Her dress is made of little trapitos hand sewn together.

Titi says that every patch on Negrita's dress has a magical story that Negrita will tell me if I take good care of her. Titi says that Negrita is well traveled, having come all the way from Ayití. "They were the first Black slave revolutionaries to liberate themselves. Your Negrita comes from great people. She's a fighter, just like you." I don't know exactly where Ayití is, only that Mami had lived on the border, on the Dominican side. We don't have any maps at home. El Reverendo says he went there as a missionary and was almost eaten by cannibals, but that Jesus saved him. I think they probably ate Jesus, just like the Catholics do, over and over again. Nobody seems to understand how gross that is no matter who does it. And priests are supposed to do it every day, even if nobody else is around. Anyway, I think El Reverendo is telling fibs, to make Jesus his personal hero so people will go to his church. Jesus doesn't really need the publicity. Anyhow, I like that Titi calls me a fighter like it's something good.

Negrita has no shoes because she doesn't have feet. Not like Barbie with her humpy arches and heels that make her look like she has a stick up her ass. That's what Mami says about El Reverendo's wife, because she acts very proper and whispers when she talks. Negrita is beautiful and dignified and doesn't need to prove anything to anybody. Like Barbie, she doesn't have a toto either. She's just here for me, and part of me, from the minute I opened that little box.

Negrita wouldn't be caught dead with Ken. Ken is a snot, a real jelly apple sonuvabigshot, and Negrita and I know it. It oozes from every thread of his tennis outfit. He has a bump where his dick should be. Boy dolls have no dicks and girl dolls have no totos and nobody has curlies. It's like down there is dirty and something to hide. Dolls don't get periods and even G.I. Joe doesn't get "wood," like I heard Papi talk about one time when he asked El Reverendo why he had so many kids. Negrita never pees, poops or burps or farts, but I teach her all about it. She should know things, just in case. There is one doll that pees, Sun Dee, so us girls can learn how to change diapers.

Our bodies became objects of fear in secrecy and shame. There's a vaccine for measles, but there is no inoculation from body shame and erasure, like the people hidden away at the Last Supper. I know, I already mentioned it, but hell, it gets to me. The cooks, the winemakers, the potters of bowls and chalices, the tailors, the jewelers, the growers of food, the builders, furniture makers, the bakers of bread, the cobblers, the sweepers and broom makers, the launderers, the servants who carried it all in and took it all out. And no flush toilets. Who cleans up the barf? Throughout history, hidden witnesses of everything; I so want to meet you.

Clearly, DaVinci—for all his famously fancy brains—never thought about it. Or perhaps he feared reprisal from his patrons? I'd expect a bent neck from other kiss-ass painters of the crustaceous class, but my Da V? Servants and workers beyond his brush. Indelible moments remain: the Judas kiss; Peter and the cock that snitched three times. Ken and Barbie: everyone and their brother knows about them. Me, I wouldn't give a second look to a grown man in short pants especially one without a penis; unless of course he lost it saving lives, not taking them. All Kens are created equal, but not every soldier's a hero. "Mami, why were there no Puerto Ricans at the Last Supper?" Sneer. "Ask your uncle." Sigh. "He told me to ask you." Thank God and Jesus and my Titi Angela for Negrita. And all the bullet, bottle and brick revolutionaries of Ayití. Whatever it took.

Rubber skin. No real feet or hands. No articulation in her neck; stuffed to immobility. There would be no bending, no running. I don't remember her having a mouth. Other dolls had all moving parts. They could sit up straight. Patty Playpal could walk and talk; she was quite the celebrity among other dolls until she was replaced by newer, less lumbering models. She soon learned that ultimately society will always favor the petite.

Not one doll could do it all. They bored me. When we played, I did most of the talking. Negrita was the only one who could converse. We talked inside each other's minds about real things like how Abraham counted every star, and why anyone would waste their time counting them, and how come there were no Black or Chino people at the Last Supper. No Black or Chino angels. No Indian angels even though they have more feathers than anybody. Adults made no sense. We wondered where the women were and who had set the table and prepared the food since all the white Apostles were sitting on their butts. There's one Black King Magi guy but he's expected to kneel at the feet of white baby Jesus and bring him gifts. I could only tell these feelings to Negrita. She never called me a blast-feemer. We talked about Judas and how sorry he felt for being a rotten friend. I told Negrita that Señora Dorca, my Sunday School teacher, said it was planned by God that Judas be a snitch. El Reverendo and Señora Dorca talked about *free will*; at the same time they told us that God planned everything. We talked about how come I wasn't Black on the outside like I felt on the inside. And how come the fun Black cousins were sent away and the sorta-white-looking ones got to live with us? Negrita, me, and any guests, all on the Castro Convertible, feet to face. Negrita pointed out to me that the Americanos hated Castro but named a couch after him.

Negrita told me people were scared of Black people because if God was white and Man was made in his image, then in whose image was the Black man made? Negrita said that stupid people think the devil made them Black in the fires of Hell where they all came from. Human smores. I cried when she said that. I held her tight and told her I loved her and not to believe all those horrible lies. I told her she was beautiful and that our onyx Black cousins with green eyes were so kind and beautiful they got sent away because of Mami's mala leche nature. Mami was always jealous of anyone who wasn't as miserable as she was, and prettier. My Black cousins felt like sunshine and looked like mermaids. Mami always felt like a constipated gray sky trying to squeeze out hail and snow. She was cursed with the face of someone always pujando; at least when she looked at me.

I felt weird naming my little friend Negrita, but Titi Angela told me that was her name. The family called me Blanquita and I didn't like that either. I do know that if I didn't have Negrita in those early years, I might not have made it. I had learned to talk and walk really late, but once I started, I knew too much, felt too much, and talked too much. Mami told me to shut up all the time. Whenever I said something she didn't like or when she didn't understand, she slapped me. I got spanked for repeating the swears she and Papi said all the time. Mami sounded like hairspray with all her mean shhhhhhhushes. She threatened to sew my lips together, the upstairs and the downstairs, and have me put away for being loca.

Mami almost had me locked up for good one time. She was busy sorting through a pile of bargain panties at Hearn's Department Store across from an Alexander's store when I was closer to eight than seven. Trips to the South Bronx Third Avenue shopping hub were exhausting, as Mami hunted for the lowest prices, dragging me through every shop without so much as a candy bar. She always decided when I was hungry. She hated my striped baseball jacket, "pareces un macho," and not just because she thought it made me look like a boy, but because Papi was the one who bought if for me and she knew I liked it more than anything she'd ever made for me and I insisted on wearing it all the time. She could only smack me so much over a jacket.

I wandered over to a stack of Barbie Dolls. I hated the way they stared at me and wanted to take their heads off, but didn't want to get caught. It was a lot easier to take off their shoes. They had tiny feet like Mami and high heels. I wanted high heels, but Mami said not until I graduated from Junior High School, and that was a really long way off. After I stuffed as many Barbie shoes as I could in my pocket, I noticed some tiny harmonicas. I wanted one for Negrita. I blew into a bunch of them, and none of them sounded right. Mami was buried in pantaletas and didn't pay attention. I took a fistful of them, so Negrita could pick out her own. Mami always picked out everything for me. There was no way I would do that to Negrita and especially not with a harmonica. Negrita had to figure out which one sounded right to her.

With bargains in hand, Mami rattled off the price she paid for her treasures and how she would have enough panties for a year. She grabbed my hand to cross the street between shops and noticed my stuffed pockets. "What you have in there?" I sucked in my stomach hoping my pockets would flatten out. "Nothing, Mami." She slapped my hands away and dug into my pockets to find a stash of Barbie's high heels in one, and tiny harmonicas in the other. "Nothing? You tell me this is nothing? ¡Ladrona y embustera!" She nearly dismembered my arm dragging me over to the nearest police officer.

"Escuse me. My daughter is a teef and I want you take her to jail." The officer looked at me and smiled. Mami was not pleased. She held the contraband up to his face. "Look at this. Look in her pockets. She left all those poor dolls with no shoes." The officer spoke to Mami in the soft tones of trying to calm a rabid dog. I don't think he liked Barbie either. "Well, Mrs., I have an idea. Why don't you take your daughter back to the store, have her confess to the manager and return everything? What do you think?" He was so handsome Mami would have sent me to the electric chair if he'd asked. I interpreted back and forth and changed the manager part to cashier. Mami fell for it. I figured that managers were usually men who thought they were Napolean or something like that, like Papi had told me, and that one of the school kids working a register might go easier on me.

I was right. Mami went to a white boy, figuring he had more authority. "Sure, lady, no problem." He handed Mami a plastic bucket without even looking at her and told me to throw everything I took into it. Mami made me apologize. "Sure kid, no problem." Mami liked him just for being white. Mami shook a finger in my face. "He nice boy. You be nice if you want to find somebody like that." In that moment, jail sounded a whole lot better. It looked like one way or another, I would grow up to be somebody's bitch. I could hear Negrita whisper: "Remember Ayití."

FORTY-ONE/ROUGE

As it turned out, I admired almost every woman Mami called "loca." Iris Chacón; Mirta Silva; Marilyn Monroe; Titi Angela; and Flor with big hair, big purse, big butt, who rented a room from Los Aleluyas next door. These "locas" were smart, beautiful and original. I think that's what Mami hated the most. Her brain had been damaged, but not enough to be oblivious. She knew how dreadfully limited she was, but never how cruel.

According to her Book of Mami, Flor was the most loca of all because she was "bembona" and "vulgar" and threw her head way back when she laughed, almost always dropping her purse. I loved when that happened because all the fun stuff in her purse would spill out, and she'd always find something to give me as a present: gum; a chocolate; a near empty spray bottle of perfume, or a tiny lipstick sample; that was my favorite.

Mami would thank her flatly and wait until our apartment door shut behind us. "That has her germs, nena, throw that garbage out before you catch something disgusting down there." I didn't know what Mami meant, but I knew it was bad whenever she pointed to my toto with her lips. "Pero Mami, look, it's brand new." She would slap it out of my hand and make me throw it out. The apartment was too small and creaky for me to dig it out of the trash after Mami had fallen asleep. Papi said that Mami could "hear a mouse piss on cotton." She never heard them when they pissed on me.

FORTY-TWO/MESH

Mary M. has fleshy bracelets up both arms from suicide attempts. Mary calls herself an artist as she languishes in the locked ward of Bellevue Psychiatric in Manhattan. It's my junior year of high school; my brain maps out all the ways I will escape my own captivity from beneath Mami's contagious fears and rage. Curds and Whey Contrary Mary must have quite a Mami herself. Her face made up like an aging diva with leaky eyes. My cousin Emilio's been locked up since shortly after his military discharge from Vietnam. His war flashbacks and delusions of being Charles Manson keep me on the visitor's list most weekends. Emilio trusts me, and I love him like a brother. He's El Reverendo's first born.

"You know what I was forced to do over there? I was embalming dead bodies, lots of them with missing parts. My friends. My brothers. We're killing women and babies over there. Too many civilians getting lit up. There's little girls selling themselves to Americans just for something to eat—and let me tell you cuz, we're not all heroes. I started dropping acid to escape. Better than what they give us here. Like Timothy Leary had sent it over. Cuz, can you get me some?"

Emilio never waits for my response. He talks, I lean, my hand on his knee, so he knows I'm listening. "Did you see I made the papers?" Manson's written up in the Times. Emilio lights a cigarette. His smile is more of a grimace and he folds and refolds the paper until he can slip it into his drooping robe pocket. "Mary's a nice lady, gives me her papers when she's done. She's a really good painter. They took away her things because she painted a naked woman with nipples and pubes. They say she's a dyke. I can't believe you're sixteen already. I don't believe it. After she painted the naked woman she told me she got raped by some orderlies. Lots of perverts in this cage. I believe her. The real nut jobs are the ones who get a paycheck. All kinds of things happen here, especially at night. Like Nam without Napalm. God, you're beautiful, cuz. You look like a full grown woman. Mary always wears that Russian fur hat. She paints good, though."

I always bring my portable Califone record player and a pink 45's case full of Motown and a little Johnny Thunder. I like talking with the patients; they're smarter and definitely more interesting than anyone I've ever met on the outside. Robert, "Never call me Bob! He's the other one!" informs me that he's here studying to be an astronaut. Mary had all of them painting, until the attendants confiscated her supplies. They were allowed to keep the paintings they'd made as long as they didn't have any "unsavory or homosexual images. Nothing that incites." It must be like being back in school for them, but these students are definitely smarter than their teachers. It's 1970 and people are still being locked up for being queer. I just don't get it—it's not contagious. I wish it was. This feeling of being in-between, of not being male or female, of thinking that falling in love has nothing to do with having a bicho or a toto, well, there's really no one I can talk to about it. There are people I can maybe tell, but I'm not sure yet.

Robert shows me the planets he painted; little circular globs of pink and green paint, each with a white dot in the middle. "You see here, that's the inner light of the planet. Every planet has a piece of the sun inside and that's what makes them keep spinning. The Milky Way is the boss that keeps everybody in line. Orion is a show-off. Take away his club and shield and he's a nobody. I want to go to Mars first and ask him why he started war." A long silence. "You know your cousin is nuts, right?" I stand up, my eyes lingering on the midnight blue landscape of Robert's universe, where Mars is pink like the case for my 45s. "Wanna to hear some music, Robert?" He nods yes and covers his ears. "Hahahahaha! Just kidding. It drives the moron social workers nuts when I do stuff like that and they have to fill out their stupid forms. You're not a social worker, are you? Nah, of course not. You're a kid. Yeah, go ahead, music is groovy. What the fuck is groovy? Oh, sorry, pardon my French." I wonder why the French always get blamed when people swear in English.

The Four Tops are very popular on the ward, especially, "Shake Me, Wake Me." Emilio sings to me and dances a little, his hospital pajama bottoms dragging on the unwaxed floor. The drugs shut down his moves and rhythm.

Emilio never asks me to dance; he just grabs me. Attendants roll their eyes and go back to their wrinkled magazines and juvenile word puzzles. I whisper to calm Emilio down. "All will be well. You are good, you are kind, just a little sadness in your mind." I always turn to poetry and rhymes in times of stress. Rhymes in times of grime and slime like here where even roaches hide, all high on crumbs of phenobarbital can't find their antennae like a man can't find his thumbs.

Papi making me watch and listen to Mohammed Ali always gets me thinking in new ways. I still can rise up on the worst of days with "float like a butterfly, sting like a bee." Emilio softens from my whispers and gently pulls me close. Always a slow dance to fast music. "You know, Emilio, Papi is the one who buys all the records for me." Emilio gives me a half smile, which for a person bombed out on Vietnam and Thorazine, is like Flor throwing back her head and dropping her purse. "How is my unc doing?" It's a question I don't know how to answer, since Papi is so full of secrets and achaques. "Papi still tells good stories and jokes. He told me to say hello to you and that when you get out you can live with us if you don't have a place."

I don't think Papi understands how far gone Emilio is. He feels guilty that he can't visit him since he started working seven days a week "to make a little extra," which means covering his gambling debts. Mami always makes sure to let me know that Papi doesn't have anything saved, except for the five dollars she forces him to give her for the savings account every week. She doesn't need to tell me since I'm her weekly interpreter at the bank and fill out the deposit slips. When the teller stamps her savings book, she eyes it with suspicion, just in case the teller is trying to cheat her. When we get outside she makes me look it over and reassure her that the account is up to date.

Mami always does her best to keep her jobs on the side, swearing me to secrecy, so she can have her own little stash of money in a sock hidden in a shoe box in the closet. She points it out to me weekly. "If I drop dead, that is for you." I remember the first time she made twenty dollars and felt like she had won a lottery. It was an elaborate flamenco outfit for the doll of a neighbor's daughter. By the time Mami's done with one of her dolls, it looks more like La Virgen de la Macarena than a flamenco dancer. All white and gold and lace. Tiny pearls stitched on like a sprinkling of stars and doll-size hoop earrings made from scraps of wire. Mami makes tiny flamenco shoes from cardboard and gold nail polish. She hand-hems the mantilla with a tight little ruffle all the way around. They're so perfect they always end up as unloved bed decorations.

Mami is proud to earn beyond the grip of a bully sweatshop foreman. She can't be creative in a factory; only do as she is told, repeating the same pattern twelve hours a day. Paid by the piece, she revs up her sewing machine like a Harley. When Papi's not home, she still does, cleaning up her sewing area before he walks in, asking about dinner. Mami knows how proud Papi is and how he needs to be the only one who brings home the bacon, no matter how skinny the pig.

Mami's mind is more screwed up than anyone's in the locked ward. Her glamorous beauty and tiny body distract from all the secrets she drags around, keeping her undetected and untreated. Maybe that's a good thing, since locas don't get too much respect in public hospitals.

Mary M. is so kind to me, as if she knows I need a mother's love. "Come here, dear." She pats the folding chair next to hers. "Emilio tells me you're a poet." "I try, Miss Mary." She winces and a thousand wrinkles surround her fuchsia lips. "Try? Well, you either are or you aren't. Which is it?" I freeze. I didn't want to lie and pretend to believe in myself. "Okay. Let's just imagine that you are a poet. Do you think you might write one for me?" Deep breath. Fluttering heart. "Yes, Miss Mary. I know I can."

I know right away that I can write about the her mink Cossack style hat, and how she looks like a queen, or maybe a character in Doctor Zhivago. "Next weekend then? Will you have it for me? Saturday?" Reddening cheeks. Fluttering nostrils. "Yes, Saturday. I promise." She waves me back to the Califone. "Did you bring anything classical?" Sinking stomach. "I don't think they put those on 45s." I never want to disappoint my Empress of the Locked Ward. "How about Mahalia Jackson?" Miss Mary looks away, then back again. "Yes, of course! Nothing in this world is more classic than Miss Mahalia Jackson!" I play "Trouble of the World" and Miss Mary sobs so much that the orderlies drag her back to her room, like somehow crying is bad, or shameful, or crazy. Miss Mary fights back hard. Fighting back is not allowed once they call you "crazy."

Emilio whispers, "Mary can't take this place anymore. She's too beautiful for this world." I secretly wonder if it's my fault for playing Mahalia Jackson. Emilio and I keep our eyes, as best we can, on a spinning 45 as the pills cart rolls out with a limp and mispronounced names jab into the air.

FORTY-THREE/ZIPPERS

In the ward, I remember a time Mami was distracted, digging through her purse in search of gum. I waddled away in my snowsuit and fat cotton diaper to the edge of the El train platform on Simpson Street. I looked down and in a flash had the thought that if I jumped Mami could never hit me again. People are always nice to dead people and say nice things. I thought that maybe Mami wouldn't hate me and maybe even love me just because I was dead. Light-speed thoughts, a tornado of images, my heart a Black Hole, the train's face a silver angel. Freedom roared towards me as I closed my eyes and gravity opened her arms to embrace my tiny, cocooned body. BAM!

Mami grabbed me by the scruff and gave me a public spanking until fevered skin sucked my soul back in, too big for me, too old. I stumbled dazed, trapped in a bargain basement snowsuit, drowning with every breath as I disappointedly returned to the ugly world of Mami.

Strangers sideglanced without a word. Mami's hands were chicken feet, clawing me back into her bitterness. A pack of schoolgirls stared like it was a show, snapping gum and sucking on lollipops and candy necklaces. I imagined myself sticking darts into their nasty bitch eyes so they could never shame anyone else. Sí, violated children can't help but have violent thoughts. The stench of El Vivero on Mami's breath. Plucked chickens hung where her pupils should be. Mami was lucky that Carmen La Maricona worked the street under the train and couldn't hear me wailing, or it wouldn't have been me that got a beating. Carmen would stick up for me. I knew that for sure.

Fever in my legs
begins at the knees
spreads quickly
I could be sewing a hole
in the crotch of my pants

usually while still wearing them,
watching TV.
Flabbiness
stretch marks
varicose veins
and not even a baby
to show for it.
Abandoned body,
sludge of sad flesh
found still breathing.
He has kind hands,
raised to be a gentleman
in Poland.
We share the same birthdate
and look like siblings.
A kiss for each bruise.
A card for every holiday.
Love is so hard to believe.
I got through algebra.
Mami will never be Abuela
I am left with that impostor
Pythagoras.
The price of a key
that is only mine.

As the locked-ward weekends and months pass, Emilio is becoming increasingly subdued and doughy. His pre-war luminosity and humor are completely gone. Even the Four Tops can't lift his spirits. He looks at me through electro-shocked eyes, taking my hand to walk over to the window bars. "See that tree down there?" I nod, barely able to see it through the screen and filth. "She keeps me alive, the one good thing I can see from here now that Mary's gone. And you, cuz. Your visits. I don't know what I'd do." She painted a naked woman. They called her a dyke. That was the end of her. "The branches on that tree are Mary's brushes, cuz, and when the sun hits through these bars just right, I can feel it paint me with Mary's long fingers all the way from Russia. That hat. I miss that hat. Cuz, you get prettier every time I see you."

Mami never lets me visit alone, and quickly loses patience waiting in the lobby, taking advantage of the cheap coffee cart prices. Once in while she gets me a glazed donut and keeps it in her purse wrapped in a napkin where most of the glaze rubs off. In those moments I almost believe she loves me. Emilio, being El Reverendo's kid, makes Mami feels obligated, resenting every visit and interrogating me on the subway ride home about "los locos" and her only living brother's son. Those endless rides where I learned the meaning of "yes'em to death."

There was a special room for Nick
locked up by his family
to "get fixed"
Jesus, it seemed
had failed.
All them holy rollers
can kiss my Black ass
I am a faggot
fag-gut
don't like it?
lick it!
We laughed.
I cheered.
Looked around.
Walls the color of school.
Air thick as wool.
Nick for President.
A better world for sure.
We laughed.
I cheered.
I could leave.
Nick still visits
my dreams.
Head full of drill holes.
Temples worn to skull.
Lick my dick!
Dial turns,
paddles burn.

Lick my dick!
Lick my dick!
Honky muthafuckas!
Holy Roller Bitches!
Nurse Cunt!
Dr. Mengele!
Saint Nick never cried.
Still twitches
in my every Christmas.
Saint Nick
Like Miss Mary;
No one ever saw them die.

FORTY-FOUR/SILICONE

When the younger cousins or neighbor's kids come to visit, I give away my toys, especially the dolls. I used to snap their heads off and spit inside them, then put their heads back on so that only Negrita and I would know about it. I was trying to give them dolly dengue. I didn't know I'd have to get it first.

My favorite toys are tiny things, like miniature cameras you once could get for a dime: plastic tiny babies you can hide in your pocket; Thumbelina tea sets from the jonkería store that smell like cheap plastic shower curtains and onions. I find really good toys there that are perfect for Negrita to play with, like marbles and jacks; even without fingers, she does better than any of the other dolls. I got Negrita a tiny camera too; we keep the pictures in our heads. There are entire albums in my folds of fat.

The jonkería place has Bolo Bats, a wooden paddle with a ball attached to a long rubber band. I beat the hell out of that ball; sometimes over a hundred times in a row. All that counting makes me think of Abraham and his stars. There's a good chance I've counted more whacks than Abraham did constellations. Sometimes I think that the Bolo Bat keeps me from killing my mother. I like chunky chalk so I can write anything I want on sidewalks just before the rain. My whole life has been more linoleum than sidewalk, but it's the sidewalks that will change your life.

Step on a crack
break your mother's back
I want to know who said it first
and in what language
rock
belt
fist
rope

cage
I want to feel
less alone.
Who was the first bad mother?
I want to know
who made her that way
and break his back
before the job gets done
its why I have a time machine.

Papi's Demon never talks bad about kids, except when he feels threatened that some boy has his eye on me, in which case anyone with a dick and a sideglance is fair game, "sonuvumbiche bastardo me cago en su madre payo malparido." Kikes, micks, spics, crackers, niggers, honkies, hinchos, gringos, jankees, and chino boys alike. Papi has the most slurs for white boys. I think Lenny Bruce is Papi's son and Carmen La Maricona his mother. I wish. That would mean I have a brother and a loving mother. Only problem is, then Lenny and Carmen might not change the world. There's a reason my time machine doesn't always work.

Papi likes to feed pigeons at el parque de banquitos, behind the Hunts Point subway station. Benches, a public toilet, a drinking fountain and nothing else. A park for tired feet and bochinche. Downtown at Battery Park Papi always has some treats for the seagulls, who spot him all the way from the ferry piers. Papi gives them all names like Shep, Fu Manchu, Boston Blackie, Harpo, Moe, Larry, Curly. Papi likes really scary rides and carousels. Sometimes he buys coffee and donuts or a pizza slice for random people on the street. I know the Demon will never win.

Papi likes my school friends. Most of them are church girls, like Sheila Fabares, who lets me cheat off her in math. She knows how scared I am of a bad grade. Mami would beat the skin off me with la correa. Not that she can read my report card, but she always knows how to extract information from anybody. "¡Huele la correa!"

Sheila and I look out for each other. She is a true Jesus girl and doesn't believe in cheating, but being in Fourth Grade, we both know that with a Mami like mine, this could be a life or death situation. All the kids at school cringe at the sight of Mami, who is way shorter than most of the

Sixth Graders. They can feel her suffocating heat from across the street. An air vent with mites that bite while flying through.

Sheila is all starch and talcum and Vaseline, but by the end of a school day those of us with nervios look ragged and desert dry. I kicked some ass when the mean bitches made fun of Sheila's after school scuffed up saddle shoes and ashy legs. She's the nicest and smartest kid in that whole damn school, with a face like Jesus lit it from the inside out. At recess, we lock fingers and call them our piano keys and we sing some Motown, but never too long for fear of getting jumped. We hold on just long enough to get the giggles and forget that we're sad all the time. I'd kick the Principal's ass if I had to for Sheila. Nobody gets to hurt my friend. Not when I'm around. Not even Jesus. He's a bully sometimes by not showing up.

Whenever it gets back to Papi that I've been a fistfight he goes to find the girl and takes us on a walk to the hot dog cart. He tell us to be friends and that friends are better than money. I can tell he's proud when the other girl gets the worst of it; they usually get a second Yoo-Hoo for their troubles. But mostly he invites Sheila. She's never had the heart to tell him she hates hot dogs. "They look like a man's thing." The first time Sheila told me that I laughed so hard I lost my breath. Sheila didn't. She was dead serious. I didn't want to ask her how she knew what a man's thing looked like. I had a really bad feeling it was the same reason that I knew. It made me want to kill somebody. It made me want to find the man that did it to her and cut his thing off and feed it to some wild, mangy dog; there are plenty of them in the neighborhood. I'm never really sure who did it to me, and I don't think Sheila remembers either, so that's that.

The boxing lessons Papi gives me in the kitchen keep me in one piece. I keep the fights real short. I still have Arlina Jackson's pencil point in my wrist; blindsiding or stabbing me with whatever's handy is the only way my opponents can get over on me. Arlina stashed razor blades in her hair. I'll remember her until I'm dead and maybe even after that.

Arlina and I never kissed and made up; Papi never found out. Good thing. I lost the pencil fight. Winter gloves over cuts. Papi was used to seeing me wear gloves indoors through winter. "Tigers, mi'ja; built like boxers. You can learn from their timing." Papi says I move from to room to room at night like a "Ben-Gay in a cage."

What does he expect? I can't sleep with all the snoring, but mostly it's because of the dreams, detonating like bombs over a foxhole. More like hallucinations than dreams. No drugs need apply. Christ all bloody on the cross hanging from the window gates. Warp speed trips to kill Hitler and save Malcolm X; I've never liked kiddie books. Disney makes people like Mr. Pagán the custodian look lazy and stupid, and Bambi makes me cry. Enough extra misery. Mad or sad is no place for a kid, and most of the time it's all I've got. My dream world, except for Carmen, is mostly nightmares, but Disney is worse, in cahoots with Jim Crow. Day terrors. I feel ashamed that I played Disney in Third Grade. Did Mrs. Lewis know how mean it all was? Disney, Universal Pictures and Warner Brothers have the Demon. Worse than Papi. I really think Peter Pan is an asshole too. Who wouldn't want to grow up and do something important with their lives? Wendy, you can definitely do better. Tinker Bell and Carmen La Maricona. Pixie dust. Trust. Dead. Forgotten. Cute kills. Nice denies. The Andrews Sisters are Jim Crow's bimbos. Too much lipstick, not enough brains. Papi's sayings are contagious. "Scrub Me Mama with a Boogie Beat."

FORTY-FIVE/KERATIN

There was only one Jaguar in the Bronx Zoo, all by herself, across from the tigers. She prowled, like she knew she could get out at any moment and take ten men down on her way out the gate. She was sleek and smooth and walked by me more than she did anybody else. She could read my mind like the elephant. She left with me. Stayed close, stayed young. Fur and purr my marrow, growl and fangs my secrets. Amazonian veins of transport, my skin thick for the naked climb, the canopy dance, intimate lessons from Orion, the Equator—my hula hoop Jaguar in a time machine on our way to kill Hitler and Mussolini before they got the Double Demon to the 35th Power. Their crew, closer to home. We're putting tacks and gum on every seat of 20,000 Nazis gathered like pirana at Madison Square Garden, 1939; called it "Pro America Rally."

Walt Disney, Paramount, Warner Brothers, Universal Pictures, all of you—those of you I know and those I don't. The ones I remember. The ones I forget. You're coming with us, me and Jaguar, to Nigeria, you jelly apple pendejo sonuvumbiches. Meet the double-headed axe of Changó, see that Black people aren't cartoons and Africa is a continent, not a country. Popeye lost his eye at twelve playing craps. He is no Bodhisattva of spinach and the sea, but a bigot and a bigger bully than his nemesis Bluto. Moron. Olive Oyl, get yourself a better boyfriend. We'll take you to Asia so you can learn that's a continent, too, and not everyone is the same and there are a zillion languages and different people and nicer than you.

The swivel Philco TV was sick of hearing all those insults and lies and swiveled itself, turned to show me where the tubes were. "Put me out of my misery! One tube is all it takes. Have mercy, the Philco cried. Holy Mary, Mother of God, pray for my channels now and at the hour of my death. Take the foil off my antenna, let me die with some dignity." Jaguar saved President Kennedy. I was the Marilyn Monroe who didn't give a damn about Kennedy boys and their bourbon good looks. I was the Marilyn who was never without a book. Another woman to be saved by the Library.

Those Kennedys didn't look as good to me as Mohammed Ali, all ripples and rain. A beautiful brain. Deep Black Sea.

Jaguar, the first woman President, presses her paw into law. De-feathers Jim Crow, eats the entrails, claws apart the "No Colored" signs. Tells McCarthy "Hell, no!" Fire Keeper Snow Leopard pokes out the eyes of Mount Rushmore. Do-Over. Takes back the Sacred. Jaguar puts on some tap pants, shoes with holes for her claws and a top hat. Builds herself a Cotton Club in the sky, free for all to see. Just raise your eyes. Changes her spots to hide among the clouds when the white man comes to collect the rent. She keeps on dancing and laughing among the stars. Some can still see her. The ones who can't find their own eyes, hate our laughter, certain we're laughing at them, pull their wallets close. Check pant zippers. Food on their teeth. Don't believe in Freedom of Speech unless it's in English. Me, I become Mahalia Jackson to feel my sadness. Cry or die. Mahalia's tears fall on the tracks of La Maricona's arms, where hummingbirds defy their nature and land in stillness to celebrate and mourn, all at once.

Jaguar swims the sky, her claws deflate Hitler's flying balloon, his windpipe forever a kazoo on display at the Smithsonian. We take flight against hurricanes and tornados of flying cows, and poverty's tsunamis of blue babies; we give the cows wings and the babies oxygen, hide them inside our hearts until the dangers pass. No one will ever know how the world got better, or why it even still exists.

Revenge is always on my mind. Lots of kids are vigilantes at heart, because we can see injustice. Born with laser eyeballs. Its why grownups can't stop looking at us when we're babies. Like they see something they recognize from before they were born but got beaten out of them. ¡Huele la correa! Write on the board 500 times I WILL NOT TALK IN CLASS. Neat. Perfect BOLD letters or you will do it again. DO YOU HEAR ME? You're five minutes late. Its coming out of your paycheck. ¡Huele la correa! Semper Fie. Present Arms. Total Control. Balls to the Wall.

We hear through the silences of apathy. Men in white hats have complejos. White Knights only show their eyes in the dark. Adults fumble around belching and scratching their asses through wars across the world and around the block. They buy chocolate bars. Suck on sour balls. Suckle highballs. Commit cigarette suicide. Jaguar and me. We save the world.

And then. Hate gets a curtain call. Turns body hair into needles straining to shoot themselves into space, where there are no cages, no zoos.

And then. Eyes. A sadness I keep to myself. Eyes. Papi's. When he comes home from eighteen-hour days of cutting, boiling, frying, baking. Eyes. When he closes the bedroom door behind him, looks back at us kids, making sure we've got enough blankets, full bellies. Then. Looks back again. Reminding us to make pee-pee and brush our teeth. Mami always asleep before him, rolled up into an angry ball. Their backs always to each other. Then. Adults can be all the sad they want. Kids are not allowed. "Smile." "What worries do you have?" "Roof." "Table." "Food." "Children starving in China." "These are the best days of your life." The air shaft grabs my attention. Grownups fear sad children. We're the broken mirrors everywhere. They can't escape. "What would people think?" And then. And then. And then. ¡Huele la correa! Mami. Papi. Can hurt you worse than anybody ever will.

The scent of cotton candy and meao de gato. And then. This cat. The most beautiful cat I've ever seen. Cat like no cat. We lock in deep. Her pain is mine. She's no Jaguar. Different planet, same thread. Laplace's Demon. Her eyes a dream that return to comfort or burn. There's always an itch she can't reach. She hunches. Stretches her legs for a Balanchine who doesn't see her. I latch onto the steel handrail that helps me restrain the desire to touch her and feel the violet electrical spirals of our inner tellings. No words possible. Tight knuckling, afraid of falling or worse; that I might close my eyes and look away. I bury my face into Papi's knees and beg to leave. No. Not this cat. She is no one to run from. Not me. We understand each other. Releaser. Primer. Signaler. Modulator. Our pheromones moan with the bliss of biting into one root. She was, she is, the beating heart of the Himalayas. Ancestral nomadic sisters. Her soul slips into mine between beats. We prowl each other's bones, dig through marrow, drink from arteries. No touch required.

The signage on the cage coldly printed in black on white: Snow Leopard. I notice the same type of sign over the door of the Ladies Room. I've always hated the word "Ladies." Mouth shut. Legs closed. Bra biting down. Panties too small. Hair stiff with perfectionism. Too much perfume. Disinfecting your toto with poisons hiding in the scent of a virginal spring.

Communicating with the dead has always felt natural to me. No Ouija Board, no rising table, no candles or incantations, no money changing hands; no child is a pimp of the flesh or the spirit. We are all born Espiritistas. Most will learn to run from it; others will become crystal ball purveyors of the dead. Like Papi, I can smell the fakes from miles away. Snow Leopard will never know the meaning of fake. Ralph Waldo understands me, us.

Exiled from her rightful place, Snow Leopard's eyes plead their way into me and remain there, resting inside my lungs, her memory in my every breath. My soul twin whom I left there to die, flattened by grief. That horrible place where she was the forced entertainment, the exotic, the endangered. I could tell she didn't like people very much; no one had given her a reason. I was helpless to free her. The lock on her cage, triple the size of my fist. Maybe Malcolm X would come back and take her someplace where good people never die and bad ones never get born.

Papi feels guilty about how sad I am and talks a zookeeper into getting me a free camel ride. The leather straps that hold down the seats are slack with age. I grab onto fistfuls of coarse camel hair and pretend to be happy as I always do, especially for Papi. I whisper loudly inside my head so that kid in front won't think I'm loca, like Mami does. Loud enough so Mr. Camel can hear—skull-to-skull communication. "I'm so sorry, Mr. Camel. I hope I'm not hurting you. I'm sorry to pull your hair. I'm sorry you have to give me a ride. I'm sorry I eat too many Twinkies and Ring Dings that have made me fat and too heavy on your back.

I crank up my neck to reach closer to his ear. "I'll bet it was people full of demonios that gave you humps in the first place. I'm sorry, Mr. Camel, so sorry you're a slave. I wish I could leave you alone. Or we could just be friends walking the desert, where no one would say we have pelo malo. Not that you do. You don't. It just feels like mine and... this wasn't my idea. Papi just doesn't know how to think like a camel yet. I don't think he really gets animals, except for bullfights. And then I'm not really sure whose side he's on. I am so sorry, Mr. Camel. I'm really sorry if you're a girl camel and I'm calling you mister." I whisper endless apologies, hand over mouth, widening my eyes, to play the cute, scared little girl, considered an adorable quality in females. I'm already in lockup at home; no need to tempt fate any further.

Every thing and every one is "mister" when I'm not sure. I have no idea how to tell boy and girl camels apart. I like animals who show off their dicks so I can be sure who is Dick and who is Jane. Yeah, kids think about things like that, much more than adults imagine. Kids think about pubic hair and masturbation and we'll find the tetas y culos no matter where you hide them, so don't just lock away your guns. Kids know that everything has feelings. I apologize to dishes when I wash them if I think the water is too hot. I beg forgiveness of my shoes when I walk too much or step on a turd.

I drag Mr. Camel's sadness with me over to Snow Leopard. I skip a little bit to convince Papi of how good it all was. Smile up at him. He believes and looks proud that he hustled me a free camel ride. Snow Leopard has slipped into her lair. The Black Panther paces; Papi says I remind him of her. Her? Did he know, or was it just that we were so similar? It was one of the best things he ever said to me. Better than when he said I paced like a Ben-Gay. And then. "You're so inquieta. Always moving. Looking at everything. You have to stop sometimes, mi'ja. You can't be a panther forever or you'll die too young. Nervios like that will kill you. You have nervios, just like your mother." And "just like your mother" is the worst thing he could say. I dissolve into water for Snow Leopard, become her tears, live in her cells, breathe in her, sleep in her, rage in her, our growls draw blood from the air's invisible body. Panther keeps watch.

FORTY-SEVEN/PLUMBUM

Days after the zoo odyssey, I'm alone in the house with Mami, I sob un-controllably, for what Mami decides is no good reason. Snow Leopard. Mr. Camel. Ben Gay. Black Panther. "It's just stupid animals, puñeta." I can't catch my breath long enough to explain. "Los animales, Mami, los animales son..." is as far as I get. She yanks me by the ponytail into whip-lash. "Stop it or I'll give you something to cry about." I feel her hate of my Papi's looks as she stares in a sneering disbelief that I'd cry over those she dumps into her "Eso" hamper. Even my hair disgusts her. *Pelo malo*. The "bad hair" that gives away secrets of the family tree. I am the permanent stain on perfection's white carpet. I am the wire hanger abortion attempt that failed. Mami refers to me as the "macho asesino en mi vientre," the one who tried to kill her on my way out; breached and kicking like a feral beast. "¡Ani-mal!"

I survived her umbilical noose. She swears I was born with teeth and talons and ate through it, clawed my way out of her. Born in a puddle of blood and shit. Snow Leopard is hunched inside the parts of me that must daily resist the regret of being alive. I know that Snow Leopard and I will one day be extinct. I won't make any babies. I squeeze my eyes shut when we pass the storks. There would be no more zoos for me after that.

There are two places I can hide from Mami for little spurts of time: The bathroom and the library. The bathroom, not so much. There's no locks on either of the doors inside our apartment and Mami takes full advantage. The only way to keep her out of the bathroom are three magic words: "I'm making caqui." I say it no matter what I'm doing. Nothing like a fried Spam shit to defeat your opponent. I figured that out by Seventh Grade. Some skanks came into the school bathroom to kick my ass for lunch money and I let it rip. They flew out of there with their eyeballs on fire.

Eventually Mami caught onto my scheme and barged in on me as I wrote *Fuck You* with Noxema on the medicine cabinet mirror. She can't read, so I told her it means God Bless You. She smacked me anyway for sticking my fingers "full of ass" into her face cream. I wised up and started writing it on my body; ephemeral tattoos. *Fuck You Bitch. I Hope You Die.* On my chest, over my thighs and the parts of my big culo I could reach.

Mami approves of library visits on account of the mean-spirited white woman in orthopedic shoes who runs things. She shushes us with a nunnish glare that keeps kids silent and buried in their books. The other librarians aren't so bad, but they're scared of Attila the Nun too. You can tell she's a big shot by the way she puts a hand on her hip and pushes out her stomach when she's being official.

"You should be in the children's section."

Attila wags a Hormel sausage finger at me like I'm breaking the law. My cuteness falls off my face from the sheer exhaustion of not screaming.

"I don't like children's books. I have enough comic books at home."

I give her the finger inside my jacket pocket.

She leans in so close I can smell the contents of her stomach.

"Well-well-well, you're too smart for our books, eh?"

I look at my feet.

"No, Missy, just the stupid ones."

Attila expands like a sedentary aquatic invertebrate soaked in fat sweat.

"If you're so smart, what's your phone number?"
My response is the speed of light.
"KI2-5000." I practice for emergencies.
I realize immediately what I've done.
"Does your mother speak English?"
I shake my head hopefully,
"No."

Attila calls over El Señor Viejito who comes in to read the newspaper every day to save money and stay warm. Attila dials my number and hands El Señor Viejito the receiver. He does as he's told; probably scared that Attila will throw him out and he'd have to buy the paper every day for the rest of his life, suffocate in summer heat and freeze in winter. He looks up at me, his shoulders sag with remorse. "I save my nickels so my grandson can go to college some day, nena." The veins of his hands tabanuco roots of El Yunque. His fingers bamboo, his feet river stones. Ancient waterfalls quiver in his smoky blue-ringed eyes. "Childrens need to listen to los mayores so they can grow up derechito. Straight up and down like a tree." I don't want to tell him there's no such thing as a straight line, not even on trees, especially in front of Attila, who glares at him like he owes her. Grownups mean well when they say they want us to be like trees, but they don't think enough about the roots and branches.

I'm cold and clammy, my heart punching me from the inside out. Attila commands El Señor Viejito to summon Mami to come and get me. Attila never says "please." Never says thank you. El Señor Viejito feels like a milkman's donkey in Bayamón. They do so much, are so intelligent and Americanos think they're stupid. Few ever think to honor a donkey, except for maybe Juan Ramón Jiménez and the people who depend on them, like desert-living Bedouins and Jesus entering Jerusalem.

Mami arrives in her high neck, ruffly church blouse. She makes me interpret into English that all the librarians have her permission to smack me if I misbehave, get fresh or talk to hoodlums—code for any boy. I try to say something different, but my lips quiver and nostrils flap. Heat rises past my eyebrows. El Señor Viejito looms like a half-starved gargoyle, making sure I'm on the up and up. Mami calms her wormy eyebrows to make a good impression. The stacks of books intimidate her, scared to death that someone might ask her to read or help them find something on the shelves. It's why she never stays.

"The library ladies are like your teachers. Treat them with respect."
I learned early on that respect means bowing my head when spoken to
by any adult, no eye contact, express no opinions of my own, not ask
too many annoying questions, and try not to breathe too loud and never
through my mouth. That last one is a Houdini act for a scared asthmatic.

The librarian nods her head approvingly at Mami's mandates with
folded arms that look like what Papi calls Christmas hams. "My mommy
wants you to know that you can hit me if I'm bad." I say mommy like a
white girl. "She said to use a ruler if you have to." I replace "shoe" with
"ruler." A smack from Attila the Nun's shoe could cause permanent brain
damage and Mami isn't specific on what parts of me Attila gets to smack. I
wonder what libraries are like for kids who live in real houses in the parts
of Queens that have lots of tree shade in summer, and smell like bakeries
on Sunday. I heard Mr. Lipschitz once telling Papi about it.

Mami says, "thank you" to Atilla and "muchas gracias" to El Señor
Viejito. She gulps down curses as she drags me towards the exit by my
upper arm, leaving fingernail tattoos. The librarian rewards herself with a
green sour ball from the jar on her desk only she touches, and goes back to
her catalogues, spectacles balanced on the hook of her nose. Mami allows
me to go back two weeks later under threat of being thrown out a window
for any infraction. Attila's word over mine. Punto.

FORTY-NINE/PULPWOOD

Attila clearly missed me and walks over to me and my pile of Emerson, Poe and Thoreau. "Young lady, do you know that you're reading aloud under your breath? Eyes open, lips closed. You're disturbing the other patrons." She has a sardine-like mustache and smells like she turned her panties inside out one too many times.

"I remember better when I can hear what I'm reading." Her doughy face looms at my neck. "Bad habits can be broken. Here's a Chiclet; try that instead." I'm surprised by the Chiclet. I guess controlling me would be easier than kicking me out and having to deal with me as an interpreter again. She flips through my books, puts them down, and steps back, hands on hips. "What would you think about Nancy Drew?" I freeze my eyes so they won't roll. How do I tell her you had to have money to be Nancy Drew—all those costumes and props and make-up. You don't need money to become a better person or a poet. She's so sincere, I almost like her. "Sure, why not? Thank you for the idea." I return to Emerson. "The secret of education lies in respecting the pupil. It is not for you to choose what he shall know, what he shall do." It was like a message from God. I used to open books in all the sections. They had magic readings in them, like Doña Ramona with her cards. There was no one I could tell about how Ralph Waldo would talk to me. Not even the nice teachers. It's kind of like an insult to them, since its their job to tell us what to do. I'm not supposed to be reading these books. Puerto Rican kids aren't expected to be reading at all. Maybe when I get to junior high.

El Señor Viejito is at his table, like always, reading day-old news. I'm reading aloud again. He puts a finger to his lips in warning and rolls his eyes in the direction of Attila. He'd heard Mami give Attila permission to smack me. Attila could probably tell by my stutter and trembling hands that I'd been smacked enough. I guess she wasn't so bad and the chewing gum did help me focus better. It was nice that El Señor Viejito was looking out for me.

I've always loved books and their otherworldly aromas. As a kid they made me think of summer camps and fireplaces like I'd seen in magazines, movies or TV. For a long time the only reading materials we had at home was a zippered Holy Bible, Papi's newspapers, comic books, Prevention Magazine and the TV Guide. So the library was paradise. Books; magazines; newspapers in different languages; photography books; National Geographic. The whole world was there.

I learned about books from a TV show called Romper Room, where the teacher would read to the kids. A few months into first grade, I was daring to read aloud. It was brutal. I had a thick Puerto Rican accent, stutter, and a lisp that I'd gotten from listening to Papi speak Castillian mixed with Basque and Caló and Mami a sancocho of dialects, malaprops, and her own invented words. The kids ridiculed me, and I caught the teacher exhaling through her mouth, then telling me what a great job I did. Nothing stopped me where books were concerned. Not reading would be like being dead. I wondered if that was how Mami felt, and then I forgot about it.

Papi had taught me to read using the "funnies" in the Sunday paper and bought me Classics Illustrated comic books where I learned about Joan of Arc and was excited by butch haircuts for women. Before I could read I'd look at the drawings and laugh, mostly because I thought that was what was expected of me, even if it was Joan going up in flames. I'd make up what I thought the story was and take on different voices for the characters. My father would tell me I was doing "berry good" as he laughed along with me. At home he relaxed his B's and V's but still made fun of the "Chinos" and their R's, which gave me a gag reflex at the sight of rice and made me mad at him and his Demon. But, still, going through the funnies with Papi was one of childhood's few highlights.

Mami, resentful of anything that resembled joy would just call us sanganos and dismiss us with a sharp wave of her bony hand. She had never learned to read or write anything except her first name. I taught her how to write mine one letter at a time a week after I started school. Shame is a big component in the building of monsters. It's a miracle I haven't turned into one.

Books and the heft of carpenter-built oak tables, chairs that required both hands to budge, and towering shelves filled with universes, made me feel a little drunk, like the Geritol shots Papi had me knock back for anemia. Besides Attila the Sausage, the other scary thing in the midst of my paradise was the Dewey Decimal System. No matter how I tried, I couldn't understand how it worked. I knew how to alphabetize, as long as I could mutter under my breath, but once numbers and decimals were involved, my brain froze. The sound of a drawer of catalogue cards being extracted was enough to send me into a cold sweat. There had to be another way to find books that were meant for me. The "Children's Section" was sickeningly blonde.

Roaming the shelves, I could narrow my search to sections: Poetry. Biographies. Essays. History. Medicine. In one medical book I could see that the heart looks like a fist. That was disappointing. I really had thought it looked like a Valentine. I wasn't big on titles or covers. Just the Table of Contents. I wanted to know right away what was inside a book, and didn't need anyone else's opinion about it. No waste of my library time. Mami always had a way of showing up just when I'd get to the good parts. Only once in a great while was I allowed to check out a book or two, since she was certain I would lose them and she would have to pay for them out of the rent money. Sometimes I got smacked just for asking.

I found a way to get around the Dewey Decimal System, which didn't matter much to an eight-year-old anyway. I had to know what was out there so I could find out what I wanted in the first place. We read lots of dead white guy poets in school; I had fun rewriting them. Frost: "Walking through the alley on a creepy evening." Poe: "Annabelle Lee, she always had to pee, the chilling was squeezing her bladder, you see." Some dead white guys are better than others. I discovered Ogden Nash after that and was sure he was un copión who stole my ideas. I thought about writing him a letter. Another big thing that happened in Third Grade was when my teacher, Mrs. Lewis, with the Buster Brown haircut, brown bread loaf shoes and hands of a steelworker, cast me in the lead role of the school play, A Tribute to Walt Disney. Well, it wasn't really a play, but Mrs. Lewis called it that and it had dialogue.

Playing a male felt perfectly natural to me. I never questioned getting that part and loved wearing a boy's suit and tie. It was my chance to make Disney a better man and let him feel what it might be like to be a little Puerto Rican Xitana girl. Few boys in our macho school, that felt and looked like a prison, wanted to be in a play, terrified of being called *bitches* or *maricones*. I had become one of the top readers in the school—stutter, lisp and all. Mrs. Lewis could probably tell I wasn't like other girls and more like herself than the Shirley Temple my mother tried to make of me. Anyway, that's how I learned to search the stacks for the plays section. Melvil Dewey did for books what Abraham tried to do with the stars.

Plays. Okay. Walk the aisle with eyes closed. Hand facing books inches away. Feel for the heat. O'Neil. Ionesco. Genet. Behan. Pirandello. Lorca. Miller. Arrabal. Artaud. Jarry. All men. But Lorca, he was so much more than a man. I read his poem "The Little Mute Boy" in a book forced between the plays, and fell in love. I whisper into the book, "You look so much like my Papi."

Poetry. Feel for the heat. More than a voice guiding me. Not a voice at all. A feeling like the bottom of the ocean, welcoming me to walk, to breathe. Teaching me that the "impossible" is just a bad idea, not a reality. Chinese Women Poets. Thank you, Arthur Waley. Robert Frost. Tennyson. Keats. Essays. Feel for the heat. A collection of poetry edited by Ralph Waldo Emerson falls open to words by poet William Cowper: "I would not enter in my list of friends, Who needlessly sets foot upon a worm." Those words set my moral compass in a steadfast direction. Ralph Waldo and me. A red pencil heart in my notebook. Lorca is a different love; I don't know why. His hands fit perfectly inside of mine. I can wear his shoes. He fits into mine. We share a hat. We both like it when rust spreads on cement, barnacles live on wood, scars form on flesh. None of the other kids know about Lorca or Ralph Waldo. At least, not the way I do. I can't tell anyone.

I find Lorca in English only, except when we meet in the spaces between words. Not taught, not learned, not preached. Born to know what others don't want to know.

FIFTY/GAS

I never heard happy sounds from my parent's bedroom. Perhaps a grunt or two that made its way into my dream haze. If there was anything going on, they waited until I was asleep. There were plenty of farts, snoring and belching, and complaints about everything from money problems to the Kennedy assassination. Papi always said it was planned by "the sonu-vumbiches who hated his brains and that is why they shot him in the head." Papi always said the government wanted leaders they could control, so there were no real leaders. "They kill the good ones. If you want to do something good, you have to do it in secret. Never let them see your hand or read your face."

I never saw my parents kiss or hug or cry together. Mami only cried with rage when she was beating me, yelling at Papi or remembering some horrible thing from her childhood that she just had to dump on me at bedtime. Papi cried when Titi Angela died. For years Mami would bring it up. "The only time your Papi cried was when your Titi died." She bent each word to imply it was a bad thing and I should hate him for it. Like he only loved Titi Angela and no one else.

Mami reluctantly reassured me of Papi's love. "He cried for you one time. One time. Te dió uno de tus ataques epilépticos, your eyes turned white this time and espuma was coming out of your mouth like too much soap in the washing machine. That's why I can never trust you with the laundry. You broke Mr. Lui's machine, remember?" Like she would ever let me forget. "Anyway, Papi llamó al doctor and he told Papi to put you in the cold shower right away not to wait for him this time. You came back como una retaldá." Mami mimicked what she remembered as the "retarded" look on my face. "Con esa cara de 'Wha? Wha? Wha happen to me'?" She turned her face away. "Your Papi was crying. I had to take care of you all night to make sure you didn't die. Ohmaiga! So many stupid questions from you. That was a terrible night for me. One of the worst days of my life." All that was missing was her crown of thorns and evening gloves.

Papi made a pronouncement in reference to women when Mami's favorite telenovela interfered with a boxing match on UHF, the independent educational channel. "All women are whores." He looked in Mami's direction when he said it. I saw her shoulders meet her ears as if about to be beaten. Papi never raised a hand to her; he didn't have to. My entire being shook with rage as I moved into him. "What kind of whore was your mother?" His slap sent me across the living room. To a Xitano born in Andalucía, his mother is like La Virgen María; La Virgen del Rocío; and La Macarena; all meant to be revered, less for their miracles than for their virtue. It's a miracle that Xitanos have not gone the way of the Shakers. It was okay for him to cagarse en la ostía, or damn the mother who shit you, or any other barrage of his version of maledictions, as long as the words never came near *his* mother. I glared up at him from the floor with all the rage I could muster: "If you ever talk to Mami like that again, I'll kill you." He was stricken, but not by my words; by his own actions. He had never raised a hand to me before, except for an aguaje of a single spanking for mimicking his curses. Always the bystander of Mami's brutality, but rarely put a hand on me, not with rage, or love.

Papi maintained absolute loyalty to God's commandment regarding parents. Mothers always got top billing. Thanks a lot, Moses.

FIFTY-ONE/GAUZE

Mami had a stepbrother, Porfirio, at the House of Calvary, an institutional hospice in the Bronx. I was twelve and passed for sixteen, the age at which they allowed young visitors into the wards. I would be meeting this half uncle for the first time. I wondered what the other half was. We got to his door and Mami told me to wait outside. I wandered off within earshot. In the corridor, a cadaverous patient in sunglasses and a faded yellow nightgown dragged a heavy oxygen tank. She sniffed her way to me and looked over my head. "Hey, sweetie, can you sneak me in some cigarettes? Nice perfume. Smells high class." I was relieved that I didn't smell like bacalao. "Maja from the drugstore. I borrowed it from my mother." "Oh yeah, I remember that. Toilet water. I grew up with Spanish people, they loved that shit and the Florida water. One thing about those Puerto Rican women, they always smell good and dress sharp. They got this look all the time, like they just got out of the shower. At least they did when my eyes worked. I can still smell 'em, though. I'll bet you're a cutie. I had my eyes until a few years ago, now I can't see shit. Pardon my French, honey bunch. My nose still works good though, and I can hear a rat pissing on cotton."

Jenny coughed violently and spit blood into a tissue. I didn't gag or flinch. Like nothing happened. I helped her sit to catch her breath. Her arm reminded me of a pterodactyl or maybe a big chicken wing. "So can you get me some cigarettes or not?" "Sorry, ma'am. I'm not old enough." "Name's Jenny. Don't ma'am me if you wanna be friends. You got a suckin' candy or somethin'?" "Uh, I got some Lifesavers." Jenny laughed. "That shit won't work here. I'll be toast in less than a month. Lifesavers, ha, you're a funny little shit." I didn't mean to be. Craning her neck with childlike hope, she asked: "Butterscotch?" "No, the fruit kind." "Better than nothin'. Gimme one." Jenny stuck out her rolled tongue and I dropped one in. She sucked on it for a few seconds and exploded into a gagging cough. "Lemon! I hate lemon! Disgusting, tastes like crap!" I put my hand beneath her chin. "Spit it out. Go ahead, spit it into my hand."

It was so easy for me. As natural as friendships with the dead. I saw a small wastebasket just outside a patient's room. Wiped my hand on the side of my dress as I snuck a peek inside. It was an elderly Black man, his hair all gray, with bandaged ankles where his feet had been. Mr. Bascomb. I'd never heard that name before. I whispered, "Jenny, what happened to Mr. Bascomb?" "Diabetes and cancer. Poor bastard. Worked twenty years with Sanitation. He'll be forty tomorrow. We should get him a cake." I took note he had a checkerboard on his night table. I realized he was younger than Mami. I felt God pinch my heart.

Mami came out to get me, grabbed me by the hand and introduced me to Porfirio. He reached for my hand and kissed it and said I was "una princesa." Mami pulled me away from him and wiped my hand with her spit and a hankie. She told me he had stomach cancer on account of he didn't eat his vegetables and that it could happen to me if I didn't watch my step. She said he'd drop dead any day so we should come back tomorrow. It was so mean, the way she said and did all that right in front of him. He closed his eyes pretending to fall asleep. Tears escaped, into the pillow that flattened under the weight of unbearable thoughts. Mami pretended not to notice. "Nos vemos mañana."

Mami kept her promises, whether to beat you or to meet you. We returned to Calvary the next day, and this time Mami ordered me to stay in the room. Porfirio was bereft and I figured it was the damn ugly face of the Grim Reaper coming to take him too soon, too young. When Mr. Reaper stands between you and sunlight, you get old real fast. I think people can outrun him for a while if they spend time by the sea. Papi always said that salt air and breathing like a yogi would keep you young. It worked for him until the alcohol drained his face and drowned his body.

Something besides Death was catching up with Porfirio. I could feel it.

He sobbed like a little boy, not like a pendejo, as Mami would say. At first she sat there and just stared at him, almost like she enjoyed seeing him suffer. I started thinking about Mr. Bascomb and if he had anyone to play checkers with. Porfirio was getting more and more agitated, and Mami sinking deeper into her gray silence. She finally sent me away with her dismissive hand gesture, which meant to wait outside the door. I skipped over to Mr. Bascomb's room.

"Hi, Mr. Bascomb. Wanna play checkers?" With pained effort he leaned on his side to get a better look at me. "And who are you, young lady?"

"I'm a friend of Jenny's." He smiled and rolled his eyes simultaneously. "Well any friend of Jenny's is a friend of mine. Pull over that chair. Red or Black?" "Black." "You have a name, Miss?" "Yes, but most can't say my name right and I don't want to put you to any trouble." I took a really deep breath. "Would you mind calling me Mrs. Emerson?" Mr. Bascomb laughed. "All right then, Mrs. Emerson it is."

I had almost said Mrs. Lorca, but I was scared he might hear it as Loca, since it wasn't a very common name. Strangers usually felt like they had the right to change my name. I didn't want Mr. Bascomb to be like anyone else, because he wasn't. He respected what I wanted. It created a dizzying haze, admiration for a real gentleman that I'd just met. My body became a field of dandelions, my brain, Papi's victrola spinning out "Claire de Lune." Mr. Bascomb was an angel or maybe a secret super hero.

"Well, Mrs. Emerson, would you like to play or dream?" "Let's play, Mr. Bascomb." He didn't know that being with him was the dream. I forgot Mami and Porfirio existed by the third round. I lost all three. Mr. Bascomb's smile made me happier than winning. By the time Mami found me, Mr. Bascomb was looking younger and I felt ferryboat-happy. Mami dragged me by my upper arm and gave Mr. Bascomb a really dirty look of disgust. She set my dream on fire and the first thing to go was my face. Wagner's Valkeries clawed through my stomach. Chopin fled at the sight of her. I would return to Mr. Bascomb to apologize if she would visit Porfirio again. "Please, God, let me see Mr. Bascomb again. Mami tried to kill him with her eyes."

Dream, March 11, 1980

A drunk is sprawled in front of an Upper West Side shrine to the Blessed Mother. Blood ribbons from his mouth, his face a carved ivory cameo. The passing faithful bless themselves, mutter the Memorare, and walk over his body on their way to the petty details of life.

FIFTY-TWO/MATTRESS

Mami got the news that Porfirio didn't have much longer. She made me wear knees socks out of respect. "Dress nice when person is dying. I'll straighten your hair." All that meant was hard yanks until she could subdue it into braids with ribbons. "White ones, like an angel." It was time for me to be an angel to a dying man I barely knew. "Pray for him 23 in Spanish." She was referring to the 23rd Psalm, which I had committed to memory as part of my Sunday School obligations. I felt bad for Porfirio, but I didn't really know him. All Mami said was that he was the one who took her to the Dominican Republic when she was a little girl. And all I knew was that lots of horrible things had happened to her there. I didn't know if they were his fault, but I thought that maybe they were.

I pretended to need the bathroom and snuck over to Mr. Bascomb's room. He wasn't there and the checkers were gone. The bed looked freshly made, as if he'd never been there. An empty slot by the door where his name had been. I knew he was dead. I closed my eyes to imagine his smile but all I could see was green blood seeping through the bandages on his stumps. I talked to the pillow: "Mr. Bascomb, I know your feet will grow back in Heaven. You won't be alone. I'm going to ask my friend Carmen to find you and play checkers with you. She has dragon tattoos on her legs. I know you'll find each other." I pushed back tears so Mami wouldn't hate me for crying for a stranger. "Please, Mr. Bascomb, please tell Carmen I will never forget her. I'm sure you'll find each other. Carmen's dragons have wings, Mr. Bascomb. I'll never forget you either and I will never forgive Mami for the way she looked at you." Yes, Jesus, I know what you're thinking, but there are some things you just can't fix. Like your Papi, and what he did with Adam and Eve. And since you are your Papi, then you did that too. What Mami did is a lot worse. Case closed.

A nurse walked in. "Are you looking for Mr. Bascomb?" I looked up at the ceiling. "No, thank you. I just got lost. Where's the Ladies Room?" She was all in white, like an angel, and offered to walk me to the bathroom. I guess in hospitals for the almost dead, it's important that everybody look like an angel. I never understood the white thing since taking care of almost dead people is messy work.

On the way to the bathroom I found a black checker in the hallway. I thought that maybe Mr. Bascomb was holding it just before he died and that maybe he was thinking of me. I thought it might be a sign that Mr. Bascomb would become my guardian angel. The first time we played he let me choose black. I still have that old wooden checker, somewhere secret and safe, where only I can see it, touch it, speak to it. And let it speak to me.

I heard Mr. Bascomb's whisper from the other side of nothing and everything: "You were the only person who never once called me by my first name." It took decades before his words detonated inside me. So many people hide inside a fiction of first name friendliness. Mr. Bascomb had his fill of them.

I got back to Porfirio's room just as Mami's rage at my leaving was about to flare up like a rash. "Tell your Tío Porfirio about school." Why would he care about that? He was almost dead. No matter, questioning Mami was an invitation for a slap. I bullshitted like a bandit. "I love school. Math especially. All my teachers are nice, and we get to sing." Porfirio asked to me sing something and all I could think of was *Red River Valley*. The minute I opened my mouth I knew it was the wrong song. So stupid, I wished I would die instead.

From this valley they say you are going
I shall miss your sweet face and your smile
for they say you are taking the sunshine
that would brighten our lives for a while.
Come and sit by my side if you love me
do not hasten to bid me adieu
just remember the Red River Valley
and the one who has loved you so true.

Porfirio cried until he couldn't breathe. I felt terrible. Mami told me to sit in a chair and be quiet. Mami stroked Porfirio's hair until he calmed down. I didn't remember her ever doing that for me. They spoke in whispers. Mami told me to listen to my transistor radio and mind my own business. It was a cheap little radio with pretty good sound. I had begged Papi to get it for me. It had a single earphone and I could listen to all the pop tunes. I made believe I had it turned on, and moved my head like I was into the music, so I could hear what Mami and Porfirio were talking about. I was relieved to hear him call me "nena dulce." Porfirio went silent, his anxious breathing gone. The last thing I heard was Mami's voice, in a whisper, her hand tenderly on Porfirio's cheek. I touched my own face and wondered what that would feel like.

FIFTY-THREE/CRUMBS

Mrs. Ralph Waldo Emerson. Mrs. Federico García Lorca. Little widow of the Spirits. I don't mind Federico going away for long periods. He was robbed of so much by the damn fascists and the Mother Church. I always thought that to be dead meant no more favorites. It isn't true. My Federico will always chase his Dalí. Emily Dickinson remains livid over Ralph Waldo and me. No one has written about this. How could they? It's my secret. Ralph Waldo guided me towards Parnassus.

Hunts Point Library. I didn't even know what a willow tree was or how it looked, or how to find New England on a map, or why it was called New England. I looked it all up. I learned so much. My Ralph Waldo influenced Emily, but its me he still loves. My life, all heat and intuition.

I can see Emily's tidy house. Clean air. We have doilies in common. Mami's are more intricate. She has an innate genius for the math her elaborate symmetries demand. Emily. Flowers in a dainty vase on her writing desk. A gray mouse scrambles across mine. Soot on every sill, my finger sliding across unable to resist writing the name of a current crush. Raging neighbors. No clear windows. No quiet. No peace. We have Ralph Waldo in common. And a need for secrets.

I envy Emily looking into his eyes, their discussions of life beyond flesh, her touching the saucer where his hands have been. I envy the secret wetting of her finger, stealing a crumb from his gold-rimmed dish to her lips as he turns to catch a moment of dusk through her hideously cautious curtains. Discreetly folding her lips, swallowing, her stomach a swirl of trapped, unborn baby grackles, her manner, outwardly polite. Oblivious of her complicity in the lauding of Lord Jeffrey Amherst for allowing herself to be the Belle of that toxic place she never denounced. Not one poem about the stolen land across which she paced, and dipped her pen, and dreamt her dreams. Not one.

I envy her. I hate her. I obliterate her. Ralph Waldo's mouth roughly

finds mine, he smells of a musty autumn, spiked cider as the world dis-
solves and he is forever my Emerson, as he has been from the day that
musty book dropped open at my feet as Atilla sucked on one of her sour
balls. Those words that stared up between my legs and forced their way
inside. Dubhe and Merak, guiding me to Polaris. Words he didn't write,
but had the wisdom to honor. Imaginings of Ralph Waldo. Another bond
Emily and I share. Conjecture. Mythologies. Realities. Love. Hate. Honor.
Obliterate. Pleasure. Shame. Emily, you and I. Maybe another time. It all
feels so different. So the same.

FIFTY-FOUR/MESENTERY

I kept an iodine bottle hidden in my writing desk. The skull and cross-bones reminded me whose side I was on when it came to pirates. Papi surprised me with the desk on my ninth birthday, "a nice place to do your homework." After every beating, I'd sit at my desk to write a poem. I would slip into a body from another time. Marlene Dietrich; Ella Fitzgerald; Lotte Lenya; Billie Holliday; voices that made flesh out of air from records spinning on the Victrola. Ravel's "Bolero" would take me away so far, returning got harder every time. The poem would call and bring me back. I read my own words to myself and the dead, since there was no one else listening. With every poem, a swallowing of grief, every new body, a beautiful forgetting. Milk of Amnesia for the pain in my stomach.

"Again? What is going on with you?"
Mami's questions always accusatory.
"Blood, Mami."
I stared at the linoluem floor.
"From where?"

I pointed to my culo. Mami had rushed me to the doctor many times following a significant amount of blood from my culo pooling in the toilet. Male doctor after doctor would touch my vagina with a tongue depressor or point with a finger and ask "Are you sure it didn't come from here?" I'd insist that it didn't. The response was always, "I don't know why she's bleeding. There doesn't seem to be anything wrong. She's too young for menstruation. Let's keep an eye on it." I convinced myself it was holy. Stigmata por el culo. I can hear Mami now "¡Señor te reprenda!"

At that same time I was having dramatic grand mal seizures, eyeballs rolling to white, foaming, clenching—a job for an exorcist. A housecall doctor Papi knew from the bar would come and put me under a cold shower and Mami told me that it always worked. Mami was a liar, so who knows? Milk of Amnesia. "Sometimes younger children have seizures for no explicable reason. Most of them just outgrow it. I wouldn't worry about it. Give her a little chicken soup. She'll be all right. If it happens again, just make sure she doesn't swallow her tongue." The only way to swallow your tongue is if someone cuts it out first. I'm certain that idea had crossed Mami's mind more than once. I couldn't find anything about it at the library because I didn't know where to look and didn't have the nerve to ask, terrified of being sent to the card catalogue, a foreign language in my land of dyslexia. "Missy, there's blood coming out of my culo and nobody knows why. Do you have a book about it?" Yeah, right.

FIFTY-FIVE/MANDALA

Dream, July, 1970

There is a Goddess in a cage. I'm somewhere in India. She is holding a paper baby and a paper donkey. She is real, her skin and hair obsidian. She is so beautiful I can barely breathe. I smell oranges. When I let her out of the cage, a snow blizzard begins, the poor begin to freeze. I see Papi, he is untouched by the storm, in a black coat and suit, white shirt and tie. A black Stetson hat. Two old homeless, alcoholic white guys are suffering so much I can feel it in my body. They are elderly male lovers. They agree to kiss in front of all of us out of necessity. They tell everyone to kiss and not be afraid. One of them says that kissing is the only way to stay alive. The blizzard gets worse and all of the people glow like the sun. A river of blood pours from the mouth of the Goddess and the donkey and baby become real. I will take the baby home. Keep him safe.

I wake up and my bedsheets are bloody. Thank God for Fels-Naptha soap. I can already hear Mami calling me a cochina for sleeping naked. Papi already left for work and there's no school. I hope Mami is in one of her shopping moods. I need to hear the subway wheels grinding, to look out of the windows. The big John 3:16 sign at the church that used to be a theater. I hate the tunnels. No cramps. Thank you, Jesus. God, I hate Kotex. Better wear all black like Papi. Please, Jesus, make this a shopping day. Big purse, lots of Kotex. Midol just in case. Bronx Mary never has to worry about having a period. Good for her. I miss her. A lot.

FIFTY-SIX/GOLD

A few steps from the Crosstown Bar was the Hunts Point Palace, a ballroom hosting the best of all Latin music anywhere. It stood proudly around the corner from a once golden washed Boulevard, now lined in a visual litany of human suffering and commerce. Los Esos withering beneath a pewter sky; the round-ups from the 41st Precinct. They hate us and we can all feel it. Even us goody two-shoes.

Tito Puente conjured magical realms from timbales. Eddie Palmieri and his piano wizardry erased the vermin-infested suffering of an abused and abandoned community, a Brown and Black sea of the unseen.

My code-switching soul wrote songs unheard by anyone except in my whisperings to Negrita; old words inside a child's body. My imaginings, burned at the stake by Mami. My songs hid in the air to survive, sometimes curled inside my lungs beside Snow Leopard. Negrita danced as I whispered: "Tico Tico Tan Tan; Tico Tico Tan Tan; entre los muertos y los vivos los heridos están, por falta de cariño, letras, y pan. Ni Mai, Ni Pai, el zero pesa más que to' lo que hay. Tico Tico Tan Tan; Tico Tico Tan." I found it years later hidden on a napkin smeared with lipstick and tucked into the page that separates Ezekiel from Matthew. I never even felt the pen in my hand.

FIFTY-SEVEN/ROSEWOOD

Papi's union dues got me into a ballet class, The instructor, Señorita R., glared at me with disgust from beneath perfectly straight monastic bangs in her Hunts Point Palace studio. I was the fat girl, and at age nine, looking twelve, one of the oldest. Definitely the fattest. The girl in her madre's red bathing suit because her familia couldn't afford the Danskin leotard. The folding, purse chancletas that would have to pass for ballet slippers.

I became the example of how not to plié, my ass and thighs tapped with a baton, highlighting the offending bulges. This public shaming among my peers completed the desecration of my body, which became a battlefield of self loathing. That day I officially became "La Gordita." I joined the legions of other "gorditas" "flacas" "enclencas" "panzonas" "culonas" y "barrigonas."

Papi's restaurant worker union dues also covered the piano teacher, who I secretly called Don Cojito, because he walked with a cane on account of his corns. He was a clean shaven hobbit in a bow-tie, sweaty wool suit and Castilian lisp. He was also attached to his baton. As I was forced to count beats like a human metronome, to Don Cojito's precise taps on the beleaguered old Brinkerhoff, the notes on the scale began to look like the rolling eyes that started fistfights in the schoolyard.

I dropped out with no questions, encouragements to stay or arguments from anyone. Mami seemed relieved. "Give me back my bathing suit before you stretch it out of shape." I turned to the Victrola and Motown 45s, inventing my own choreography. Wanting to be Diana Ross, knowing I'd always be Cindy Birdsong. Didn't matter how much better Cindy sang. In those days skinny was expected of "desirable women." A little skinny and a lot of surrender would get you the man and the job. Fat was considered not only unattractive, but a chosen moral deficit. I became determined. No one was going to stop this Gordita from loving music and dance, even if it meant dancing in socks across uncooperative, sad linoleum, while singing into a hairbrush microphone.

The year following the demise of my life as a "professionally trained" artist, Papi sacrificed for a full set of the Encyclopedia Britannica. Papi probably figured that if the artistic gifts of xitanería had eluded me, surely God must have doubled down on our Romani intelligence and wit. One book at a time, on time. Lay-away. When the first book arrived, Mami decided then and there was no more reason for me to go to the library where I might be "distracted." I suppose her random and loud reprimands, the crackling of plantains in hot oil, the whining of the electric can opener, neighbors rocking the bed springs, records spinning on the Victrola and telenovelas at full tilt, were no match for the occasional glance I might get from one of those Brown or Black boys who she was certain would distract, disgrace and defile me before marriage. My virginity in exchange for her deferred American Dream; a quenepa in the sun.

I took up table space with my backbreaking school books, tapped my pencil, sang my homework, asked Mami for help, knowing she couldn't give me any, and became such a nuisance, that I was allowed back in the library. The battle to get back to the library was worth the soplamocos and sting of the strap.

FIFTY-EIGHT/MARROW

Besides serving drinks at the Crosstown Bar, Papi was also the bouncer, his chiseled upper body sharply contrasting his underdeveloped legs and badly deformed feet that kept him out of the military. The story was that Papi had been healed of polio at the blessed Springs of Lourdes, France. Men from the family took him by horse-drawn vardo from Sevilla to Barcelona, where he was met by a wealthy male cousin who, with an enterprising charm and regal bearing, had assimilated into Spanish society. He took Papi the rest of the way to Lourdes in a Ford Model-T. His mother Manuela's husband, Manuel, had died at age twenty-nine of some illness my father refused to name. I guessed Manuel died of syphilis or some other disease that would bring dishonor to the family. Whenever I asked Papi how abuelo died, he always said the same thing: "Nobody knew, mi'jita."

I always knew when Papi was lying as he used the hyper-diminutive to place me in his bubble of my imagined innocence. Papi did his best to protect me from what he saw as past family disgraces. No sense in adding to the ones that afflicted the here and now. Except for daily alcohol consumption and smoking his cognac-dipped, frozen and thawed "guinea stinker" cigars, Papi was a health fanatic who practiced Yoga, took vitamins and was a big fan of Jack LaLanne.

Papi was brutally handsome and could charm anyone, male or female. He could also make you want to flee his presence with a look and weighted silence. More than once I'd overheard him talking with his good friend, Mr. Lipschitz, about owing money to the "Shellac" which is how Papi heard "Shylock." He knew nothing about the Merchant of Venice, nor did he understand that he was insulting Mr. Lipschitz, who was also one of his penuchle playing buddies. His spine so curved that he reserved the strain of making eye contact for only a select few. When I was still the right height I could see movies of sadness and ghosts in his eyes, even when he smiled. "Such a cute little cookie you are." He'd give my chin a loving little squeeze and slide his eyes in Papi's direction.

"Virgilio, G_d has blessed you with a good girl. She's a smart one that little bubala, I can see it. And such a punum! She's just like her Papi, only better!" Papi rarely smiled, but Mr. Lipschitz always coaxed one out of him. Papi admired his good humor and always treated him with affection and respect. Mr. Lipschitz was the only one of his family to survive Auschwitz. He reminded Papi of how much he had to be grateful for, no matter how much the weather made his bunions and joints ache or how much he owed the *shellac*. "No time for all the schmegegge. Family and good health are everything." No one knew that better than Mr. Lipschitz.

FIFTY-NINE/CHALK

I'd been waitlisted for P.S. 77, an IGC school (Intelligently Gifted Children) but didn't have any mentors to pull strings. Papi, who had the bartender goods on most of the South Bronx politicians, could have made it happen. But being overprotective, he preferred having me in a school that was walking distance, rather than risk my riding the subways or buses alone. Mostly, he feared that beyond his periphery, I might cease to be a "good girl." The thought that I might not finish college and become a "jelly apple" instead was always in the forefront of his mind. He feared the influences that surrounded me. He feared I'd get knocked up and end up the "whore" he and Mami most feared I'd become.

Neither of my parents ever realized that they were the cheerleaders of all my failures. Their lack of trust in me, their suffocatingly overprotective ways, my mother's correasos y chancletasos and my Papi's fluctuations between emotional distance and borrachera love who allowed the daily beatings, were the perfect brew for raising a child with poor judgment and debilitating trauma.

Papi truly believed himself to be a good father; brainwashed by mythologies of what it meant to be a "family man," which he had become at a tender age on the streets of Andalucía and at sea, making his way to Ellis Island. Our family was nuclear, alright; every day another mushroom cloud. I felt nothing. Not even numbness. I moved through life in a state of unreality. Like any benevolent sociopath, I could mimic whatever the moment required. I harmed myself only enough to know I wasn't dead, just broken. It was always clear to me that doing good for and with others was my salvation. A well-managed crazy was my glue. My name remained a hieroglyph beneath the wrong skin; the colonizer's melanin. Inane and repetitive writing assignments in school were penance, not being the perfect daughter, student, or child. I was the malignant tumor in the lives of Mami y Papi.

The Horses Followed

Fatherhood stepped
on Papi's Xitano toes.
The vardo of his youth
limps on three wheels;
colors bleed to shadow
by the changing of seasons.
Carvings worn shapeless
from acts of living.

Belligerent children
of payos haunt the hollow shells
of long abandoned carriages
in search of histories unknown;
the ghosts they find, their own.
Our people have moved on.

Faithful horses vigilant
at Heaven's Gates
made by Xitano hands
formed on anvils
forged and carried
on fires of persistence;
the will to live and wander
to follow the voice of God.

Our horses no fools
to the Reaper's guise;
our blood and theirs
spill markers of arrival and return.
Find us. Carry us home.

SIXTY/SOAP

Papi was a lefty who was forced to use his right hand during the two years he had of schooling; he did the same to me. He'd seen the treatment of lefties, like we are children of the Devil; he wanted to spare me the misery. Right: diestre. Left: siniestre. It was rare that his people had the opportunity for schooling (not to be mistaken for education, which they gave to themselves) and that little boy made the most of it. In two years he learned to read and write with beautiful penmanship and over the years became a polyglot, reading newspapers in three languages every morning with his espresso while most people slept. Able to defenderse en siete idiomas: Spanish; English; Italian; Sicilian; Portuguese; Caló and Basque. Papi was determined to make his eighteen-hour work day more interesting for himself and everyone around him. "Just because you don't go to school you don't have to be an ignorante. Intelligence is learning to love what you must do when what you want to do is not possible." He'd leave his cup on the table for Mami to pick up, and finish his papers on the subway ride to work. He never told me what he really wanted to do in life. Papi had kept that secret, even from himself.

At the Crosstown Bar Papi talked politics and ponies. He owned the spotlight in any conversation, speaking multiple languages at once; code switching like he was mixing drinks for a party of seven. When friends came uptown to visit from Little Spain in Greenwich Village, Papi moved effortlessly from one dialect to the next. The bar gleamed, the spinning red leather stools had no rips, or stains, the chrome frames glistened like a new Cadillac and I'm certain that the black and white marble tile floor he scrubbed daily was where the "ten-second rule" was invented. "Is not my bar. So what? Is my reputation. What else does a man like me, who has no box in which to drop dead, or two nickels for his eyes, have for his name? Work is never dishonorable mi'ja. If you clean toilets, make them the cleanest toilets in the world. Take pride in whatever you do.Then you are something. Someone of importance. Have dignidad like a Queen, no matter where you are. You don't need a kingdom when you know it is only yourself you must rule. Isabella y Fernando were sonuvumbiches and Columbus was their lambe ojo. Los imperialistas are only for themselves. We must be for the people or we are for nobody, not even for ourselves." Papi's spontaneous and random speeches were like Saturdays at the movies, or walking on the ceiling. They always took you someplace strange and wonderful.

Teatro Puerto Rico

Boulevard Theater
Isla Theater
President Theater
Freeman Theater
Movies in Spanish
Little Heavens. Beautifully Made.
Angels. Gargoyles. Birds. Sirens.
Jokes and Sorrows
Written for Us
Our Faces on the Screen
Gathering Spaces
Our Voices
Cheers. Boos. Whistles.
Warnings. ¡Escondete! ¡Corre!
Neighbors. Spaces. Gathering. Joys.
Where We Saw Us. Laugh. Weep. Love.
Limited Run.
Gone.

Spinning on those perfect bar stools was one of the few pleasures of my childhood. Papi's friends were charmed by my painstakingly created Shirley Temple curls and home-sewn outfits made from fabric remnants that rivaled anything in Bonwit Teller's window. Mami was a genius at designing in her head and cutting newspapers into patterns from the images she saw by closing her eyes and recalling what we'd seen in all the best Fifth Avenue displays. Ideas arrived in Manhattan to be conjured in the Bronx. She couldn't draw beyond a four-year-old's perspective. Daisies always taller than the house, amputated bodies, and maimed pentagrams for stars.

Like Nikola Tesla, Mami's visions were rendered on invisible walls suspended in the air. In place of words or numbers, there were shapes and designs. She couldn't draw or read instructions on any ready-made pattern, yet every piece she conjured from Papi's discarded newspapers, and neatly folded brown grocery bags, she devised into flawless completion, fully lined with seam binding, patterns aligned at seams, with flap button holes done by hand with equidistant stitches. She sometimes made origami cranes along the way. "I saw them one time on a Crisma tree en Manhattan." But she couldn't make me a leotard no matter how much I begged. The material was too unnatural and she just couldn't make sense of it. God spoke to her as bobbins spun. She decided she didn't want me dancing ballet like a putika anyway. That pronouncement arrived a day late and a dollar short. I wished I'd never walked into that ballet class in that hideous bargain basement bathing suit. The very sight of it made me want to drown myself. "First position. Second Position. Plié. Hold. Hold. Hold." I was terrified of farting.

Mr. Georgie, the police detective, was my favorite of Papi's regulars at the Crosstown. "Hey, Chico, how about a cherry Coke for my friend here? Extra cherries." Papi's friends called him Chico because he was short. The first man to ever call him "shorty" was also the last. The same word in Spanish carries undertones of endearment and respect, an area where the English language is threadbare. Papi reserved *Virgilio* for medical matters and people he didn't trust. Mr. Lipschitz used it and pronounced it perfectly, out of respect. His Xitano name, El Curro, or just Curro was used mostly when in the company of anti-Franco Spaniards or Xitano allies like Don Ramiro at La Marqueta. Mami used it when she wanted something from Papi, like to fix the toilet or make a big, fancy cheesecake to bring to Titi Angela's on holidays.

Mr. Georgie, who Papi called Georgie Porgie, would always slip me a quarter for the jukebox. "Hey, Georgie-Porgie, no spoiling my little girl!" In those days, a quarter got you six songs. "So, your Papi tells me you're doin' good in school. Yeah?" It excited me to know Papi talked about me since he never told me he loved me. Not ever. "Yes, I'm doing really *well*, thank you. Thank you for the soda and the quarter, Mr. Georgie. Papi says you're a big shot detective."

His Marío Moreno half smile sent me spinning on the stool, so he couldn't see the blood heating up my face. I climbed down and looked for something by Papi's favorites, the Mills Brothers or Nat King Cole. Papi was still a bigot when it came to Black folks he considered "hoodlums" and "jelly apples." I was secretly hoping Mr. Georgie didn't think I was a little stuck up snot because I knew the difference between "good" and "well." I was always tormented when I thought I'd come off as Papi called me a "wise guy," not like a mobster, but like a smartass, or like Mami would say, "una present'a." The jukebox wasn't kept up to date, but close enough. It didn't have anything in Spanish even though most everybody in the neighborhood was Puerto Rican, Dominican or Cuban. There was

Doris Day singing K Say-rah, Say-rah. I didn't realize that was supposed to be Spanish, *Que Será Será*, until after I graduated high school. There wasn't much by women. I didn't like the cutesy pie Maguire Sisters and had an aversion to all things soaked in pink.

My jukebox favorites before Motown exploded in 1961: Harry Belafonte's "Angelique O;" Frank Sinatra's "Castle Rock;" Ernie Ford's "Sixteen Tons;" The Penguins' "Earth Angel" and anything by Muddy Waters, especially, "Got My Mojo Working." I loved learning new words from the time I could talk, since it took me so long to get there. "Developmentally delayed," I then rode my brain rocket to make up for lost time. Mojo is still one of my favorites. I find a word I like and latch on; a cat chasing a penlight.

"So Chico, you told your chiquita banana o'va here that I'm a big shot, eh?" Papi checked a wine glass for water stains. "Nope. Just didn't want to say 'shit' in front of my daughter." Mr. Georgie left Papi an extra dollar tip. I didn't know there was money in swearing. "Take good care of this one, Chico. The boys will be lining up." Papi pointed with his lips to the signed Roberto Clemente baseball bat mounted on the wall. Mr. Georgie winked at me. "You got yourself a good Papi, chiquita. You'll be alright." I thought of Mami and her belt. Papi's silence. His face behind a newspaper. His aching juanetes. "See you tomorrow, Georgie Porgie. First one's on the house." Papi checked every glass for stains.

Papi had a DJ friend he called "Payola Pat." Papi explained all about the corruption of payola in the music and radio business. "Buncha racketeers." If you have the money to pay off the DJ you get your song on the radio. How do you think un ladrón de cultura like Elvis Presley got up there? Pan-pan, vino-vino. I rest my face."

Radio was a huge deal when television was still fairly new and not everyone could afford those hefty consoles. Papi swore Pat never took payola, but Papi called him "Payola Pat" anyway. He liked alliterating. We had stacks of vinyl and shellac records from all genres: 45s, 78s, 16s and 33⅓ revolutions per minute. Revolution was one of those latch-on words for me; so many meanings inside one word. I made revolutions with my body, turning like the Temptations; I linked two circles to make my 8s, which I later read in Reader's Digest were part of the sociopathic profile. I was raised to be perfect and form an 8 in one swipe; I seldom did, because the bottom part always came out too skinny, and I liked circles better anyway. No mess, less stress—a kid's gotta find their "fuck you" place somewhere, or implode.

Maybe I just wished I had a smaller culo like my one swipe 8s. I like the word culo. If I had a son, that is what I'd name him, along with enrolling him into martial arts classes from the moment he could walk. Maybe I am a sociopath. But if you say culo out loud you'll see what I mean. Don Culo. It's crass and dignified all at once. If I hit the Lotto I'll buy an island and name it Isla del Culo. My son can be a real Papi Culo.

Anyway, my theme song became Sy Oliver's "I Ain't Got Nobody." I sang it after every beating. I sang it in my head at church. I sang it in the tub as Mami scrubbed my vagina a little too long. I heard it when I had to eat runny eggs, and just before a fist fight. "Mi'ja, listen to La Boheme, Rigoletto, listen to Harry Belafonte, Sam Cooke, Ethel Waters, the Japanese Koto, (I thought he said toto and had to turn away) Cante Jondo, Pablo Casals, Eartha Kitt, not just comemierda rock and roll. Elvis copied everything from los morenos. He is nothing original. Listen to everything, this way you can learn about the world. We can read and travel the world with our ears. I love the Sicilian and Italian people, pero I think they can do better than Bobby Vinton. Parece un gato pel'ao. Too skinny. Too much Vaselina in his voice. No cojones. Oh, and don't forget *The Barber of Sevilla*, of course."

Papi usually got jobs with Italians or Sicilians; they liked the fact that he spoke their languages and took pride in their food like he was born to it. Some of the guys admitted that Papi made a better "gravy" than their mothers. Papi could summarize the story lines of La Traviata, Rigoletto and the Barber of Seville. "Sevilla, coño! Seville is not a word, cabrones!" Papi sang what he called the Xitano's opera and blues all in one, Cante Jondo, the "deep song," while he prepped at work before any customers arrived. "Chico, your songs are so depressing the basement rats are hanging themselves." Papi grinned like a born trouble maker. "No rats in this basement. Trust me." That was Joe's Pizza in Greenwich Village, one of many places Papi made sure had no rats—at least nowhere near the food.

All of Papi's really close friends were Jewish, like Mr. Lipschitz, who was Papi's best audience, next to me. When Papi sang, the songs did all his crying for him. I think they did for Mr. Lipschitz too.

Mr. Lipschitz refused to leave the neighborhood when all the "Se Habla Español" signs started showing up in store windows and scaring off "los Americanos" as Mami called white people. Mr. Lipschitz said, "Puerto Ricans are as American as anybody. We have apple pie, they have flan. Big deal. We all have to break a few eggs." I thought that maybe Mr. Lipschitz was catching some of Papi's sayings.

"I was forced to leave my home once. Never again." Mr. Lipschitz said this whenever Papi complained about neighborhood crime and the arson fires that had started showing up earlier than most people think. Papi admired his courage. Despite all of his maladies, Mr. Lipschitz "never takes baloney from nobody. Not even Hitler. He survived the camps, mi'ja. He is protected by the right hand of God. Always respect Mr. Lipschitz, mi'jita. He is a holy man who is too humble to know he is holy." I did respect him. And still do. The veil is thinnest for the saints. Todavía le pido la bendición a Mr. Lipschitz y a Papi.

SIXTY-THREE/ROCOCO

Our building, known as the Professional Building, rested on three city blocks. In its pre-arson-for-profit heyday, it rented mostly offices for doctors, lawyers, realtors, and other white-collar professionals. The expansive and elegant marble lobby was filled with heavy, carved furniture that retained a Spanish Inquisition redolence; like Doña V.'s brownstone shrine, but without the frankincense and piss. As you passed through the glass doors fitted into ornate wrought iron swirls at the main entrance, you were greeted by a concierge. Miss Dotty, "la jamona," as Mami called her, and Mr. Joe, el "moreno buena gente," as Papi called him. They forwarded calls to all of the apartments at the building's main switchboard and placed mail into appointed wooden slots.

I don't remember anyone from the late shift because I rarely felt the night air unless I snuck into the kitchen to open a window and nibble an undetectable sliver of bitter Cortés chocolate. In bed by 8:00 p.m., except on Sundays when we squeezed onto the sofa with any visiting family members to watch the Ed Sullivan Show. Couch potatoes are not a new crop. The advent of television stretched the taproot from fingerlings to meaty russetts. The dreaded end of Ed Sullivan at 9:00 p.m. meant the weekend was officially over. Papi's blindingly white, starched shirt and chef's apron hung from the shower rod; flags of unavoidable surrender.

SIXTY-FOUR/CRAYON

Mami's jonkería store list for the day is on the table with her drawings. A horizontal rectangle for a bar of Fels Naptha soap (three cents less than at the A&P); a circle for whatever scouring powder was on sale; a crown and upwards pointed arrow for the tallest King Pine; (which means the floors are getting done and I'll be walking on my bare heels for most of the day) a whistling stick bird with giraffe legs for a new tea kettle. A red mark next to it hoping to find one like she'd seen on display in Macy's window. "Is that beautiful color like the Chino restaurant your Papi takes us in Pa'chesta."

Eating out is the only time I don't see my parents fight and the only time I'm allowed to speak at the table. Papi loves Chow Mein and Mami loves ribs. They always make me a special plate from theirs, and we still have leftovers to take home. Those little white boxes with the wire handles are so beautiful. Papi lets me carry a little one with the leftover rice. On the train ride home I swing it between my fingers and pretend I'm on the Coney Island Wonder Wheel, staring out over the ocean, trying to hitch a ride on a seagull to a place Mami will never find me. As if she can read my mind, she reaches around Papi to slap my hand. "Deja eso. Con la comida no se juega."

Papi has Sundays off. It's family and Church day for Italians. He goes in a little later on Mondays and comes home late. "The boss is sleeping it off. Too much cannoli and Grappa." He says that every Monday, with a twinkle, as if he's getting away with something by going into work an hour later. Before walking me to school he chats with Miss Dotty at the switchboard. Miss Dotty keeps her crisp lady shirt collar turned up and her slim waist snugly belted around her I Love Lucy dresses, perky with petticoats. Her perfect makeup and teeth, well curled hair, the scent of Lanvin's Arpege and funny innuendos (which she and Papi think I don't get), keep Papi lingering at the desk.

The almost-late walk to school is a sweaty exercise. I don't mind; it's worth everything to see Papi laugh *before* having a drink. Papi and Mr. Joe laugh a lot too, but their heads laugh downward with lots of shoulder action, not thrown back with lots of chest like when he laughs with Miss Dotty. Man talk and flirting is like two Papis in one.

Mr. Joe lights up from the inside out when we talk. He's very tall and bends a little and I look up. He always asks about school. I never have the heart to tell him how rotten it is and how much I'd rather be dead than walk into that haze of old urine, cigarette breath, and spoiled milk. I tell him about my good grades and how I'm in Fifth Grade now and almost got skipped a grade, and how I always get jobs like erasing the board or being the milk and pretzel stick snack monitor. Talking makes us both a little happier. I always call him Mr. Joe out of respect, like Papi does, and let him know how much I like his striped bow tie and his Cross of Jesus cuff links. He owns one tie clip he keeps in his pocket. Art Deco style in gold and black. He tells me more than once that he got it for being the first in his family to graduate high school as he taps it three times and looks upwards.

Mr. Joe is more professional than Dr. B., whose prescription for every aliment is the same: "a nice cup of tea, two aspirins, go to sleep and call me in the morning." Dr. B. makes house calls for five dollars, which is half our weekly grocery budget. He never really looks at me.

Mami says I pissed on him once when I had a seizure. Papi calls him Dr. CuppaTea. Mami calls him Aspirinita. The way she says it makes him sound like he has a tiny dick and brain to match. Puerto Rican women are the queens of talking with and without words. There are always at least three conversations going on at once.

Mami doesn't like too many people, especially Black ones who remind her of where she comes from. Of the little Black Haitian girls lined up beside her for the tourist perverts on the border in what she calls the "cicatriz" between Haiti and the Dominican Republic. Mami got punished with things shoved inside and got bruises where they wouldn't show, so when the perverts were sizing her up they wouldn't ask for a discount. Her skinny, tiny, pearly body kept her marketable longer than the other children. "I was a berry, berry bad girl who did terrible things." She brought in more money, and it gave her a better chance to survive. Later came the Masak nan Pèsil or Masacre de Perejil; a lingering terror of death by association. Her fear and denial of Blackness, her permanent grudge moratorium against rolling her "R's" in Spanish—those snitches for

Trujillo's genocidal soldiers who were *just following orders*.

Details arrive piecemeal and in color as my bedtime stories. Told and retold until I lose the ability to cringe, or the desire to vomit. The barely negligible difference between a slap and a caress. A longneck beer bottle up the ass? What else is new? I don't need a nightlight; I keep a steak knife under my pillow and talk to God by repeating the Pledge of Allegiance over and over. Invisible under God. It's one more thing I learned on the television school, Romper Room.

Sometimes instead of praying I draw pictures of cats on brown paper bags to keep the mice out of my bed.

Mami has the goods on everybody, whether it's true or not, but never a bad word about Mr. Joe. "A nice man of God." She tolerates Miss Dotty and whispers to me that she's just a "pobre jamona enclenca" who can't get a man; probably because she "gave away her toto like a little putika when she was your age. A man can smell it if you are not a virgin. They're like dogs looking for bones in the garbage." I didn't know men could smell it. Fifth grade doesn't teach you anything. I'm going to wash my own toto from now on, in case Mami misses a spot. Next time Kruschev is on TV I'm going to listen if he says *Putika*—it sounds Russian to me.

SIXTY-FIVE/PILLS

After Dr. Aspirinita permanently fled north on the Hutchinson Parkway,
whenever I had pus in my tonsils or really bad nervios that made me
either puke or get diarrhea, Mami insisted on the Lincoln Hospital emergency room. The hospital was known as "un toile" and I always came out
sicker than I went in. I can still see blood splatter on bile-colored wall of
the emergency room. It's where I always ended up if Papi wasn't home. It
was the only hospital Mami knew how to get to on the bus. "Nena, the bus
comes faster than the ambulance in our neighborhood." If Papi was home
when I got sick we took two buses to see his doctor friend, a pediatrician
he called "Dr. Albert Schweitzer."

Dr. Schweitzer had an office in his own house on what felt like a moun-
tain in a part of the Bronx where you had to climb endless concrete steps
and battle thick sumac branches on the way. He was worth the trouble. I
always knew everything would be okay no matter what, with Dr. S. "He's
a real doctor, mi'ja, not spaghettis and meatballs." Papi thought of spa-
ghetti with heavily breaded meatballs in a thick sauce as an insult to real
Italians; an impostor dish for Americanos barrigones. Dr. S. was nobody's
meatball.

Dr. S. always refused Papi's money and gave me a green lollipop. I
always thought he was famous, but it was just Papi doing what he always
did, re-naming people. Sometimes he would slip Dr. S. a bottle of what
Papi called "real medicine." Dr. S. never objected since Papi did it with
his Xitano flair. Sometimes it was rum. On special holidays it was a brand
new penuchle deck and five bucks to get the game started "after the turkey." He would also mention that chestnut stuffing was the way to go. Dr.
S. never mentioned having a family or turkey, and I didn't see any photos
in his office, except one of a handsome, young man in WWII Army gear
slipped into a really fancy frame.

Papi could give you an old sock or tell you to go fuck yourself and
name you Uncle Bonzo (he loved opera) with so much charm that it felt

like flirtation or sounded like a compliment. People took whatever he gave. Papi was above the laws of society and made his own rules. I had to take not only what he gave me, but also what he didn't.

It was always a mystery how Dr. Schweitzer and Papi knew each other and how come he never had Mami come along after the first visit. They were both so handsome and manly in that Art Deco-leading-man kind of way, with an irresistible womanliness in the way they side-glanced and smiled. They talked without words and the room would feel soft; a gossamer Persian silk, fragrant with sandalwood. I could feel Morocco from all the stories Papi told me about swimming there from Gibraltar, as a Quinine smuggler during a malaria outbreak. Sometimes my visions alighted on a hand-embroidered quilt catching me in mid-air, as winged camels (atá Allah) flew past me. The veil was always thin in the realities Papi unknowingly conjured, even in his sober silences.

When Papi was with Dr. Schweitzer, he wasn't sober or drunk. He became someone I didn't recognize. Someone I wished would always show up. Someone who could see the flying camels and make me know they're real. Pour Maghrebi mint tea from sixty centimeters above the glass, my initials in the froth. Our bodies Bedouin, ready for all manner of cruelty; resilient, content. We both always felt better after we left Dr. S. Papi felt even better when Dr. S. gave us a prescription—making it really official to Papi that I would get well.

Papi, a socialist at heart, had his own lexicon and made up words for the social strata. The rich were the "hightónes comemierdas", and the only thing worse than those high tone shit eaters were the poverty pimp "jelly apples" who looked good on the outside but were rotten inside. "They dip the bad apples in burnt sugar water and sell them to suckers like it's something special. Never fall for a jelly apple, mi'ja. A good apple doesn't need dipping. Better to have one good friend than ten jelly apples. Once you swallow a worm more grow inside you and it is very hard to get them out. Always smell your food before you eat it. ¿Capiche?"

One of Papi's favorite sayings was: "Tell me who your friends are and I'll tell you who you are." Papi didn't have a lot of friends, but I liked all the ones he had. Like Mr. Detective Georgie Porgie, Dr. Albert Schweitzer, and Mr. Lipschitz. Papi would always say goodbye to Mr. Lipschitz the same way: "If your lip shits, my ass whistles." I'd turn red and give Papi the Mami hate look, but Mr. Lipschitz always chuckled and shook his head. Friends have their own rules. "Chico, you're meshuggeneh! Hadran Alach."

I'd get so excited when Mr. Joe would tell me I had mail, which was usually a card from Titi, or when I got sick and the teacher would force the kids to make "get well" cards. Sun discolored cheap manila construction paper, with pencil and crayon drawings, carried the stale classroom air and windowsill dust to my sickbed. A sickly kid, I received cards for having "chicken pops" "diarears" "missels" and "the flew." I only felt loved and safe when I was sick. It was the only time Mami didn't hit me and Papi bought me extra comic books. A part of me still enjoys having a cold.

With forty-five kids to a class, every ledge, shelf, available tabletop and doorknob was used for storage. The dandruff of old erasers with one foot in the grave landed everywhere when I smacked them together in my official capacity as the Blackboard Monitor. Broken, chewed-up pencils in a ratty cigar box and broken or half-eaten crayons in old mayonnaise jars were passed around when it was time for art or card making. Ragged, racist textbooks with broken spines, rulers, lined paper, and canisters of pink barf-sucking crystals were everywhere. Confiscated airplane glue and BB guns were petty larceny temptations in the teacher's locked desk drawer next to her emergency bourbon. Teachers having to make something from nothing is an old magic show still on the circuit.

Once in a while Titi Angela sent me a dollar or two in a perfumed pharmacy card, the kind with flowers, glitter, and sappy rhymes in Spanish or English. Titi's favorite toilet waters were Lily of the Valley and Violets. She never treated herself to Eau of anything, saving every penny she could for her kids' education. When I'd call to thank her, she'd make me promise I would use the money to get something for Mami at the jonkería store, or maybe a nice Maja soap from Mr. Saul's farmacia, where Papi bought us big, five-cent green tinted glass bottles of Vichy water, "God's real Holy Water. Good for the kidneys." It took me years to realize that Titi was teaching me how to kiss Mami's ass so she might let up on the daily beatings. Titi didn't know that nothing I did ever pleased Mami. She never gave me a real smile; couldn't find one, and I know she tried. I still get anxiety sweats when buying gifts for anyone, and finally called it quits on Christmas and birthdays from the sheer panic of it all.

Mr. Joe was my Jesus. The gentle one, the shepherd; not the pull out the whips and tumble the tables of exploitation Jesus. Nope, that Jesus was up in Harlem. "Well, Miss, I think Mr. Malcolm is a fine young man." Mr. Joe looked away and out of the small, bright window that looked out onto the street. "I just don't like the company he keeps. Going to get him in trouble some day." I was going to ask him what the X meant, but whenever I asked one of my "bobería" questions, as Mami called them, I usually got into trouble. I was happy that sometimes Papi only took the sports pages for his long ride to work, leaving the news behind so that I could learn about important people. No one told me Mr. X was Jesus of Harlem. I just figured it out. He stood up to the racketeers and jelly apples, and the crooked politicians, just like Jesus did with the Romans and the hightones y los comemierdas. Besides, God couldn't have just one body with so much work to get done. If you read the Bible and look at how people behave, you can always figure out which ones are Jesus. Sometimes it's a woman. The big shot Las Vegas lights and fireworks Jesus is supposed to be coming again, and I look forward to the show.

Mr. Joe would tease with a search through stacks of solicitation mail. "Hmmm, young lady, it was just here a minute ago. Don't see it. Wait. Let me look in a few more places." Mr. Joe would lift up papers, fan the pages in a phone book, lift up the trash can, and then finally, always find my mail on some high shelf. He'd smile and watch me pull out a bobby pin, chew off and spit out the rubber tip, and carefully open the envelope after sniffing it for Titi's cologne.

"Watcha got there, Miss? Something good?" I'd do a spin and show him the card from Titi Angela and offer him half of the money, "Here Mr. Joe, so you can get some candy." He would give me a look like I had offered him the whole world, smiling really big with both hands on his heart. "Thank you, Miss. That's very kind of you but it would make me happy to see you buy yourself something nice. With all that money you can get a whole lot of candy and some good toys too."

He was right —those were the days of penny candy and Woolworth's, that everyone called "The Five and Dime." Mr. Joe always reminded me about the "Young folks at that Woolworth's counter in Greensboro, North Carolina." He told me he was leaving out the really bad parts so I wouldn't get too sad. "Miss, you are never too young to change the world. Make sure whatever you get yourself, share a little with your friends. Friends are very important in this life." I thought about how Mami didn't really have any. I didn't fully understand about Woolworth's except that it was Black and White young folks fighting together against Jim Crow. I had already learned from Atilla that Jim Crow wasn't a bird. I was so relieved to know that there wasn't some big, evil bird out to get Black people. It was evil laws. Mr. Joe said "And too bad about that. Stopping an evil bird wouldn't take so long."

Whatever I bought, with my Titi money, I always put something aside for Mr. Joe and would slip it into his hand when I thought nobody was looking, like a penny box of Chiclets or a two-cent pilón. He would thank me with a wink and slip it in his shirt pocket tapping his heart. "Maybe you should think about putting a little aside for college, Miss. Mr. Joe got the sugar diabetes and can't eat too much candy now."

Papi always said "everything in moderation" is the best way. I don't think it applied to his palitos de ron. "Okay, Mr. Joe. Next time I'll pick up something nice for you at the Woolworth store when Mami takes me." I was thinking he might like a set of jacks, to pass the time as he waited for the phone to ring. I could get really nice ones for ten cents. I would have died of embarrassment if Mr. Joe had ever refused my little offerings of affection. There is nothing like the desprecio of a gift to wound Puerto Ricans or Xitanos of any age. Mr. Joe was a gracious recipient of anything I ever gave him in sharp contrast to my mother's drawn out, lethagric "Aaahaa. I likee" with a sneer of disgust passing for a smile, making me feel I'd given her a dog turd rolled in confectioner's sugar.

SIXTY-SEVEN/SPINDLE

Despite my fierce hatred of Shirley Temple, I did some faux tap dancing up and down the five marble lobby steps that led to the elevator. I secretly hoped Mr. Joe would dance with me one day like Mr. Bojangles did with Shirley. To me, she was the brat of an overbearing stage parent and Mr. Bojangles was a great artist who'd be better off dancing with me in a red bathing suit than with that dimpled Kewpie doll robot in way too many ruffles, her creepy Medusa head of librarian albino eels.

There were two elevators in the building. One for freight, where the most accidents happened. Two sets of stairs; one was a double in opposite directions, like in a fancy palace. Six stories. Apartments A to Z on every floor. We were 4X (like Malcolm) where my parents held me hostage. Once in a great while I was allowed to visit other kids in the building as long as their parents were home. When La Colombiana moved in next door with her two hyper-nasal, asthmatic boys, Wilfredo and Louis, Mami felt no threat. Louis was the most nasal of the two with the kind of voice that got your ass kicked in school. Louis was such a good friend that I started to believe that maybe Bronx Mary had put in a good word. She had definitely worked some mojo on Mami. Louis and Wilfredo both liked to draw and played with dolls. La Colombiana was a proud butch single mom who always made me feel welcome and liked having me over to play with her boys. They were different from other kids in the building, and nothing like the building stalker everybody called "El Chino" As far from Chino as China.

Louis braided my hair with ribbons from La Colombiana's sewing box, and Wilfredo painted my nails deep burgundy. We read to each other, made up songs and dissonant harmonies with the sound of La Colombiana's Singer sewing machine whirring in the background. Every now and then she'd shout from the next room, telling the boys to teach me to dance *Cumbia*, a dance evolved from 17th Century slaves. "Make sure you tell her it came from Magdalena, Colombia." We'd fall out in hysterics. The asthma tablets were always within reach when we got together. La Colombiana wanted them to have the joy of telling me, no matter how loud she blared it through the wall. It was nice to hear my name spoken as if I mattered: proof of my existence.

SIXTY-EIGHT/EMBROIDERY

El Chino is sixteen and still in elementary school. He prowls el building's stairwells and sometimes traps me on the way to la tiendita around the corner—the only place that at thirteen years old, I'm allowed to go alone; at least when we run low on bread or milk. "I'll stick it in you so far it'll come out your mouff, bitch." My knee, a jackhammer to El Chino's sack while pulling on his ears. El Chino to the ground, me to the air. This has happened more than once. He's a mentecato jelly apple who never learns. Mami always gives me ten minutes to get to la tiendita and back. A minute over and she threatens to come down to "agarrarte por el moño y meterte con la correa." El Diablo himself can't stop me from bringing home the Wonder Bread before the clock strikes cocotaso. Mami's scarier than getting raped in a stairwell with a splintered stick by a dozen El Chinos.

There was only one time El Chino got the better of me. He snuck up from behind and it took longer to fight him off. I got my thumbs in his eye sockets and he dropped me like a sizzling tostone. I ran back upstairs, no bread, no milk. Mami didn't ask, she just slapped me. I yelled out: "¡El Chino, Mami!"

That was all I had to say. She dragged me by the arm to La Soplona's house, a Pentecostal church lady who knew everybody's business and didn't mind telling it. Anything to take the fish eye of Jesus off herself for cheating on her husband with El Super. "Praise God." Mami concurred. "Alabado sea El Señor." They hit the "Amén" in unison." Boom!

The women and girls in the building have all heard the legends of El Chino, but since nobody ever speaks up, Mami thought he might be a myth, an excuse, someone to blame if we lost our cherry on purpose. La Soplona knows El Chino's father from her church, the something-something of the Holy Ghost. They've got a big white pigeon painted on their storefront window. El Chino's father, Señor Peña, an old school, strict Dominican, had confided in La Soplona that his son had some problems controlling his urges. "Losing his mother made him a little soft in the coconut.

Especially the way she died." La Soplona had told Mami: "He met his wife at one of those camps after la bomba en Pearl Harbor, where he was a guard. He hated the camps. He told me they were evil places where they threw innocent people, separated families and treated them like dogs. He said this Señorita muy especial always had a smile for him, no matter what. He still calls her mi *Lucecita*. Her real name was like Saka Mosca o algo así." Mami loved bochinche, but wanted to get back to El Chino.

La Soplona inhaled, like a deep sea diver. As she exhaled, I noticed one of her tetas was smaller than the other. "Pobrecita Chinita, she survived that rotten place to be killed on the street with baseball bats by idiots making believe to be soldiers. ¡Cobardes! May they rot in hell! ¡Ay! ¡El Señol me jep'enda! The cops never got them. It happened in some fancy neighborhood in Queens where she worked cleaning fish. Lo Blanco con chabo always get away with these things. Believe, me I know." La Soplona looked down and locked her hands behind her back and rocked side to side, exhaling. Mami looked away. "Me too. I know. I know. ¿Quiere un chicle?" Mami gave us both some Chiclets. She always had some in the pocket of her bata.

La Soplana told Mami that she didn't want El Chino's father to feel bad about his son being a pervert, since he was so sad already, so she advised him to ignore it. "The boy can't help it. It's not his fault, Señor Peña. It happens to a lot of boys. It's natural for young men to have these feelings so that the world can continue. It's how God made them. It's better for...um, you know...for it to be active down there if you want ever to be a grandfather. If we have another flood, we can't just put animals on the boat. It's not the Bible times anymore. People can get to the boat with the subway. Don't you want grandchildren for the boat? Déjelo quieto, pray for him. The girls have to learn better than to tease the boys. I was young once. They know men have needs. That Iris Chacón Show is raising a generation of perdidas. It takes two for Pachanga. Praise God, and give your son to him, like Abraham." My eyes hurt from listening so hard. I figured out El Chino was half Japanese.

Next La Soplona gave Mami the scripture and verse details of El Chino: Where he lived / the apartment number / how clean the place was / his father's full name with middle initial and where in the D.R. he was from / that he was good-looking / that he made good Puerto Rican coffee for a Dominican / was a snappy dresser / sang in church like Bobby Capó

/ and always smelled like Bay Rum. She repeated the entire El Chino was motherless story again / that El Chino smelled like a tecato / that he wasn't really Chinese / and how in her opinion the Chinese are smarter than the Japanese / that the Japanese are better looking / and how she can't really tell them apart except in the movies / and I tried to tell her that white people play those parts / and Mami yanked one of my trenzas half way to an August Moon / and they praised God from Genesis to Revelations. ¡Amén y Amén! La Soplona shook and sucked in hard from a brand new asthma inhaler that sounded like a cat toy. It was a new thing in poor neighborhoods, where scientists liked to experiment. Mami offered her a Lydia Pinkham pill; a little tin always in her brassiere for emergencies. The pills were for "that time of the month" but seemed to do the trick for all kinds of maladies, according to the medical advice women gave each other at the market. The pills were kept in a locked glass cabinet, which made them "official."

It seemed that La Soplona would never run out of gasolina. "Ese nene e' un Dominicano endroga'o, quel señol lo je'penda." Mami punctuated the Spic and Span air with "Um-hum. Um-hum. Um-hum." She was ready to make her exit. "Que Dios me la bendiga. Gracias por todo." Turning down an offer to keep bochinchando over pan dulce y café con leche, Mami stomped back to our apartment, squeezing my hand. "No worry. El Chino is going to get some religión today." I missed out on pan dulce because of that sonavambiche, El Chino.

SIXTY-NINE/PEAS

Mami took a fast cold shower, since the hot water had gone out again. She yanked the knots out of my hair, then heated up water on the stove and washed my body with a soapy face cloth, then rinsed me off as best she could with another one. "Take your Papi's big towel and dry yourself good." She checked me all over when I was done to make sure there was no stink, and made me put on white cotton dress she'd made from a bed sheet. She got dressed up like for a job interview with a homemade gabardine suit, full arsenal make-up, a French twist, a little Violet cologne, fresh Chiclets for her breath, deodorant, and polished church heels. As always, she picked out everything I would wear, including underwear and accessories. A hand-crocheted pink beret, a thick, itchy, retiree blue bargain basement cardigan over the sleeveless dress, and a deep navy wool poncho she'd made from an old blanket, with a hand-embroidered hem of flowers to match the sweater and beret, with interlocking gold frog closures that matched my two dollar, gold lamé penny loafers from an Alexander's bargain bin. Those shoes got my ass kicked in school more than once.

Titi Angela had given her the blanket that would become that poncho when she heard about our boiler troubles. It was a relief to be wrapped in something touched by my Titi. Mami handed me a pair of small white hand-sewn gloves, beaded with tiny pearls. Mami and I had tiny hands in common. "I made those for when I married your father, to look good in City Hall. Don't get them dirty."

It was a long, icy walk to El Chino's building on Simpson Street. It was one of those gray winter days that make everything look worse than it is. Mami stepped hard in her rubber-covered heels, I slid around in the oversized red galoshes that protected my "special shoes," steadying myself on Mami's arm.

On the way there, we passed Carmen La Maricona and I hid my face in Mami's fancy black cashmere coat that "fell off a truck" one Christmas, afraid that Carmen could read me as a snitch. Carmen would want me to kick El Chino's ass myself and throw him down like a dragon. Like the tattoo ones on the outside of her legs. I wish I could tell her I did. Tell her that I was sure he iced his balls with a bag of frozen peas for a week. That I gave him some Bugs Bunny ears. That he lost his breath and I got away. Carmen would be so proud of me. "Hey, pretty girl, you're a warrior too, huh? I wish you was my baby girl. Damn, that is some funny, badass shit." I know she would hug me and tell everybody on the block what I did. After that, girls would laugh at El Chino if he tried anything. That would be the end of El Chino. No more legend. Just another Dominican kid with nervios like a Puerto Rican girl.

At El Chino's father's apartment, Mami was uncharacteristically polite, but never lowering her guard or warming her icy demeanor. When speaking of El Chino to his father, who was even more handsome than Mami expected, she replaced de'gra'cia'o hijo de puta me cago en su alma with "su hijo tiene falta de disciplina." She could see why La Soplona had to hit Mami's Lydia Pinkham pills after talking about him. I think Mami was feeling a little bit of nervios herself. We had left our rain rubbers outside the apartment door. I wondered if they felt lonely and scared. Especially my rubbers, too big for themselves.

Nervios or not, I knew that the umbrella with the extra sharp metal tip was itching in Mami's hands. Mr. Peña excused himself and returned from the kitchen with glasses of Cherry Kool Aid he had prepared in advance, after a call, I was sure, from La Soplona. Those church ladies always tend to find loopholes in the Ten Commandments. The mere sound of Mr. Peña's voice put La Soplana's salvation at risk. Her heads up to him of the Mami invasion and Mr. Peña's "gracias, muy amable" was worth the risk of God's wrath to her, especially since forgiveness is always within reach.

"Mi Lucecita, mi Hakiri, always told me that cherry was a nice drink for the ladies. I hope you like it." Mami thanked him, and put her glass on a coaster next to another Porcelain Lady. I concentrated on keeping my glass steady, terrified to drink or to spill. There was only one coaster.

"What happened to my manners? May I hang up your coats? Please, have a seat." Mami remained standing. "Very nice, thank you. No, is okay, I'm no tired." Mami took off her coat and draped it over her arm. That was my cue not to sit either. I had no way to take off the wool poncho as cold sweat began to gather in every fold of my uncomfortable body.

Mr. Peña, called out to El Chino with a nettled voice, from the neat and well appointed living room where we all stood ill at ease. He had a "Porcelain Lady" too. Nothing like my special one, but like all the others in the full price stores. She was gleaming; her legs in perfect stillness and not an ash on her. Mr. Peña saw me staring at her and rocked her legs with a sad, little laugh, probably thinking I would like it. I smiled to be polite and looked away. "It was a gift from Hakiri, mi Lucecita, for my birthday. She thought I would like it. I didn't. She said it was a pretty American lady. No one could ever be more beautiful than my Hakiri." I didn't think I could get any sadder.

The velvet Last Supper over the sofa made me think of how women probably bruised the grapes to make the extra wine that got Jesus a reputation for miracles. Women are the saviors of our world, and now one, despite all of the cyclonic knots within her, was trying to protect me. Or maybe just my body, so my white husband, whoever he might turn out to be, wouldn't be getting damaged goods. Mami always said "if a man can smell sex on you he will never respect you. Only good girls get good man."

I couldn't get Mr. Peña's Porcelain Lady or her stupid shorts out of my head. I stared into the red Kool Aid and smelled blood, wondering if the Prince of Darkness would sneak in and drink it for me. I could hear El Chino flush the toilet and run the sink water long enough to wash all eight of his hands. I wondered if he was pulling at his thing. He entered the living room slumped over. A sharp glance from Mr. Peña straightened his spine. At the sight of Mami's death-ray, El Chino dropped his eyes, surveying his spanking new Keds. He shrunk down to just two arms and two hands.

"Señor Peña, si su hijo touches my daughter again, even looks at her, you can be sure you will never get to be a grandfather. I say this with todo respeto." Mr. Peña glared at his son as he spoke to Mami. "My son will never even look at your daughter again, se lo juro por mi Hakiri, que en paz descanse." "Muy bien." Mami gestured razor cuts up the length of her arms. "Si no, le rajo las venas y le chupo la sangre. Forgive me, but I would die for my daughter and kill for her."

Mami's bottomless rage popped like a live operatic telenovela wherever she went. It was dizzying to hear those words come from the mouth of the same person who killed a little piece of me every day. The ragingly self-possessed four foot, eleven inch demoniac with a Garrison belt who almost always looked disgusted at the sight of me, was making blood ritual threats on my behalf to a man built like the Chrysler Building. El Chino never looked up from his Keds. The look on his father's face, assured me I would never see El Chino again. I never did, but throughout my life, plenty of others came to take his place. I wondered what would happen to the poor schmuck who might accidentally step on his brand new sneakers after that beating. In our neighborhood, people died for less.

Mami made me swear not to tell Papi about El Chino. "He won't talk to those kinds of people. He will just kill them and go to jail. Then what happens to us? Welfare? Keep you mouth shut or te parto la cara." Spanish is so pliable. Parto can mean to break, crack, or to give birth. So did she threaten to break my face or give birth to it? I own a mirror. She did both. I look more like her with every passing year. Now there's a definition for Purgatory.

SEVENTY/BRASS

Papi was a neighborhood hero. No one ever said it, but everybody knew it. He was short and limped on account of his childhood bout with polio, so they never saw him coming. What he lacked in physical stature, he made up for in agility, timing, and concentrated force. If he saw a man abusing a woman or child on the street or threatening them, Papi always intervened. The biggest and most macho guys often backed off right away. A *nothing left to lose* stare was the only thing my parents had in common. Papi whispered inches from the bully's face. "Excuse me, señor, would you like to fight with a man?" Sometimes, that was all he needed to do. Other times a loud "Mind your own business" shot back at him. Mistake. "You made it everybody's business by putting it on the street. And in front of mi nena? Sonavambiche! *This is my business!*" Papi would show the guy his left fist with the broken off pinkie. "Do you want to find out how I got this?" Insinuated concrete grave. A stunned crowd. Pigeons left bald by light speed of left hook. Ambulance. Rust. Muffler drags like poverty's Christmas. Drowns the siren. The movie in Papi's double feature eyes. Camera steady. All eyes roll. Except Papi's. Dead on.

Confronting bullies made Papi hungry. If he had some jingle in his pocket, he'd get us each a pizza slice and we'd share a Coke. "Cabrones y cobardes, mi'jita. The world is a sewer. That's why I have to be strict with you. You're a beautiful girl, so smart no one believes you're only twelve years old. These pervertidos always have their eyes on you." What papi really meant was that I had big tetas for my age, but he would never say that. "That's why every weekend I send you and your mother to your Titi's house. It's quiet, like el campo over there. Clean streets, good people. Lots of trees. Good for your lungs."

Every Saturday for as long as I could remember, Papi would take five bucks he'd saved up, won at cards or borrowed, and give it to Mami so we could go to Titi Angela's house in a taxi to the Gravesend section of Brooklyn. When we didn't have cab fare we got there on the #6 and #4 trains. Next, the Sea Beach, the Culver Line trains, on the independent BMT appendage of the NYC subways. The Culver was a run of military green train cars with yellow corncob seats. The Short Line.

It was a long ride from the South Bronx to get to that Culver Line, which took us to another world. Titi had married a Sicilian bookie with mob affiliations, and they lived on a residential, tree-lined street in an attached brick duplex in a predominantly Italian neighborhood. To a South Bronx kid, it was the countryside; complete with old man Bonanno who gave us rides for a dime on his rickety hay wagon pulled with great reluctance by his flatulent horse, Fratellino. "We can ride the subway for the same money. Ese viejo hincho is a thief and beats ese pobrecito caballo." Mami dismissed me with her slapping hand. Titi Angela always came through with the dime.

When Old Man Bonanno wasn't dragging kids around, he was selling rags. Mami told me that "Los Italianos" used that wagon to dump corpses into the "Gusano Wanas Canal" and that one day it would be Papi, if he didn't pay his gambling debts. Only Mami could turn a rainbow into a garrote.

Titi's husband, Joe, was a cross between a George Raft and Omar Sharif. Always in his Fruit of the Loom blazing white tank top, chiseled guns well oiled, an unfiltered Chesterfield dangling from his full lips, and black horn rims half way down his ample nose. He commandeered the kitchen with a row of black rotary phones, a pickle jar stuffed with shorty pencils, slips of paper, stacks of cash, and brown paper bags. "Hey, sweetheart, get your Titi Joe a beer and his church key." I had called him Titi Joe once and it stuck. His beer bottle opener was next to the cookie jar. "Help yourself. Wash your hands first, peanut. Little girls should always have nice clean hands." He'd pucker his lips for a quick little kiss.

Girls kissing men on the lips was accepted in Titi Joe's family, at least when Papi wasn't around. "You're a good girl." He'd pull out a roll of Fruit Lifesavers from his coat pocket. "Take two; one for later."

Whenever I dared to ask Papi for a kiss, he always asked, "How much you want for it?" I got scared to ask him for too many kisses; didn't want him to think I didn't love him and just wanted money. Inadvertent whore training. Just as normal as the penis worship of infant boys. The informal penis kissing of newborn boys by women on Mami's side of the family had become an informal sacrament. The occasional piss in the face was considered the harbinger of La Buena Suerte. Giggles all around. Getting pissed on by a baby boy was like a promise you'd hit the number. Sometimes it actually worked. If a girl pissed on you there'd be a rumble of cussing and one more annoying diaper change and a mad dash for the blue seltzer bottle before the stain set. Diaper washing was the only option in those days. Good for the Earth, bad for the women stuck with the job. Girl piss stank. Boy piss was holy water. Blue glass seltzer bottles arrived by the case once a week.

"Go outside and play for your Titi Joe. The grownups have to talk." For Titi Joe's sister who liked to visit, Ant Pauline (only snobs had aunts) food was love and sweets were endearment. "Sweetheart, take one of those nice Italian cookies, with the rainbow sprinkles like you like." The unspoken bribes and edicts all of us kids understood. I snuck out a couple extra Piñoli cookies in case I needed to bribe a bully. I didn't like those much anyway.

The block was populated by aggressive boys. I don't remember playing with, or even seeing a girl. They were either kept indoors or it was simply an unfortunate coincidence for me. No kids of color in the neighborhood either; my dark Sicilian relatives who had married into the family via my Venezuelan born Titi of Puerto Rican parentage, referred to their dark skin as an olive complexion. I guessed they'd rather be green than Black.

When I stepped onto that sidewalk I left my girl side indoors. It was freedom and prison all at once. Mami thought it a "good neighborhood," meaning white, so I was able to play outside unattended. It was where I worked the 1950s stick ball street game and foot racing. I got good at both. Too good. I found and smoked "ciggie butts" off the street, like some little badass putz.

Sick of being outrun and outplayed by a Bronx spic, the boys were coerced by a barrel-bellied pinhead they called Patrissy, to tie me to a tree with somebody's mother's laundry rope. They pinned down my arms, legs, and throat. They called me Pocahontas. They ran circles around the tree slapping the palms of their hands against their mouths, "WOO-WOO-WOO-WOO-WOO." The object of the game was to hurl their thickest phlegm loogies into my face. I didn't scream, afraid the rope would strangle me. Once they got bored they just left me there, mumbling about something on television and stealing some beers. "Maybe the dogs'll eat'er." They barked and laughed. "Old man Banana can dump her in the

Gowanus." Or the Gusano Wana, as Mami called it. "Yeah, right next to your bitch sister."

I was almost indigo by the time Mami came out to call me in for lunch. She asked me what I had done, not who had done it to me. She untied the rope with a look on her face that told me she was sorry they didn't finish the job. Dragging me by the arm she threatened me through gritted teeth back to Titi's house. She smacked me hard on the back to stop my coughing which only made it worse. "No crying to Titi or I'll kill you. It's time to eat, not cry, llorona. Let the poor woman have a day in peace." She hustled me into the bathroom to wash up and look decente. The rules were always on the side of the white boys. Surely I must have provoked "los nice nenes Italianos; son un chorro de brutos, pero por lo meno son bruto con chabo." Stupid but with money was *nice boy* enough for Mami.

Mami never hit me when Titi was around. She'd pinch me or dig in her nails when Titi couldn't see. The look on her face letting me know not to go crying to Titi, or life could get much worse. Trapped indoors for the rest of the weekend, I tucked myself into the single bay window in Titi's bedroom. From there I could look down into the basement synagogue behind Titi's house and lose myself in the rhythm of the Hasidic men shuckling. Their reverent focus made me feel safe, even through the harsh florescent lights and wood paneling that highlighted the worn parts of their wool coats in summer, and the wiry texture of their beards, contrasted with the smoothness of their well tended payot. I added a repeating musical soundtrack to their movements and was transported to another world; Jesus loves me this I know, 'cause the Bible tells me so...time disappeared and so did my troubles.

SEVENTY-ONE/FORMALDEHYDE

Papi's rheumatic fever-damaged heart started giving him trouble. The elevator, like everything else in our landlord abandoned building was falling apart and the long four flights to our apartment were too much for him. It was time to move. I was twelve and Mami dragged me to the Public Housing Authority to sweet talk them, interpret and fill out all the necessary forms. I remember turning on the tears about my "daddy's heart condition." He was only Papi at home. I had already learned that I needed to code switch with white folks. I prayed that Mami wouldn't act "too Puerto Rican" and I spoke without contractions to sound official and not slur my words.

I could tell that the chain-smoking bleached blonde who was handling our case was looking for a man on account of too much blue eye shadow. That's another one of those things that people think kids don't know. I told her how pretty she was and how hard her job must be and how nice she was to help us. I told her my mother had mental retardation but that she did her best to be a good mother. I figured that most white people thought we were all retarded anyway, so no harm in pouring it on thick.

"My daddy works very hard to put food on the table and keep a roof over our heads" (I'd heard that line a thousand times from Papi when Mami yelled at him for drinking too much or gambling) "I'm so scared that he'll die if we can't live in a building with an elevator. If we don't get an apartment soon, my daddy is going to die." I made myself just hysterical enough to get away with "If my daddy dies it will be your fault. Oh, I'm so sorry, sorry miss, sorry, I didn't mean that. It isn't your fault my daddy is sick."

Blondie pulled out a different form. "Where do your parents want to live?" She handed me a tissue and touched my hand to console me. "Daddy says Spanish Harlem would be nice." She gave me a pitying look. "My daddy is from Spain, you know." I knew that people treated us better whenever I said that. Mami taught me that trick and experience confirmed it. She wanted me to pass for Jewish, but Spanish would have to do. I never wanted to lie about who I was. That Papi was Xitano was not up for discussion, since Papi barely talked about it. I wanted to live in El Barrio too, so I wouldn't have to interpret for Mami all the time and we could go to La Marqueta on Saturdays without having to lug the shopping cart on the subway or bus to get fresh fish and produce. The Hunts Point Market was pretty good, but everything cost less at La Marqueta because Mami could work her discount magic fluently. Papi was convinced everything was fresher, mostly because he knew almost all of the vendors from when he worked at Doña V.'s diner.

"Let me see what I can do." I could see I'd gotten Miss Blondie's eyes a little wet because the blue was smearing. We went from a three-year waiting list to an apartment in the predominantly white Northeast Bronx Pelham Parkway Houses within three months. We were among the first Latinos that made the cut and the first Puerto Ricans in our section.

Now we were living in the country, like Titi Angela. Not in a real house, but it was still brick and only a short six stories high. The hallways didn't smell like cat piss and there were no rats, mice, or roaches. I had my own room with a window that faced a play area that had a giant cement turtle. Most everyone was Jewish or Italian, with a few African American families, so I was still stuck being Mami's interpreter. Every day from my own room I sent ESP messages to the turtle to come to life, to grow wings and take me away someplace where I could forget I ever had a mother and not feel guilty about it.

SEVENTY-TWO/BRISTLES

Living in a mostly white neighborhood took some getting used to. At least the supermarket was only four blocks away, with a Laundromat even closer. Along the way was a shoe repair shop, so Papi could easily keep his one pair of good shoes. "If you only have one pair mi'ja, you keep them nice, always clean and polished. Always make sure the heels are not worn down, good laces, no scratches, no holes in the soles. If your shoes are no good you look like a bum and no one respects you. The zapatero is the best friend of a man who wants to make a good presentation wherever he goes. This is why your Papi always has work and we will never go on welfare. During the depression your Papi had to fix his own shoes with cardboard and newspaper. I had to walk very carefully to avoid mojones de perro, gargajos y chicles on the streets." Papi always made me laugh when he said mojones.

I went to Frank Whalen Junior High 135 for Ninth Grade. All I remember about my experiences there was the first time I got caught refusing to pledge allegiance at one of our general assemblies in the auditorium. I always stood respectfully, kept silent, hands at my sides, just like I had in elementary school. I never understood why we had to sing to "America the Beautiful" and pledge to the flag just before getting lectured to about toilet paper wads stuck to bathroom ceilings or the consequences of "chewing gum like cows" in class. One day, the Principal, Mr. S-Something, saw my resistance to The Pledge and called it to my attention, and that of everyone else within five rows. Custodians do the dirty work, but Principals have to do the dirtier work, like impose rules, ruin your day, call in your parents, make teachers feel inadequate and make sure the intercom works. "You have to show respect for our country, young lady." I refused with silence. He pulled me out of the row. As we walked up the aisle, I ran and he chased after me. I outran him and hid in a janitor's closet until the school day was over and I snuck out with the Eighth Graders. I told Mami what had happened. I expected the beating that would finally do me in, and instead she said: "Pal'carajo con la bandera esa. Mañana bamo pa' hablal con el goldinflón ese." Basically, she didn't like the idea of my being forced to pledge or being chased through the school building by a middle-aged blowhard.

"Mr. S., my mother says I don't have to pledge allegiance." Mami looks him up and down and sideways. Beads of sweat form just above his eyebrows. He looks at me and says: "Tell your mother that you have to pledge allegiance or people will think you're a Communist." I interpret and Mami instructs me, taking her cue from neighbors who were Jehovah's Witnesses. "Mr. S., my mother says that it's against our religion to salute the flag or kneel to fake gods or take the Lord's name in vain. She said that you might not understand because you're Jewish and she doesn't really know what they teach in Jewish school. She also said that my Papi says that there is supposed to be separation between Church and State and that since God is in The Pledge, you are forcing me to break the law." My mother never said the last part, but I had heard Papi and Mr. Lipschitz talking about it. They didn't like flags either. Mr. S.'s neck veins throbbed. He threatened to expel me. Mami kept interjecting, "This is free country." She said she'd take him to court for religious discrimination. Mr. S. understood when she called him a sweaty, fat fuck shit eater in Spanish. He sent me to class after we escorted Mami to the exit door. I think of her every time I don't pledge allegiance. It's the only time thinking about her feels good.

SEVENTY-THREE/FINGERS

I got through the Ninth Grade in one piece. I'd wanted to try out for a specialized arts high school in Manhattan, but my parents weren't having any of it. Whatever single drop of my Arawak Nation, Taíno blood remained in my DNA was repulsed that I would be attending Christopher Columbus High School, just blocks from home. My wild curls were a source of amusement for most of the girls with ironed, rolled, or burnt hair. The straighter the hair, the cooler you were. My rainy days Afro and hourglass figure guaranteed my outsider status from day one.

Mami and Papi both insisted that I dress up for school. Mami made me suits for the secretarial pool she dreamed I would one day join. Papi insisted that dressing was a way to show respect to my teachers and that they would respect me in return. "Those kids who go to school looking like beggars and bums will grow up to be jelly apples. I have only second grade because I had no chance. You will go to college and be smarter than your Papi, okay?" It was a rare moment as Papi lovingly held my face. I would have said yes to anything.

Sophomore year in high school was full of discovery. I was in three AP classes. I talked my English teacher into letting me turn one of my essay assignments into a performance monologue. Carmen had made her way back into my psyche by then. I wrote the piece about a Puerto Rican girl coming out to her mother about heroin addiction. Miss O. asked if I would perform it in front of the class. The silence in the room, the storm clouds that settled on Miss O.'s face and her shameless sobbing, reminded me why I had wanted to go to an arts high school.

I auditioned for *L'il Abner* and *Guys and Dolls* at Columbus and landed the female leads. They were musicals, so that's how I found out I could sing. Auditions were during school, rehearsals weren't. "Show business is for whores. If you go to that school for rehearsals I will drag you out by the hair!" Well, Papi, so much for Betty Hutton and Gypsy Rose Lee. I auditioned anyway just to know I could get the roles if I wanted them. I turned them down each time for fear of Papi's public shaming. I knew his word was good. The drama teacher knew, and he never stepped in. Nobody did.

The catalyst of my desire to be an actor was the same land mine that shattered the possibilities. Dramatic monologues in English class would have to suffice. The more I was abused at home, the better I got at contorting into the mask of a happy teenager. My early morning demeanor at school irritated my classmates. "I hate how you're always so fucking perky." "I can't deal with you until after coffee." I remembered milk and Bustello in my bottle then Mami hating me because I'd be up crying all night. Over decades she convinced me I'd been a repugnant, spoiled brat. At least, that's how she saw me. Home had become my default acting school. I had everyone convinced I was the happiest girl in the world and funny too. I had developed a fine tuned wit and even made my teachers laugh when I was class clown. I was such a good comic, and I never got in trouble for it. No one knew anything real about me, not even my misfit posse of friends. I knew how horrible it was to feel so much torture and despair inside. I felt a responsibility to help others feel happy. Outside I had the glow of a perfect childhood, inside, each day was filled with suicidal and murderous ideation and secrets. "What happens in this house stays in this house."

SEVENTY-FOUR/GOAT

Nothing about my life had prepared me for a meaningful relationship, but everything about it taught me who I didn't want to become. After one of her beatings, with gritted teeth and burning eyes, I looked deeply into every pore of Mami's face: "I swear to God I will never be like you." I was five. Round Two. Smacked down to the floor. She grabbed that red leather Garrison belt. I refused to cry. That was the moment I ceased to be a child, but was smart enough to not let anyone know.

Mami raised me on the horror stories of her childhood and litanies of self-loathing that some days revealed everything and others times were just allusions. In her darkest moments she referred to herself in the third person. "Mami was a very, very bad womans. She did bad things." The old woman I had become before Second Grade tried to reach her; to love her, perhaps even to heal her. "What things, Mami? You can tell me." Her eyes would disappear into another world. "I can no say these to you. Bad peoples did bad things to me. My own stepbrother." A churning silence, then long sobbing and webs of snot. Mami's face twisted into a mask of fear, then sadness, then rage. She could speak when the rage arrived, and I would be the "puta ingrata" who would get to hear it all. The things she knew she shouldn't tell, spilled over into a type of reverie, a catharsis. What she needed mattered more than what was right for her only child. I was rarely spared any gruesome detail.

Every story began with a whimpering sigh, "Ay, cha-cha..." The bruja in the family (not the good kind) was named Altagracia. High Grace. According to Mami, no one has ever outrun her name like she did. Family legend had it that Altagracia had been schooled in "Boo-Doo" by "los negros malos de Aytí." According to the Book of Mami, Altagracia was Black, practiced "Black" magic and slashed the throats of goats in front of children, forcing them to drink the blood.

Mami often showed me scars on her head where Altagracia had stabbed her repeatedly with scissors, just enough to torture but not kill.

She showed me bite marks on the upper insides of her thighs. "She put the dogs to bite me. One time, un pero Alemán almost ate my toto. You lucky to be here." She made sure to show me the dog's bite scars on her upper inner thigh.

Child torture tales were among my bedtime stories. After spitting it all out and painting her shadows on the walls, Mami would fall to her knees and sob and suffocatingly hug me, swearing to God how much she loved me. Reminding me of my good life and luck. Her desperate embraces and sudden returns to rage made me struggle to get free from the vise of her cruel love. In those moments, I was the most ungrateful of all children. Ceiling crack angels turned into smirking demons, as my soul floated away from my body.

Mami's experiences with Altagracia added to her anti-blackness, denying her own bloodline, her origins. A blindfolded child strapped to a bed for perverse sacraments cannot see herself; she will become estranged from her body; run from it and from anything that speaks of Love and Tenderness. Those two miracles everyone should know, become unknowable. False. The presence of Shadows that can never be fully identified or apprehended; impossible to touch.

Mami made sure I knew how lucky I was to have food and a bed to sleep on, even if I had to share it with three cousins on very long visits when El Reverendo was out preaching, and shaking out money from the same kind of shadows that left their teeth rattling in Mami's insides. My cousins snored, but only I wet the bed. Sometimes we'd all wake up screaming, when mice snuck in with us, crawling over our bodies, realizing we were wet with my piss too. Mami was La Reina de Pine Sol y Clorox, but the whole building was infested. Papi said they probably mistook my skinny cousins for chicken bones. It was the first time I thought that maybe, just maybe, for one second, he was calling me pretty. And then I thought that mice probably just don't eat pork.

Mami's step siblings had inherited her when her mother died in childbirth from malnutrition. Mami had been told by her Tías that she was the size of a small mango when she was born. She never grew past 4'11" or 90 pounds, but to me she was a giant with blazing red lips, talons and fangs. There were no photos of her as a little girl. That part of her life became a composite of all the monstrous stories I came to believe were my fault—no matter that they pre-existed my conception. My love would never be good enough. I would never be able to save her. It took decades before I realized that maybe I should transform all of that energy into saving myself.

All eyes to the ground in shanty town
watch every shoeless step
no time for sky
no ride to the sea
no food in her belly
nothing pretty to see
gutted little girl
now the woman with
nothing left for me

SEVENTY-FIVE/DING

By the age of nineteen I'd saved enough money to leave home. I got my first job as soon as I was the right age for working papers. I started out at Alexander's Department Store, where Mami had trained me in the art of bargain hunting. The woman who interviewed me tore up my application as I was walking out of her office. I'd seen her grimace when I told her I was Puerto Rican. The hard tear of paper. Flutter into trash. The who I am. Garbage to a bigot.

I wrote a letter to the Executive Office denouncing her actions and soon after I was hired as a cashier. I guess they figured that a fourteen-year-old with a strong signature, who could write a professional, typewritten letter and was aware of her legal rights was worth considering. The junior sized Royal typewriter in its own latched case came from the pawn shop where Papi dropped off the same "gold" watch over and over again to place his bets. Clickety Clack. Clickety Clack. Self defense. You took it away. I took it back. Clickety Clack. Clickety Clack.

They trained me as a cashier when I refused to work stock. Clickety Clack. I was friendly, polite, quick, and entertaining. If a button was loose, I'd tell the customer to ask the floor manager for a discount, "Just don't tell him I sent you. You noticed it yourself." Clickety Clack. I kept that manager busy and the customers happy. Clickety Clack. Somebody had to balance the jacked up prices of retail that weren't going anywhere near the factory workers. Clickety Clack.

My line was always long. Made the day fly. I'd wanted to work the jewelry counter with Tony the Greek who was sixteen, wore a suit and tie and had a British accent that made me swoon. We flirted on breaks, but it never amounted to anything. He was polite and engaging, but not interested. I was content to speak with someone who loved books as much as I did and could travel far and deep in a short conversation. We tasted each other's lunches. My first dolma, his first maduro.

As punishment for my main floor success, I was sent up to the Siberia of housewares. Within days, a co-worker robbed my cash box of $140 and I was blamed by the one I named "Laniard Louie, Keeper of the Keys." He was the Department Manager; Saint Peter of Bargain Hunters. His underling, the nebbish floor manager with two chins, who I named Vinny the Chins, trusted me. Chins knew I hadn't done it, and defended me to get another chance. I became my father: "Thank you, but I won't work with crooks. You lay down with dogs you get fleas." Besides, I was grossed out to know that some of the girl cashiers were giving guys blow jobs in the stock room. I was still waiting for a first kiss and it was never going to be Tony the Greek, so I quit in the middle of my shift. Let somebody else clean up the mess that had nothing to do with me. I wish I'd given Chins a better name. At the very least, more original.

I missed Tony the Greek and the elderly Jewish women who wore perfumed silky scarves and so readily hugged. "I have a nice grandson for you to meet. Are you Jewish?" They were always surprised and disappointed that I was Puerto Rican, but only because they hoped for a girl like me in the family. I never felt that my being Puerto Rican was a problem for them; it was a religious thing. Many had experienced or lost family members in the Holocaust and understood the price of being different and the importance of protecting traditions, beliefs, and culture.

Over the years I had many "Jewish Mothers" in the Bronx. They loved me, fed me, gave me trinkets, perfumes, chocolates, made me feel welcome in their homes, but there would be no hanky-panky with their well guarded young males. Mami approved of the visits, as long as she knew them as neighbors. Mami kept hoping I'd marry a Jewish professional, or someone on that track, and I kept trying, so as not to disappoint her. I could convert, but no religion ever did me any favors. I forever remained a beloved outsider. "Such a punum; a shame she's a Shiksa." "She looks more Jewish than my nieces, go figure." "Sweetheart, bring me the wax paper. I'll wrap some of this rugelach for your mother. Who doesn't like rugelach, right?" Right. Forever right. Especially the chocolate ones.

Sorrows and rage became hunger pangs; an endless hole in my stomach, always bitching for more. I became known in my family as the girl with the hollow leg. My nalgas jiggled at an early age. That old woman's body came and went and one day it stayed, as my thighs rubbed their bickering complaints against hot and humid weather. One day at school my nalgas were insulted by Joaquín, who was so handsome I had written his name chained to mine in perfect penmanship, filling pages in my notebook, just days before.

"Hey, Culona, where you goin'?" Joaquín laughed a laugh that doesn't belong anywhere near good people. I was heading to the blackboard to compare and order integers. Math was terrifying enough without hearing that mean laugh like marbles rising and falling inside him, hitting hard against each other. I wanted to call him enano, which he was. His legs formed a skinny O but an O nonetheless. Arms like flippers on a pinball machine. I thought of calling him a freak, a fucking midget; tapón; mojón. I thought of sticking needles in my nalgas to squeeze out the jigglers so Joaquín might like me and be sorry for what he said. Pricking and squeezing would take too long. Slicing them off would be better. If only I could reach.

When the starvation crisis hit Biafra during the civil war of the Igbo people's struggle for cessation from Nigeria, I got active in high school politics. Devastating images on television of starving children stayed in my body. Global starvation was nothing new, but now it was less invisible. I was disgusted by the apathy of my schoolmates and began making and plastering posters with horrific images of children with distended bellies too weak to brush away the flies eating the mucus from their eyes. I posted all over the school, concentrating mostly on the cafeteria. I placed the worst images above the ice cream freezer and stood there with a collection can. "Do you really need that ice cream?" I didn't even think of asking permission or anyone to help me with my fundraising and no one volunteered. I had grown up with that dread feeling of social exile and the false comfort of self-isolationism, that if you want it done, you'd better do it yourself. I lost the worst of my fractured cadences, surprising myself with contractions along the way. My hand reaches for another's. "Don't. You don't need it. Look at that little girl. Have your ice cream tomorrow. Today, do the right thing."

I mustered up all of my mother's skills for inducing guilt (minus the violence) and in two weeks raised $500 for humanitarian organizations that were helping with the Biafran Airlift. In those days, $500 was a good amount of money.

I told Rosie, my surrogate Italian mother, who lived on the same floor as us in the projects, about my campaign. She was proud of me and said "Let's turn it into $1,000!" She went to her bedroom and pulled out a full body, bright yellow Easter Bunny suit: ears, cotton-tail, trap door and feet. "I'll raise money on a dare at the *fack-tree*. I'll take bets that I'll wear this to work everyday for a week and ride the train in it. The bastid boss'll bet against me. He thinks he's got big balls? Wait till he sees mine! That hump thinks us women are stupid. I'll show that mameluke my kinda stupid."

I thought she was kidding. Rosie was a completely self-accepting woman, built like Quasimoto and carried herself like a Queen. "Will you really wear it on the subway too?" She responded with the confidence of a Miss Universe, posing like a 1920's Ziegfield Girl. "You kidding me? Them people on the train will go crazy for this. I'll make us some Rocke-fella money for those poor kids." She zipped on the suit and we laughed till we had to fight for who got to the toilet first. It was my first piss in a sink. In less than a week, Rosie handed me a coffee can dense with mon-ey; no singles. My first enduring lesson in the power of shamelessness.

Our fundraising efforts turned me from a brainiac isolated nerd to one of the cool kids. I ran for School Council Vice President and lost to Frank Fanelli, mostly because he was a sharper dresser, and I was hated for being the top English Honors student in the school, scoring a 99% on the English Regents exam.

"Did you cheat?" "If you're Puerto Rican, where's your knife?" That one was Larry B., who only had one arm. "Now I know how you lost it." Too many coming at me, not enough wisecracks. "You don't look Puerto Rican." "She's probably doing it with Mr. M. She laughs at all his corny jokes." "No way, he's too old. I think she's doing it with Mr. H." "Puerto Rican girls are used to doing it with their fathers, so no big deal." "How the hell does a fucking Puerto Rican get a 99% on the English Regents?" "Bitch."

SEVENTY-EIGHT/CUTICLES

My consolation prize came when Mr. H., who drove a white Stingray, asked me to join his Leadership Class. Only a few students were invited. Suddenly I was one of the top cool kids. Mr. H. and I had eyes for each other. Some of the girls could tell. I'd had a woman's body for years. Before I met Mike, I wanted Mr. H. to be my first. No chance; no matter how tempted, he was a good and decent man. He always treated me with respect, apart from the occasional slow falling wink, which I thought might be a tic.

One day at school, for no reason, some random girl yanked my hair in the hallway. I tore into her like I was on fire. Mr. H. broke it up, lifting me off of her, setting me down, then getting in that mean girl's face: "What did you do? I know you must have started it!" That was the first time in my life that an adult had shown me unconditional, unquestioned trust. He just knew the truth—that I would never start a fight—and required nothing from me, other than taking me to his office so I could sit down and catch my breath. That was the beginning of knowing that I wasn't as worthless as I was raised to believe. My high school hero teacher and first serious adult crush made me feel seen.

That night I stared at myself in the medicine cabinet mirror, wondering if Mr. H. really might like me in a kissing way. My teeth looked yellower than ever. I dragged myself to bed where I chewed and peeled my fingernails for hours.

SEVENTY-NINE/PEANUTS

Rosie's lessons in shamelessness, along with her ability to find the blessing in any situation, saved my life. "Domenic is an asshole and a lazy piece of shit, but he's got a big thing down there and he makes good chinga-chinga." The accompanying movements of her ample belly would drop me to the floor with laughter. Rosie's green eyes never looked in my direction with anything but love. She had two grown sons. "I love my boys, but you're the daughter I always wanted."

It was the first time I experienced a mother's genuine love. Titi's came close, but her funeral Mass mournful demeanor, even in laughter, kept us from ever pissing our pants with joy. Rosie always sent me running to her immaculate bathroom fragrant with flowery deodorizers. "When you come back, let's play some rummy. You get the peanuts, I'll get the cards." I knew my way around Rosie's kitchen. The bag of peanuts was in the usual place: a cracker tin from the 1950's that still looked new. Pouring un-shelled peanuts into a red bowl, was a healing ritual. Cards and peanuts in their shell with Rosie always meant swearing with abandon, a sip of her burgundy wine, seltzer with sliced lemons for me, and being a galaxy away from Mami's brutal eyes and rabid hands.

On Sundays, Rosie let me help her with family dinner. No one else was allowed in the kitchen when Rosie made her "gravy." A first gener-ation Italian, raised in Brooklyn, Rosie kept some of her mother's tradi-tions going—only they were more Brooklyn than Naples. "Get me the ol-ive earl, sweetheart, and cut the onions nice and small." Her son John's dog would come begging. Rosie could never resist. "Rocky, keep it down. Shhhh." Rosie would toss him one of the little meatballs she made just for him, put aside in a little souvenir bowl from Tuscany she bought for a dime at a church tag sale. "Don't tell your father, he'll kill me. Here, that's the last one." It never was. Rocky was her first "grandchild" and the lit-tle bowl held her dream of someday visiting Italy. It would never hap-pen on factory pay, even with a union, and her part-time elevator operator husband made just enough to keep him in white cotton tank tops and illegal cigars. "My Domenic looks like George Raft. Handsome bastid. Don't get me wrong, he's still a lazy asshole. One of these days I'm gonna flush him down the turlet." Rosie would laugh brazenly as she chopped the fresh garlic with a vengeance and glow. Domenic was clearly the love of her life.

After Alexander's Department Store, I took another job at the Grand Union Supermarket in the shadow of the Pelham Parkway train station. The market was always extra busy when the subway-fatigued workers poured out from the station. Most never touched the handrails as they ran down the long, steep metal stairs. Most were workers anxious to bring home the hard-earned groceries and drop those damn brassieres, carefully roll off the pantyhose to prevent snags, pull off their shoes, ties, and belts, dropping sport coats, blazers, jackets, wherever they might land. Uniforms to the wash bin, the day's sweat and stink soaped, rinsed, squeezed out and hung to dry for pressing. Stragglers held on tight to those handrails. The children and elderly, the weakened by illness or by life; the slow hated by the fast. "Marmolillos, coño." Mami muttered as she rushed past them, scampering the rest of the way, taking a deep breath as if just pulled from a raging sea.

At the Grand Union, neighborhood people appreciated my Robin Hood ways. I could always tell when someone's money was tight; I'd let a few things slip by on the unmonitored conveyer belt. We'd share a knowing look, a code between those of us living paycheck-to-paycheck. Our cheap shoes bound us to loyalty, even as strangers. A few years later, I did the same thing at a Gristede's on West 14th in Greenwich Village. It all started when I saw an old woman pay with pennies for cat food to feed herself and the woman behind her with a cartload of crabmeat for her cat. Maid Marian took over, telling Robin to "Step back; this job calls for a woman!" There weren't alarms on hot dogs in those days, at least not on the East Coast, and I had learned to keep an even, cool look from all those free acting lessons I got from living at home. I had become equally adept at playing the "smart good girl" and the "dumb broad;" whatever my inner warrior and the situation required.

Robin Hood was no crook and took down bullies where it hurt them most—right in the coin sack. I knew Papi wouldn't approve, so I kept my lawless ways to myself. Once I became more Marian and less Robin I felt assured no one would suspect or snitch. I was right. Being underestimated for being female has certain advantages.

EIGHTY/SAWDUST

There was this one boy who always had a book in his back pocket and waved at me through the Grand Union's big picture window. He'd shop at least three times a week for a small, single item like a candy bar and get on my line even though it was usually twice as long as the others. The manager assumed my wrap-around lines were due to my winning personality and "those big, brown eyes."

Book Boy introduced himself with a Green Card. He pronounced his name in Polish, but asked me to call him Mike. Living in the Bronx from the age of five, Mike had also learned to speak Spanish. I blushed every time I saw him and could barely get out a "Hi" without stammering. Mike was handsome, wholesome, sinuous and strong. He pressed his own shirts, and was so much a gentleman, he made me feel like I was in a movie. He was an honor student at the Bronx High School of Science and planned to become an engineer. He made polite conversation, but I could tell he was as nervous as I was and hiding behind his jokes. I wondered if he might be *the one*. I was sure Papi would like him. He was no jelly apple, and, like me, was studious and worked to earn his own money. The sight of a Vonnegut in that just tight-enough back pocket, made me sweat.

Mike finally got the courage to ask me on a date. I was terrified, suspicious why someone like him would like me, and excited all at once. The "yes" caught in my throat, and sounded like the squeal on a tightly tuned violin. Mike didn't laugh but asked in all seriousness. "Was that a yes?" I nodded and smiled with my lips closed. "Great! I'll come by tomorrow." My inner voice blared at me: "You're too fat. Your teeth are yellow. He'll dump you." My mother pulled up a lead bucket and sat on my chest. "Look at you. Grifería, barrigona; pareces un pordiosera." My heart raced to outrun Mami's insults. I carried my cash drawer to another register for shift change and watched as Mike walked away, waving to him through the window. I tripped and every coin fell through the wooden slats of the vintage floor. Mike turned his head quickly, pretending not to see, so as to not add to my humiliation.

My temple veins throbbed. I'm a such a loser. Jesus H. Christ, it's filthy between these slats. I hate my fucking mother. I wish she were dead. Jesus, forgive me. Shit. My pantyhose just ripped. I hate pantyhose. Now I'll have to waste money getting new ones. I hope he likes my legs. Oh, God, this jiggly ass! Mike. Michael. Michal. Warrior angel. Will he fight for me? Will he only step on the necks of evil men and allow dragons to fly? Oh, shit. I'm gonna get fired. Fuck my parents for being poor. For being my wardens. Maybe I won't tell them about Mike.

Rage always made me stronger.

"I'm sorry, Mr. Daly. This floor is dangerous. If I were an old lady I could have a broken hip. Should I call the Union and report it?"

That got him good.

"No, no. Its all right. Let me help you up. I'll take care of it. How are your knees? Did you twist an ankle? Did you hit your head?"

"No Mr. Daly, I'm okay. Just embarrassed."

I limped a little and made myself look like I was about to cry with "those big brown eyes." Daly's sweat rolled like a cane-cutter's in an August hell in Guánica.

"Why don't you go home, dear, and rest up? No need to call the Union. Just put some ice on your knee, sweetheart."

Daly permanently ruined "sweetheart" for me as it bobbed in the air like a lost turd.

"What about my stockings? They're all ripped. Maybe you should let us girls wear pants? What do you think, Mr. Daly? Would that be a good idea?"

I made my eyelashes grow an inch by sheer will.

"Well, I uh. Well, all right, we can try it out, as long as they are pressed and not too tight." I thought of Vonnegut.

The look in Daly's eyes reflected me bent over a Methodist Church pew. He had that pervert edge where you're not sure if the guy is creepy or was dropped on his head as a kid.

"If they're uniform issue the store will pay for them, right?"

I stared into his eyes without blinking, wetting my lips.

"Well sure. I don't see why not. But you'll have to clean and press them on your own like with your old uniform."

I looked right at his mouth, like Sophia Loren with Marcello Mastroianni.

"Thank you, Mr. Daly. You're a very nice man."

Daly was too old to care if I was fat. He cracked his neck in two directions. I would have done really well at the Performing Arts High School.

"Nice of you to say, sweetheart. Are you sure you're not from the Midwest? You've got such nice manners."

I wanted to punch him in the throat.

"Mr. Daly, I'm originally from the South, you know."

"Really?"

I leaned in.

"Yeah, South Bronx."

Daly laughed nervously and fumbled over to the blonde done up in Cleopatra makeup on Register 5 when she tapped her service bell with long hot pink nails and snapped her gum.

"I gotta void here."

She was a Sophomore at Columbus with lots of uncles, but I don't think she knew much about Vonnegut.

EIGHTY-ONE/SPACE

On my way home I grabbed up a *Daily News* someone had left in the wash-room to search the Want Ads. If I was going to see Mike, I'd better find a job a little farther from home; at least a bus ride away. Mami pinched pennies so hard I knew she'd never spend the fare to spy on me. Now a high school senior, I was allowed to ride the bus, as long as it was only the #12 bus that ran almost a straight line from our Bronx projects to the Irish Manhattan border on Dykeman Street. Straight. Lines. Everywhere.

The Want
Of what
of who
not allowed
This Want muzzled
by religiosity
nailed shut and away
from demons of Tenderness
for my own good.

Want. ed. Out. Law. Kiss.

Gun hidden beneath a counter
of scars. Mami's finger caught
in the trigger.
Silencers abound.
Want. Unheard.
Bullet to blow
my brains to Heaven's Gate
should I dare to even reach for it.
Want. Ad. Escape.
Al. Ca. Traz. Of the Projects.
Can. Not. Pro. Ject.

L.I.V.E. O.N.E. L.E.T.T.E.R. A.T. A. T.I.M.E.
I will read a book from that pocket.
He will read to me, that beautiful Polish boy.
Grass below. Sun Above. We will Want together.
Fear will leave us.
Dead or Alive.

The March of Dimes was offering phone work. I hated talking on the phone, since every time I did, Papi would hang it up and insult whoever was on the other end for keeping me from my homework, and me for raising our phone bill.

The job was to collect on pledges. I borrowed a baseball bat from Rosie for the interview, to show I was serious. I was a big believer in subliminal messaging and I really wanted the job. There'd be no more tearing up of my job applications. I made no mention of the bat, which I held at my side like a cane throughout the interview. Towards the end of our meeting, Mrs. I Can't For the Life of Me Remember Her Name (Mrs. ICFTLOM-RHN) asked: "So, what's with the bat? Baseball fan?" A nervous sarcasm. I told her I was headed to softball practice after our interview. Her shoulders receded away from her ears. I got the job.

The Grand Concourse might as well have been Paris. Close enough that my parents would let me ride the bus alone, but far enough away that penny pinching Mami couldn't walk there. While making pledge collections at the office, one of the women I called told me with a time-shredded voice that she was sitting Shivah. I didn't know the word and heard it as "sitting and shivering." A sudden fever rose from my guts and I launched into a monologue of tenants' rights, and that I'd go over to her building right then and confront the super and make sure the heat got turned on. "There is no excuse for this! I'll make it get turned on!" I'd be borrowing the bat again. "This is a disgrace! I grew up shivering in our apartment and I know how awful it is. You could get sick." When the angelically patient woman could finally get a word in, she explained the meaning of sitting Shivah. I wondered if I could flush myself down the toilet. I stuttered out my best apology. "Don't worry, honey, you meant well." "Yes ma'm, uh, Shalom and I am sorry for your loss, Mrs. Levinson." Her kindness kept me from getting caught in that toilet drainpipe with my head looking up at ass for the rest of my life. Eight days later her pledge came in, doubled.

EIGHTY-TWO/KEYS

After a few months, I'd won the trust of Mrs. ICFTLOMRHN, and offered to stay after hours. Everyone except for me and Mrs. ICFTLOFRHN were volunteers, so it was up to us to take up the slack. It was summer, and my parents didn't mind, as long as I got home before dark. I was given a key to the office, and for the first time in my life had a space all to myself that no one would invade, at least for a couple of hours. There was a working typewriter with all its keys where I could write poems, a private bathroom with a hook latch. The office had sun-yellowed brittle shades that only went down a third of the way. The cathedral windows offered a great view of the Concourse and the daily breathlessness of hustle. Those windows were too big. If I wanted to pick my nose, it was good to go into the bathroom.

Mike and I started sneaking around soon after I left Grand Union, meeting at the Botanical Garden, walking on the parkway and fancier side streets where we didn't know anyone. It didn't matter much, since all we did was hold hands and hug. Since I was getting good grades and was still a virgin, at least to anything consensual, I was allowed to walk the neighborhood. Mike would leave notes for me in our lobby mailbox on his way to school, the only other thing in my life for which I had a key. A miserable little key for a lock that could surrender to a toothpick. Mami never checked it until late afternoon, since mostly it was bills, and Papi was off to work at dawn most days anyway. I lived for those notes that always ended with "I love you." He was the first person in my life to say it to me in a way that I believed. I would have believed Titi Angela, but I can't remember her ever having said it in words. Until Mike, those words had always sounded like a beer cap hitting a courthouse floor; almost a statement, but in reality, just litter.

I stayed at the March of Dimes longer than any other job; full-time in summer. Once I was certain no one was snooping on me after hours, Mike started coming up to visit. I'd make my quota of calls soliciting pledges and learning to deal with people hanging up. I was pretty good at getting people to pledge. It was the times I had to chase unpaid pledges that I really didn't like. My survival at home depended on becoming a master manipulator, but when it came to putting the squeeze on old ladies for a couple of bucks, I just didn't have to stomach for it.

At 5:00 p.m. I'd take a deep breath, pre-count my overtime pay and plan my eventual escape. Every penny I earned was in the bank. I would get away from my parents one way or another and I wasn't going to do it by marrying Mike. I needed to know that I could save myself without the assistance of any man, no matter how good he was or how much he loved me. Besides, I only knew how to mimic human emotions. I understood the outward expectations, but mostly I lived on the adrenaline of adolescent hormones, the hypervigilance of repeated trauma, convinced I was an impostor at being genuine or even human. A lone wolf who could interact with her pack, motivated by hungers I hadn't yet named.

EIGHTY-THREE/PANEM

It was a Sunday at Titi's house in Graves End. We'd had Titi Joe's escarole soup, which always made me gag and the arancini that Titi Angela made, stuffed with extra hand-rolled mozzarella that tasted like love. "Go for ride with your Titi Joe," Mami insisted. I knew she hated the sight of me and just wanted time with her sister. Things had always been strained between them with their unspoken secret, of Papi marrying Mami only to be close to Titi. Those weekends away, Mami was glad to be away from Papi. "Men only want womans for one thing." She'd gesture with her lips toward my toto.

"Is nice day. Go for nice ride with Titi Joe in his nice new car." Mami made me hate the word "nice" like toxic men made me hate "beautiful." I didn't want to go. I hated that car with its leathery gangster smell and Tommy gun sideboard. I hated being alone with Joe but could never remember why. Mami called me an ingrate and told me to behave and respect Titi Joe.

My body remembers the hairiness and smell of his arms. The sweat smell of pistachio green bed sheets. I remember the smell of lead bookie pencils when he opened the big glass jar on his dresser. I remember the faint mothball smell of the room, and the stickiness of pomade in his hair. The cheap cologne at his neck. His hands were so big, like weather-worn baseball gloves, his fingers stained with newspaper ink checking out the pony action. Trifecta. Win. Place. Show. Horse names reveal expectations. Forced to run. Once a horse belongs to someone, there is no more running for the joy if it.

Men shout horse names, clutch racing forms, bite into fat cigar stubs; their lives flashing before them into futures that will never be. Life's purpose, an oil-slicked mermaid, that eludes the clench of despair. The horses. Fed. Brushed. A clean stable. Words of praise. An apple. A carrot. No more open sky or endless pastures of smiling dandelions and vast intrepid kingdoms of crickets and their chosen kin. The end of self-made paths by melodic rivers. The only pleasure left; the groaning of humans stepping in steaming piles of shit. Pity the puddle, the brush, the snapping twig.

The smell of wheat pennies in a thick white box on Titi's night table tempted me on every visit. Stealing helped me erase the pictures whirling in my brain. I'd think of the penny candies I would buy. If I played with the pennies long enough without getting caught, I could make myself forget anything. Spin the penny. Roll the penny. Stack the pennies. Count them. Forwards. Backwards. Spin. Roll. Count. Stack. Count down. Count up. Add. Subtract. Multiply. 1953. 1955. Add all the years together. Beg Lincoln not to tell. Put him under your shoe. "Things can get bad for you, Mr. Lincoln. Very, very bad if you're a snitch. I don't care if you're dead. Only part of you is dead. I can kill the other part. I can make you disappear."

Steal a pencil from the jar. Play hangman with Judas. It wasn't his fault, you know. Preordained is what El Reverendo called it.

> Roses are red.
> NO, NOT RED. YELLOW. PINK. ORANGE. TINTED EDGES. WHITE.
> Violets are blue.
> NO, RED, PURPLE, YELLOW. 500 NATIONS OF VIOLETS.
> Sugar is sweet.
> NO, SUGAR IS NOT SUGAR. SUGAR IS EXTRACTED BY FORCE.
> SUGAR WAS NEVER BORN. IT WAS MADE.
> SUGAR IS ANGRY. GETS EVEN. EATS INTO BONE.
> And so are you.
> NO, NOT SWEET. NO NOT SUGAR.
> Not predestined.
> Made by force.

EIGHTY-FIVE/HOPS

Papi was starting to notice that I was no longer his little nenita. His once direct looks had become side glances. His rooster walk was listing to one side. Mr. Lipschitz had been attending fewer of the Sunday penuchle sessions at Papi's Old Men's Club at the Palace, and the Crosstown had gone downhill since Papi left to be a West Side chef. Detective Georgie Porgie who sat in on the games once in a great while over the years, was getting married and had been reassigned to Staten Island. "Hey, Chico, I'm leaving for cop Siberia. Me and Angie want to make some babies. I'm getting too old to be a father, but what the hell? Look at you. You're like that actor, what's his name? That Mexican Irish guy." Papi rolled his eyes. "Lambe ojo. You mean Anthony Quinn. What do you want? I know you want something." "Nope. Not at all, just sayin' some guys get better looking the older they get. And you got yourself a beautiful girl. And smart too."

Why did Geogie's fiancé have to be named Angie? Georgie flicked a mint into his mouth like he was about to make-out in some backseat. "That little girl of yours used to love that old Jukebox at the Crosstown, and now she's in college. You must be a proud Papi, old man." Papi reached into the cooler on the floor by his feet and tossed Georgie Porgie a beer. Here, last one, for you. Congratulations, Detective." Georgie Porgie caught the can in both hands like a bridal bouquet. He got quiet and just stared down at it, then looked up at Papi like some proud kid who'd just gotten an award. "Thanks, Chico, with babies coming and buying a house for my Angela, I gotta save every dime. I'll miss you, Chico. I hope you can make it to the wedding. Bring your daughter. Leave the wife home." Papi never spoke a public bad word against Mami, but the perpetual sadness in his eyes gave it all away to anyone paying attention, especially a detective.

Titi Angie was gone, and nothing could bring her back. I couldn't help but feel a fleet of tiny white boats sailing gently through the blue canals of my arms of into the sea of my heart, as I imagine Papi's and Titi Angela's stolen kisses. I was sure of them. Arms pressed close in photos, trying too hard to look like just friends. L' amuri è come a tussi, nun si po ammucciari. I still can't help but wish they had held each other through at least one entire night. I'll never know.

For years after Titi died, two days before my ninth birthday, Mami's Top Ten Litanies of Loathing always included: "Your Titi's funeral was the only time I ever saw your Papi cry." She forgot he cried at my crise d'épilepsie.

The funeral I was not allowed to attend. "Too young." No matter how I begged every family member and reassured all the adults in the family that I was ready. Only El Reverendo was on my side. He was no match for Mami, even as the sidekick of Jesus. I didn't get to say good-bye to my Titi or see my Papi cry for her. I wish I could have seen him sob, his heart full of a grief. Papi, in a storm of feelings over someone he loved. I wrote "FUCK YOU" over the 23rd Psalm in our damn zippered Bible with a blood-red crayon. Never caught, because it was never read. The bitterness in Mami's voice tore all the sails off my little boats. The canals of my arms went flat, like Carmen's. Only there would be no hummingbirds. "It was the only time I ever saw him cry." Mami was the original broken record.

Papi pulled out another beer for Detective Geogie Porgie and a 7 UP for me. "Congratulations, Jorge. No more Georgie Porgie for you. Now your most important job is coming." I felt like it was a Bar Mitzvah when Papi signaled me to raised my soda, too. "To the new Detective Papi of Staten Island and his family. Salud. Dinero. Y Amor."

Old Blue Eyes dropped
I've got you under my skin
as Papi poured from the tap
I've got you deep in the heart of me
into a tilted glass
So deep in my heart
foam, a slow forming crown
 you're nearly a part of me
Perfect every time.
A thousand times.
Papi, cura, confessor.
Wiping towel always within reach.

Always a kindness for friend or stranger.
Even for the thief of a life
that could have been his.
The haunting name
Angela
unearthed into a body
not hers, never his.
Cantaor of ache into song.
Xitano.

EIGHTY-SIX/AMMONIA

Mami was making breakfast when from the bathroom Papi announced that he was going to color his hair. "Nobody wants to hire an old man." Even though Papi's job at Al Buon Gusto was secure as long as Pietro was alive, there was never a certainty in life that he could hold onto, or trust, except that he had a daughter. "My hair used to be color de castaña, and now it looks like mouse hair." Mami yelled. "Clairol #46. Yo te lo pinto." Papi cringed at the thought of Mami's touch almost as much as I did. "I already got it from Mr. Saulie. I can do it myself."

After breakfast, Papi grabbed a little brown bag with everything he would need to color his hair, including rubber gloves. Papi and I were never good at following directions to the letter. Our Xitano spirits demanded constant improvisation. Papi read the directions aloud, perhaps to pretend someone was helping him. Maybe Titi Angela. He said something about no Clairol needed in Heaven. As the minutes rolled out, so did the "carajos" y "coños." When it came time to wait and let the color sit, Papi sat on the toilet wearing his see-through shower cap. Papi was not good at waiting. "¡Me cago en Dios y la Ostía!" "Papi, why don't you come out and read the paper or something, while you wait." Mami called it. "Your Papi doesn't want you to see him looking like a pendejo con pelo de luto." Papi yelled out: "It's not black, it's castaña! Old people with Black hair look like mentecatos. I want my natural color back. And *I am* reading the paper!"

Mami just couldn't back off. "Vanidoso despues de viejo." "This isn't vanity. I want to keep putting food on the table. Old men are forced to retire. But with what can I retire? I have to work until I drop dead." Working at Al Buon Gusto was the most money Papi ever made outside of winning at la bolita or the track, at $150 a week. He worked 18-hour days, six days a week. No overtime, just a Christmas bonus at the end of each year.

Papi lost the battle with Clairol #46. There were streaks well beyond the hairline that couldn't be washed off and a splat of dye on his bald spot. He sat on that toilet longer than the directions called for, lost in his newspaper. Papi wore his Stetson full time for the next six weeks. Every day. Mami mocked his wearing a winter hat in Spring. "Pareces un Jasídico de'so loco en Brookleen." An unbearable shame came over his face each time he removed his hat, and a sweaty discomfort each time he wore it. Pietro surprised him at work with a new Chef's hat. It was a little too large and covered the stains just right. Papi folded some duct tape inside to keep it from slipping over his eyes. That may have been the worst heart-stabbing sadness I felt that wasn't my own. Papi's face, framed like Jesus when the crown of thorns was pressed down hard by the brutal hands of the Roman Empire.

Papi didn't know it, but, like Yeshua, he was a political prisoner too. Mami never missed a beat, even while serving his morning espresso. A hand on her hip, a sneer of disgust. "Pareces un payaso." Then off to poach his eggs and steam some greens, so he wouldn't have a heart attack. She had thrown all the salt into the trash the day she found out that a Dr. D. had put him on Nitro. "Papi, isn't nitro an explosive?" "Yes, mi'jita, it is. It is a very small explosion in my chest to keep my heart going. Is nothing, no big deal." Papi carried the little brown glass nitro bottle in his pocket wherever he went.

Soon after Dr. Aspirinita had fled the neighborhood, Papi started seeing Dr. D. He kept seeing him even after we moved to the projects. "He's a good man. He helps everybody. He's not a crook, like some doctors. He lives in the same building where he works. He helps the people." Papi took me to see him one time when Dr. Schweitzer was on vacation. My throat was on fire and my tonsils oozing pus.

Dr. D. was in one of the old, landlord-abandoned tenements, where rent was still collected by thugs and rats had the rule. Papi walked me by the long line of itchy, anxious people. "Hey, viejo, why you cuttin' the line?" "Yeah, who the fuck you think you are." One was sucking down sugar packets, another one eyed my purse. One woman had a screaming baby in her arms, wrapped in a thin blanket. No bottle, no binky, nothing. I thought about Carmen and how she seemed to always know how to take care of business. I never saw her eyeing anybody's purse.

Papi knocked and waited. He gave the crowd a look that turned their shouts to muttering. Only the baby screamed. Maybe Papi was viejo, but he still had the death-ray eyes when he needed them. Papi never liked waiting, and after the Clairol incident, he wasn't about to stay too long at any fair in that sweaty hat. Papi knocked again, and Dr. D. let us in. Come in, Chico. You too bonita, you must be Chico's daughter. You're all he ever talks about."

Those words from Dr. D. hit me hard. What did Papi say? How come some doctor I never even met gets to hear about me and I don't? "So, my friend, what's the problem?" Papi lifted his pant legs and pushed down his gleaming white socks to reveal ankles so swollen the skin was translucent. How did I not know? Dr. D. asked Papi about how the Nitro was working and a bunch of other questions. Then he asked Dr. D. to check my inflamed throat. I gagged from the tongue depressor going in too far back. "Nothing. Nothing. You're both fine. I'll give you a couple of prescriptions."

Papi didn't ask any questions. He was grateful that Dr. D. would see us any time day or night, and liked that he spoke Spanish. Papi handed him two five dollar bills "Chico, this is too much" he protested while slipping the bills into his pocket. "No, no, Dr. D. I could never do enough for you. You're a good man, you take care of the people." As we were walking out I got the red rush of courage to ask, "So, what's wrong with us, doctor?" Papi looked embarrassed. "You've got a smart one here, my friend." Dr. D. bent down a little to talk to me, His cigarette breath almost knocked me over. "Well, your Poppy has too much water, and you have an infection. He gets diuretics to help him make pee-pee more, and you get an antibiotic to kill the bacteria. Anything else my dear?" I was about to ask another question when Papi interrupted. "You have many customers waiting, Señor Doctor. Thank you and see you next time. Que Dios me lo bendiga." Dr. D. gave us a little wave. "G_d bless you too my friend, and your little chatterbox. She's a cutie." The line outside Dr. D.'s door had grown twice as long.

Papi rushed us down the stairs, taking off his hat and limping all the way. Once outside he took a while to catch his breath. "Is having too much water inside you dangerous, Papi?" Papi looked away to respond. "No, it's nothing. Your Papi just needs to make more pee-pee." I thought about all the people on the line. Was Dr. D. keeping them alive, or keeping them addicted? I didn't ever want to see Papi's ankles burst.

EIGHTY-EIGHT/QUILL

When I had finally saved enough money to leave home, I decided on doing it in a way that wouldn't terrify my parents or hurt Papi's heart. My college had a study abroad program at the University of Sevilla, Spain. I could finally meet family on my father's side. Maybe Papi could imagine them keeping an eye on me, even though he hadn't seen them in almost sixty years.

Papi and Mami's terror of losing me to the demonic forces of the world still rose to the top. "I will not let you leave. I will take away your passport." I squared off with my Papi for the first time. "You'll have to cut off my feet to stop me. I'm leaving." The image of his bloated ankles weakened my resolve for a moment. Then out poured the litanies of my ingratitude and "mala hija" accusations from both of them. I responded with a cold silence they had never experienced from their prisoner before. The hatred in my eyes scorched them. The Abuser. The Bystander. The Well-Meaning Wardens. I would be free, whatever that meant. Whatever it took. It would be a plane ticket or a butcher's knife. Either way, I'd made up my mind to be gone.

I went to my room to speak with the ghost of Federico García Lorca about his love for Andalucía. That beautiful genius whose work brought me closer to Papi's people than Papi ever dared. My literary hero in what he wrote and how he lived.

His remains were never found. I have found them over and over in my dreams, hidden within a steeple where a rooster's crow has replaced the bells. He is a fistful of gold dust, a bow tie, a bloody quill. I hear a step on a loose board, I turn, he kisses my mouth and I always wake up before finding my tongue, before I can swear it's really him.

Dear Federico

Men following orders
ended your flesh
in fields of fallen bluebirds
who like you, swallowed great evil
to save the few
so the People might believe
that good is possible.

May it give you solace to know
you saved this life;
your hand on mine
holding the knife
that had vowed to bleed
out the sadness, the needle
to suture light into flesh,
making beauty of scars
your lessons to gut
my worthless
faith in humanity
infuse my bones
with the sea
for the suckling of
forgotten fish.

You, Federico are my faith.
What do I care that you love men?
I am neither man nor woman.
You could love me.

As these words arrive
I find courage
to step beyond dreams;
you Federico, you
your courage my black quill
of a dawn that rewrites me as ululations
rise from these fingers now tongues.

When Papi realized I wouldn't back down, he relented by removing his cloth shoes and mended socks to rub his bunions. Code for surrender. Mami went full metal Armadillo, keeping out any thought of reason or love. "If anything happen to my daughter it will be you fault. I kill you." The poor kitchen walls cringed from the unmuted, desperate voices of pots and pans, casualties of Mami's inner war.

Papi and I remained uncomfortably silent. He called out for his vitamins. Sweet sound of running water. Mami's slippers slapped out her annoyance as she brought him the pills and glass. No thanks. Just the sound of swallowing. Mami waited for the empty glass and disappeared into the making of arroz con pollo. Papi's thanks seldom reached for her.

Papi looked up at me. "I have a few old letters, photos; they will help you find our family." Papi's Xitano feet deformed by his insistence to force roots from a nomad. His sad eyes looked up at me, defeated; his only child, for whom he tended to those twisted roots, was set to wander. "There is an old cigar box en mi armario. Please go get it for your papi. Next to my good hat." The chocolate brown, wool Stetson was his only hat, protected from moths in its original box. The streaks from his crown of Clairol #46, almost faded. No worse than the Vitiligo now.

The onion skin paper, the postmark-cancelled stamps on thin airmail envelopes when mail was a very serious endeavor, were passports to a secret world, reviled and segregated from the rest of Franco's Spain. Papi had me sit beside him on the sofa. He gently rested his little treasure chest on one of Mami's hand crocheted doilies. "The one on the left is my sister, Pepita." He spoke as if I hadn't seen the photo many times before. Papi always brought it out for family and company, to brag that he once had a beautiful sister. If a question was asked, he'd offer the curious a drink "para fortificar los huesos." Papi had fortified a lot of people's bones.

"Ya ella no es parte de la familia, mi'ja. Ella se fue. Hizo cosas." I was listening intently to what Papi didn't say like he always didn't say. Maybe he'd let something slip. I wanted to know more about Pepita and who the beautiful woman next to her was; the answer always the same. "Una prima." The two women leaned into each other, heads touching. Radiant. Happy. Like the hidden circumstances of his father's death, Pepita and her story had been erased, as was most of his family.

Papi shared his past in bits of fragmented shadow. That cedar box was the one thing I had never dared to touch or even think of snooping into. It would be like sneaking into a Sacristy and prying open a Monstrance to touch the Body of Christ. A dread fear of feeling nothing but a dry wafer kept me from the ultimate sacrilege—the loss of wonder. I wanted to know who Papi and Mami had been before the absence of tenderness in their lives had left them unprotected from the barbarism of unfulfilled longings. Childhood's instinctive desire to fly and the incomprehensible absence of wings. Or worse, wings severed at their tendons, that left lungs too scarred for the full breaths required for a healthy mind. There would be no breaking or entering into sequestered recuerdos. There were no images of Mami y Papi as children. Undocumented lives take many forms.

NINETY/BÉNÉDICTINE

My escape to Spain was near. Spain, which I arranged for Papi and Mami's comfort as one of those asinine "Study Abroad" trips with people you might like or not. We all met with our trip chaperone at a party at the Program Director's apartment in Greenwich Village. Dr. Olga Catán. She was a suffocatingly proper Franco type and still managed to have a heart. She singled me out as the only one in the room who knew "how to properly dress for this occasion." I remember feeling proud and hiding my face. I had also shown up with two pounds of Italian cookies I picked up on Arthur Avenue, "Little Italy" of the Bronx. It set me back a bit, but "never show up to someone's home empty handed" had been drilled into me by Mami and Papi. Our trip chaperone, Mr. José Capoté, was fond of a good Tinto and had a way of making life feel easy, and anything possible.

Papi took me to JFK airport in a cab. After breaking both legs as a Moto-cross daredevil, he never got behind the wheel of anything again. Papi decided that it was time for us to sit down and drink together at the airport bar to calm *my* nerves. Papi was trying to smile and be easy going about it all. He had never been able to conjure that demeanor without alcohol and that was not the day.

Papi introduced me to the Singapore Sling. "This is a very nice drink for a young lady. You are old enough to drink now. It is nice for you. Like a fancy punch. Salud. Dinero. Amor." The toast was Papi's version of la bendición: Health. Money. Love. He saved it for special occasions. The clink of our tall glasses fluttered inside me like a first kiss. The drink was liquid candy. I couldn't believe Papi chose to have a "lady's" cocktail with me. We sucked down one after another. I took to it easily. Papi acted like he was giving me a Shirley Temple. At the end of it, I was buzzed but still standing. Papi got wobbly and a little teary-eyed. Our final toast was one usually reserved for New Year's Eve. It was August. "Dicen que uva, pan y queso saben a beso," to be followed by a midnight kiss for cheer and good fortune. I thought that maybe this would be the time Papi finally told me he loved me. I settled for a quick hug and the kiss on my forehead, his watching me as I walked through the gate. He knew he'd lost his mi'ji-ta, possibly for good.

I met up with a distant cousin, María C-something on the plane who was part of our travel group who didn't make it to Dr. Catán's event. Some bullshit about her "menstrual." She was a fastidiously dressed, prep school sycophant of a white male canon and virginal abuela all at once. She'd straightened her nappy hair into smooth, Lois Lane curls and a clear manicure. She adorned her monotone with gelatinous hand gestures that occasionally came up for air. She was a CUNY kid just like me, but looked down her nose at my jeans, t-shirt, and men's blazer. She had no idea how hard I had to fight not to become just like her, what it took to dress like me and not how my parents wanted me to. If it were up to Mami, I would have been yanking up my pantyhose and pulling on a girdle the entire trip, the home-sewn pencil skirt of my gold buttoned burnt red business suit eating me alive.

Before buckling my seat belt, I removed my bra through a sleeve; María buried her face and shook her head. I slept through most of the flight in a narcoleptic haze of Singapore Slings and María's incessant babble about how we must have churros y chocolate at the station in Madrid before we get on the train to Sevilla. She would ride First Class. I chose Third, since I knew it would be more fun. I was right; there were full wineskins, live chickens, and music on the ride.

María got her premade churros y chocolate at an upscale cafe full of tourists. I stayed outside with an amputee street vendor who made them fresh for each customer, shaping the dough on the bare stump of her left arm and dropping it in the fryer. The confidence and sense of self-acceptance of this proudly indigenous Maya woman made me feel that there was hope for me to some day find out who the hell I was, even in the presence of my colonizers. She ladled the dense chocolate into a thick mug, just like the one Papi had brought me home from work. Papi would have flirted with the churros Goddess, showing off his broken pinkie and post Polio legs. I knew they would laugh at what others shunned or feared to discuss. His leather bota of Tempranillo would have been passed around the train car and he would have re-named everyone, including the chickens.

The churros Goddess and I chatted about our love of animals, nature, friends, and the creative spirit. We both cried when I told her about Snow Leopard. "Animals don't belong in cages. We should live in friendship with them. I get treated the same way without the cage. When they taste my churros, then everything changes." She spoke to me in Nahuatl. I didn't need an interpretation, and am not certain I got it right or even close, but I could feel the simultaneous rage and compassion in her voice. Her eyes traveled my face. "They don't become more human after that first taste, they just give me bigger tips!" The way she said it was funny, but the content wasn't. I bought extra churros to bring on the train to Sevilla. I could watch her roll that dough all day long. Her confidence and dexterity were hypnotic. The churros became snakes and let me know I was in the presence of Ix Chel. She had embroidered every inch of the coarse cotton huipil she wore. A regal work of art bursting with Hisbiscus flowers. I handed back the mug and left with a greasy paper bag full of churros I could share for a fraction of the price María paid for one and an inch of espresso with a dried up lemon rind.

María assured me the cafe was "pure elegance" and "worth every peseta." Yeah, right. Her fat-free body bored me as much as her speech.

The train car was overcrowded and fragrant with home-cooked food and the musk of hard labor. There was laughter and camaraderie and café negro passed around from thermoses to have with the churros that were happily torn for sharing. As a first-timer to their country, I was offered a window seat. Mesmerizing landscapes of castles, arid plains, and hills brought Don Quixote that much closer to my heart that already adored him. We sang and swore on that train car until Franco's disciple, the train cop, gave us the fascist look of disgust while stroking his leather baton. As soon as he left I called out "policía de palito" and the roar rose again. I wished I'd said it to him, but Papi had warned me well about Spanish prisons and how little it took to get locked up. Your chances tripled in third class. Some things never change, whatever the government.

"Here, mi'ja, take this." Before I'd gone through that airport gate at JFK, Papi slipped me an envelope of cash, like he was conferring with a bookie. "First Class train only, mi'ja, okay?" "Sí, Papi." I saved the money and my soul instead. I know that Papi would have done the same.

When I stepped out into the air and dusk orange light of Sevilla, my luggage dropped from my hands. My arms rose up, and every part of my being joyously submitted to el embrujo de Sevilla. I had never felt a place incarnate, pull me into itself and fill me with rivers from every continent. Such fevered mysticism often swept me away, but this was the first time it filled me, the first time I could feel my body where my feet reached into the ground and the ground rose up to meet me.

I caught a glimpse of stick-up-the-ass María, and hid myself from her. Let her call for a fancy car, or whatever it is snobs do. I would make my way to the women's pensión where I would be staying with thirteen other women, given directions by the best of all concierges, a street cleaner. Who could know the labyrinth of Sevilla better than the persecuted and exploited workers of a fascist regime? I made my way with sage guidance from a man who referred to himself only by his surname, as he had been named for the Dictator by his "poor, illiterate, bamboozled parents." "So your name is Francisco?" He spit on the sidewalk, risking a severe summons and said, "¡Mejor que me llames Mierda!" I felt Papi smile inside me, Mami turn away in disgust.

At the pensión, the thick brown toilet paper gave me hemorrhoids and the potato omelets made me fat. The women taught me how to insert a tampon when they saw the wad in my pants. I was adopted by a pack of fascist-loathing, Communist students. We broke as many insidious laws as we could—from curfews, to public displays of French sensibilities, our tongues and voices dancing the roar of disobedience. We outran the Civil Guard on foot and on motorcycles and I learned I had wings.

ACKNOWLEDGMENTS

I wish I could write all of these names in a circle. Every one of you is another heart that has kept me, and keeps me vibrant, creating, and thriving. All of you helped me to write this book, my poems, and all the books that are being written, whether you know it or not. Not everyone is listed here—that would take an entire book. It may be decades or even a single moment when you have brought the alchemy of your presence into my life, and it lives within me. Please know that you have all activated my imagination, inspired my work, uplifted my heart, and have strengthened my upstream swims during the worst of storms.

Thank you, Naomi Rosenblatt and all of the Heliotrope Books familia, for being my loving and brilliant doulas, breathing with me all the way from cover to cover. You bring new depth and meaning to the world of publishing, with your deep and abiding respect and genuine support of authors. Judith Rosenblatt, you are a role model for aging like a Goddess; Leah Wells, you are a road model for staying young at the soul's core. Thanks to Jennifer Maguire, publicist, for your relentless support of *Mi'ja*.

Special thanks to the Academy of American Poets for the Poets Laureate Fellowship funded by the Andrew W. Mellon Foundation, that allowed me the undisturbed time to complete this memoir, and also a new collection of poems. The Springfield Cultural Council, for helping to seed big creative visions. Mass MoCA's Assets for Artists with Briana Halpin, for supporting my vision for the life of this book.

James J. Lescault, the life in my love, guardian of my dreams, archivist of my work, healer of the deepest wounds. A true revolutionary of radical love and action throughout your life has made you a formidable opponent of bigots, gaslighters, and greed mongers. Carry on, you slayer of demons, and remember the words of our ancestral brother, Oscar Wilde, as you battle the small-minded: "Mediocrity always detests ability, and loathes genius."

Lauren Johnson, two flames, one orbit, in this life and the next. Nuff said.

Michael Surdej, a constant in my life since high school. Always a book in his back pocket; secret warrior. One of my heroes. E.S.P. love.

The late Frances Goldin and Fred Ho, for encouraging me to write the parts of Papi that live in this book. Fred, you brought a new world of loving friends and creative prowess into my life.

Iris Morales, who invited me to publish my first printed volume of poetry and for morning cafecitos y batas in times of struggle.

José Angel Figueroa, for the gifts of friendship, support and venue throughout my literary life.

Rhina Valentín, for being a dear friend, producing my work, and celebrating my being since the day we met. Dr. Jane Gabriels for introducing us. The late poets, Emilie Glen; Barbara A. Holland; Pedro Pietri; Louis Reyes Rivera; Sheldon Bieber; Peter and Patricia Fillingham; and Judith Ortiz-Cofer, for inspiration and guidance on my poetry writing journey. I stand on your shoulders and can still feel my hands inside of yours.

Sandra María Esteves, and all of the Ordinary Women / Mujeres Comunes; Michael Devlin; Jeffrey W. Meyer; Richard Spiegel and Barbara Fisher; and Ron San Marchi for showing me in my youth that my work was worthy of publication, and then helping me get it published.

Eric Johnson and Nina Olff for our second home and retreats into the joys of friendship and mutually inspired creativity. Always in my corner.

Readers y Familia: María Luisa Arroyo Cruzado; Dr. Diana Alvarez; Dr. Priscilla María Page; Dr. Lisa Aronson Fontes; Dr. Robert Spivey; Naomi Jacobson; Beverly Naidus; John Lescault; Dr. Li Yun Alvarado; Urayoán Noel. James J. Lescault. Your feedback, support, loyalty and unconditional love keep me going and always will. I never have to doubt that you will tell it to me like it is, and like it isn't. That is love. I see you.

Rosemary Tracy Woods, we are Sisters of the Flying Broom; we carry the Moon along with all of the Ferocious Women: Kim Parlengas; Samalid Hogan; Norma Nunnally; Janis Astor Del Valle; Jean Canosa Albano; Francheska Morales; Eilish Thompson; Narelle Thomas.

The late Dr. Roger N. Buckley, for being a true friend and champion of my work. My favorite seagull. See you at the beach.

Angela Rola, for friendship and family holidays; for laughter and telephone seances.

Magaly Cardona, muse to some of my best poems; giver of keys to my NYC home.

Sara Littlecrow-Russell, they don't know you like I do. For being a constant light and love on my journey. For medicine that always heals.

Pelonomi Khumoetsile-Taylor, for bringing María Luisa Arroyo into my life.

Matthew King, for being a 4:00 a.m. friend, loyal and true.

Leah Poller, for birthday pancakes in her sunny Harlem kitchen and haircuts in her Parisian bedroom that make me feel like a beloved child and limitless warrior all at once. For never using the word "maybe". For spontaneous rave events wherever we go.

Maestres Dr. Ben Barson; Dr. Diana Alvarez (aka Dra. Xingona); Desmar Guevara; Abraham Gomez-Delgado; Matthew King and Kevin Scott, for believing my work and marrying it to their vibrant and rebellious compositions.

Wendy Porter-Coste for decades of friendship, camaraderie and support in my work as a teaching artist.

Marina Celander for your luscious art-making with my words.

Ruthanne M. Deutsch, because it is and always will be, OUR thing. Super Shero.

The Late Miriam Colón, First Lady of Latinx Theater, who called me out of the blue to tell me how much she respected my work and showed up for me in unforgettable ways; a secret magic between us.

Marjorie and Frederick Hurst, for welcoming me as a writer into my second decade with *An African American Point of View*.

Michelle LeTendre, always a presence of love, support and inspiration in my life. Badass B.S. Buster.

Embraces of Gratitude:

Dr. Gloria Caballer-Arce; Rosalba Rolón; Muriel Fox; Gizelxanth Rodriguez; Masaru Koga; William "Billy" Myers; Dr. Royal Hartigan; Dr. Stephanie Athey; Dr. Myrna Nieves; Kathy McKean; Donald Sanders; Tian Hui Ng; Charles Rice-Gonzalez; Evan Plotkin; Ashanta Smith; Sarah K. Steiner; Melanie West; Janice and Rolando Curtis; Ed Cohen; Tim Rooke; With Margraff; Gricelides Saex; Luisa Cardaropoli and family; Mariclaire Smith; Pam Racine; Kenisha Lillian Nicole; Dr. Henry Julio East-Trou Kathryn Neel; Dorca Iris Gómez;María Aponte; Janis Ian; Zoe Rinchen Lemos; Ed Cohen; Jezabel Montero; Rich Villar; Margo Singaliese; Oscar Bermeo; Fish Vargas; George Goodwin; Galen Passen; Elizabeth Wills-Ogilvie; Commissioner Helen R. Caulton-Harris; Daniel Jáquez Pritchett; George Malave; Taylor Ho Bynum; Dan Bisaccio; Nancy Mercado; Steve Bloom; Nejma Nefertiti; Majora Carter; Keli Garrett; Eileen Mackin; Dr. Robert Mackin; Dr. Janice Defrances, Dr. Alvilda Sophia Anaya-Alegría; Dr. Raúl Gutierrez; Peggy Robles-Alvarado; Natalia Eugenia Muñoz; Damaris Pérez Pizarro; Elizabeth Roman; Tinky Weisblat; Alice Kociemba; Zydalis Bauer; Mayor Domenic Sarno; Titus Kaphar; Thomas J. Putnam; Barbra Ilten; Dr. Christine Dinsmore; Ruth Levine; Glenda Jasso Aquino; María Aponte; Rick Kearns Morales; Pablo Delano; Dr. Geri Gutwein; Marco Dermith; Dr. Demetria Shabazz; Dr. Amilcar Shabazz; Ela Alpi; Raquel Obregón; Shel Horowitz; D. Dina Friedman; Myriam Quiñones; Jossie Valentín; Lydia Pérez; Felicia Lundquist; Dr. Faythe Turner; Dr. Noe Montez; Nicole M. Young-Martin; Janine Fondon; Dr. Yadilette Rivera-Colón; Dr. Trevor Boffone; Perry Yung; Dr. Henry Julio East-Trou; Kristina Scott; Caridad De La Luz (a.k.a. La Bruja), the Ign!te the M!c Collective, and all of the adults and youth who continuously inspire me.

Dr. Andrew B. Torres; Abigail Santiago; Ilhan Braxton; Deanna Chrislip and Brian Hale; for their support in harnessing the liberating power of intergenerational artistic collaborations.

My beloveds from around the globe who are Jazz Ready listeners and extraordinary artists. Special shout out to our official Jazz Ready Angel, Dr. Luis A. Marentes.

Local, national and global supporters of my work who have consistently amplified my voice, and provided me with fiscal support and/or venue —books grow within us over time and the art we create is sustained and nurtured by countless people—whether we know it or not:

Art for the Soul Gallery; Senator Joanne M. Comerford, Massachusetts Legislature; National Organization of Latino Arts and Cultures; Pregones/PRTT theater; Thomas J. Dodd Research Center, University of Connecticut, Storrs; Amherst Media; Asian American Cultural Center and the Puerto Rican/Latin American Cultural Center at University of Connecticut, Storrs; Library Land; The Black and Latino Legislative Caucus of Massachusetts; Latino Breakfast Club; Sleeping Weazel Theater; Springfield Public Library; Regie Cabico; Black Women Playwrights, Washington, DC; Brooklyn Academy of Music G.A.L.A. Theater. D.C.; Mass Poetry; Los Angeles Theater Company; OPEN/Bronx-Net; Massachusetts International Festival of the Arts; Massachusetts Cultural Council; The Progressive; Community Foundation of Western Mass; New England Public Media; Red Sugarcane Press; Rotary Records, MA; P.R.I.D.A.; Afro Yaqui Music Collective; Putnam Vocational High School, Springfield, MA; Out/Spoken Word Poets; Seeds of Solidarity Farm; Afro-Asian Music Ensemble; Bing Arts Center; Latinx Theater Commons; Augusta Savage Gallery, Dr. Terry Jenoure; New England Poetry Club; New England Arts Hub; Goddard College, Vermont, with special thanks to Dr. Otto Muller, Jacqueline Batten, Dr. Myrna Miranda-ONeill; Manuel O'Neill; Sui Yee Wong; Karen Nicole of the Goddard College family in Vermont. Design WorkShop, Inc. Springfield, MA.

Each and every one of my students for over four decades.

These acknowledgments do not even begin to name all of the people and institutions who are part of all of who I am and all that I do and will continue to do. If I haven't named you, know that I have felt you and I see you. Your heart inside of mine.

ABOUT THE AUTHOR

Magdalena Gómez is Poet Laureate of Springfield, MA, where she co-founded Teatro V!da, a performing arts collective; she is also an Academy of American Poets Laureate Fellow, the author of *Shameless Woman* (Red Sugarcane Press) and the co-editor of *Bullying: Replies, Rebuttals, Confessions, and Catharsis* (Skyhorse). In 2019 she received the Latinas 50 Plus Literature Award at Fordham University, and the Latinx Excellence on the Hill Award from the Black and Latino Legislative Caucus of MA at the State House. The nationally acclaimed musical *Dancing in My Cockroach Killers*, based on a dozen of her poems and produced by Pregones/PRTT, has been performed in Los Angeles, DC, Massachusetts, and Off-Broadway in New York City.

Born to a Puerto Rican mother and Spanish Romá father, Gómez has been writing, performing and telling stories since early childhood. A devotee of Lorca, Emerson, and Chinese women poets since the third grade, this eclectic thinker is at once fierce and tender, one who creates a mystical bond with every audience.

9 781956 474053